Valuing Older People

Valuing Older People

Positive Psychological Practice

Elspeth Stirling

A John Wiley & Sons, Ltd., Publication

5/20/10
Lan
$39.95

This edition first published 2010
© 2010 John Wiley & Sons Ltd.

Wiley-Blackwell is an imprint of John Wiley & Sons, formed by the merger of Wiley's global Scientific, Technical, and Medical business with Blackwell Publishing.

Registered Office
John Wiley & Sons Ltd, The Atrium, Southern Gate, Chichester, West Sussex, PO19 8SQ, UK

Editorial Offices
The Atrium, Southern Gate, Chichester, West Sussex, PO19 8SQ, UK
9600 Garsington Road, Oxford, OX4 2DQ, UK
350 Main Street, Malden, MA 02148-5020, USA

For details of our global editorial offices, for customer services, and for information about how to apply for permission to reuse the copyright material in this book please see our website at www.wiley.com/wiley-blackwell.

The right of the author to be identified as the author of this work has been asserted in accordance with the UK Copyright, Designs and Patents Act 1988.

All rights reserved. No part of this publication may be reproduced, stored in a retrieval system, or transmitted, in any form or by any means, electronic, mechanical, photocopying, recording or otherwise, except as permitted by the UK Copyright, Designs and Patents Act 1988, without the prior permission of the publisher.

Wiley also publishes its books in a variety of electronic formats. Some content that appears in print may not be available in electronic books.

Designations used by companies to distinguish their products are often claimed as trademarks. All brand names and product names used in this book are trade names, service marks, trademarks or registered trademarks of their respective owners. The publisher is not associated with any product or vendor mentioned in this book. This publication is designed to provide accurate and authoritative information in regard to the subject matter covered. It is sold on the understanding that the publisher is not engaged in rendering professional services. If professional advice or other expert assistance is required, the services of a competent professional should be sought.

Library of Congress Cataloging-in-Publication Data

Stirling, Elspeth.
   Valuing older people : positive psychological practice / Elspeth Stirling.
        p.   cm.
   Includes bibliographical references and index.
   ISBN 978-0-470-68335-4 (cloth) – ISBN 978-0-470-68334-7 (pbk.)   1. Older people–Psychology.
2. Aging–Psychological aspects.   3. Positive psychology.   I. Title.
   BF724.8.S75 2010
   155.67–dc22

                                                                        2009043713

A catalogue record for this book is available from the British Library.

Typeset in 11/13pt Minion by Aptara Inc., New Delhi, India.
Printed in Singapore by Markono Print Media Pte Ltd

Impression   2010

Contents

List of Tables and Figures

About the Author and Book

Elspeth Stirling is a practising clinical psychologist who has specialized in work with older people in the National Health Service in the United Kingdom for 28 years. She has also trained in social role valorization (SRV)-based service design.

This book applies SRV principles to our thinking about how we as clinicians can contribute to better humanitarian care for people who have ongoing disabilities, illnesses and end-of-life issues. It examines the impact of devaluation of older people's lives in the context of technology-dependent societies. Like all sciences, applied psychology now exists in a global context dominated by imperatives for achieving ecological sustainability and regenerativity of resources. Using SRV and positive psychology principles, the book indicates how more age-inclusive societies and open awareness of later life issues are fundamental to strong communities as well as to personal happiness and resilience.

1
The Psychology and Ecology of Ageing

Ageing in a Global Context

There is a common belief that certain societies, namely 'western' or 'northern hemisphere', represent the epitome of human social and economic development. Hence they are referred to commonly as the 'developed' societies. By implication, other societies are described as 'developing', and indeed these other societies are rapidly staking their claim to what they see as their share in the 'good things' that the Western cultures take for granted. As biosphere science has shown, however, the planet could not support human (or any other) life if all societies were to function with the same levels of consumption and lifestyle as the so-called 'developed' societies. It is more accurate and realistic to say that these 'developed' societies are actually *technologically dependent* societies – who can only afford their dependence and affluence because they are the few. Consumption of energy sources such as oil and gas, and of food, water and forests is already known to be resulting in net irreversible depletion of world resources and irreversible changes in the patterns and behaviour of the earth's systems, namely sea level, fresh water, temperature, and air (Worldwatch Institute, 2004; Princen, Maniates and Conca, 2002; de Souza, Williams and Frederick, 2003; Meadows, 1995). Such high levels of resource consumption are not sustainable for the technologically dependent societies, and certainly cannot be sustained if extended more widely.

This is also the first period in history when longevity is occurring en masse – at least in some societies (Bond, Dittman-Kohli, Peace, and Westerhof, 2007). It is timely to explore and explain those societies' responses and the changing experience of ageing. In particular, to pursue a positive understanding of ageing, including of individual achievements and social transactions, is an important matter in the wider ecology of the planet. A current and very negative response is to blame 'the old' for taking up a share of scarce material resources. Western societies already transact their business towards frail older people through institutional containment and socially engineered separation. This has been explained as repression of fear about death, being enacted through unconscious social processes of control (Sudnow, 1967; Smith, 1999, 2003). It has also been the case that with the growth of technology societies have focused on the creation of the 'perfect individual' and 'eternal life', further fuelling denial and defensive eugenic measures against frail older people. However, such negative and blaming attitudes about 'the old' can only deflect attention from the real issues. Effective responses to the current ecological imperatives will include revising downwards our expectations about our material lifestyle for example, reducing our consumption of energy and water, hand in hand with learning how to achieve happiness, pro-social behaviour, and a sense of environmental mastery and purpose in life without dependence on material consumption or technological fixes. Traditionally these 'higher virtues' have been seen as the territory of the few – perhaps those who live a long and spiritually guided life. However it seems as if they will become the desirable goal for all ages as we learn to adapt to sustainable lifestyles. Positive psychology, being the science of those processes that contribute to thriving and resilience, whether in late life or early life, may be growing at a critical time ecologically, and may benefit from the changing population demographics.

Positive Psychology

It has been argued that the pre-occupation of clinical psychology since World War II has largely been with the disease model, and that as a result traditional psychological theories grossly overpredict psychopathology (Bandura, 2001). Positive psychology is the scientific study and theory of those factors and processes that contribute to positive, personal outcomes and development, despite adverse life conditions and experiences (Seligman, 2005; Seligman and Csikszentmihalyi, 2000). These include the following:

1. Positive subjective experiences such as well-being, life satisfaction, flow, hope, pleasure and happiness.
2. Positive individual attributes such as expectancy, resilience, self-efficacy, optimism, creativity, coping, future-mindedness, knowing and wisdom.
3. Group level attributes that is, relationships that foster pro-social behaviour, responsiveness, responsibility, nurturance, altruism, civility, moderation, tolerance, civic virtues and citizenship.

Positive psychology is concerned with the accomplishment of positive desirable life goals, such as well-being, optimism, happiness and pro-social behaviours – *irrespective of* adversity or disability. Rather than being tied to the 'reduction' of pathologies or symptoms its primary focus is on accomplishing positive humanitarian competencies, such as future-mindedness, responsibility, nurturance, altruism and other civic virtues. In doing so, it does not ignore special needs, disability, distress or pain – on the contrary, it distinguishes mental illness from psychological well-being, and adversity from resilience, as separate and distinct dimensions. Accordingly, applied positive psychology goals 'go beyond the baseline' (Keyes and Lopez, 2005) – this means *not* limiting our goals to symptom reduction (such as reducing depression or minimizing challenging behaviours) but establishing plans to reach positive desirable humanitarian goals irrespective of disability or adversity. Positive psychology directs us to learn from the scientific study of how individuals adapt and recover naturally (natural resilience). A positive psychology intervention is one that aims to recreate those conditions to strengthen capacity for coping and to optimize the likelihood of successful adaptation of an individual in the face of challenge and difficulties. Both individual and social factors and processes are of relevance to positive psychology (Wrzesniewski, 2005).

In later life the individual is more likely to encounter challenges and adverse life conditions – particularly in the areas of health, relationships, roles and routines. In addition, the senior adult is more likely to be free from the focus on occupational and child-rearing tasks that can predominate earlier adult life. It could be argued that technologically-dependent, production-focused societies extend the earlier adult life pre-occupation with work and production goals, and delay development in other positive traits and competencies, namely prosocial and civic competencies and experiences. Accordingly, senior adult life could be thought of as potentially an opportunity for developing and expressing those other positive psychological traits and competencies (such as optimism, future focus and pro-social behaviour), which positive psychology identifies as of particular importance to human functioning.

In the present historical context of ecological crisis, there is an imperative for societies to foster pro-social behaviours and attitudes, to change high-consumption patterns of behaviour and to enhance collaborative behaviours and beliefs. For biological survival to be achieved it seems that human societies will require to foster new and significantly different social and personal behaviours. Therefore, societies will increasingly need citizens with just such positive psychological capacities and traits. This 'ecological' concept sees later life as having a unique purpose in the cycle of life, and necessary to regeneration of sustainable life across the generations; it sees later life as an opportunity for the development of positive psychological traits (e.g. future focus, capacity for reflection, and responsiveness in relationships) and humanitarian competencies (e.g. pro-social behaviours and investment in community/group beliefs and activities) and freedom from the material and production concerns of earlier adult life. On this line of reasoning, successful psychological development in later life can provide powerful models of different ways of thinking about the purpose and value of life for succeeding generations. The capacity to see value in life that transcends the individual lifespan is similar to spiritual beliefs but, unlike particular faith systems, it is not transacted through belief in an entity (e.g. a god) but through belief in the continuity of universal human values (such as responsibility, nurturance, altruism and community-mindedness) and the sustainability of life for succeeding generations.

The study and understanding of positive psychological development in later life is not the study of 'adult life – but more of the same'; on the contrary, it addresses different life experiences and accomplishments. Because these later life issues are more likely to focus on values that transcend the individual, they may be pivotal in our species' progress towards creating a sustainable relationship with each other and with the global environment on which we all rely. Later life brings opportunities for transforming the experience of self, and the value of self, in the cycle of life – to envisage a future that transcends the self laterally (i.e. across community) and vertically (i.e. across generations). These transcendent forces give personal meaning to late life beyond the more material matters and experiences characteristically valued in earlier adult life. They move us towards the competencies needed for enduring communities – communities that can sustain hope, optimism, spirituality, morality, ethical behaviour, altruism, empathy and resilience.

Positive ageing is the reality for most people (Williamson, 2005) – yet in contrast the emphasis in research has been on the pathologies. Clinical psychologists working with older people have always implemented positive approaches such as person-centred care and functional analysis (which focuses on the environment and the social context of the individual). This book aims to drive forward these insights and knowledge, and to place them in a firm alliance with the 'new' positive psychology and the existing understanding given to us by social role valorization (SRV).

Positive psychology: a synthesis with social role valorization

In taking a positive route to conceptualizing ageing the content of the book draws significantly on the work of Wolf Wolfensberger on the normalization principle and social role valorization (Race, 2003; Wolfensberger, 1994, 1998, 2000, 2003; Wolfensberger and Thomas, 1983; Wolfensberger and Glenn, 1975) and of John O'Brien on the framework for accomplishment (O'Brien and Lyle, 1986). Although they focused on the life situations of people with learning disabilities, the principles are just as applicable to understanding the life situations of other groups in society who may be vulnerable to social exclusion or disadvantage associated with a impairment or a negative interpretation (such as 'not a life worth living').

SRV and positive psychology have some key common themes in understanding peoples' experience of their difficulty. These include the following:

1. A focus on *roles* and *relationships*, which influence well-being and are protective as a buffer against adversity (Lemay, 1999).
2. Recognition of the importance of the *competent community*. An age-competent community is one that fosters an optimistic outlook on ageing for everyone and that is conducive to older individuals achieving fulfilment, including people with disabilities.
3. Recognition that the *presence* in the community of persons with disabilities or who are close to their death has the potential to evoke strength and resilience in others. Opportunities to share life-defining experiences themselves foster pro-social competencies and hope in community members of all ages.
4. Countering the pathology culture – instead seeing adversity as 'normal' and people as benefiting from opportunities to learn from and live with adversity. People whose adverse life circumstances are severe are not seen as the 'unfixables' but as examples for others to learn from.

The Three Levels of Ageing

Wolfensberger's 'three levels of impairment' provides a useful model for understanding how ageing is more than a physical event:

First level: Physical changes that occur with ageing – the most recent understanding of this is that 'ageing' is a result of an accumulation of tiny errors in the cell DNA repair mechanism (Kirkwood, 1999, 2004; Finch and Kirkwood, 2000).
Second level: Negative beliefs about ageing result in lowered expectations of the ageing person.
Third level: The person internalizes negative beliefs about ageing, and even more seriously reduces their own opportunities for fulfilling their life.

On the other hand, this vicious circle can be made a virtuous circle – such that life satisfaction, happiness and positive cognitions about the future regenerate energy and support a continuing fulfilment of life potential. An age- and disability- 'competent' community has the capacity to see strengths in the inclusion of aged and disabled citizens – as well as having the competence to support the specific needs. Competent communities have no need to expend energy on denial and defensive measures (such as segregation and separation) against people who are old or disabled. Age-competent communities have the capacity to function in a manner that connects individuals of different age cohorts while valuing their different experiences, skills and capacities – tensions and differences will not be denied but openly acknowledged and regarded as opportunities for learning and progress.

How is Ageing Responded to in the Societies of the Technologically Dependent World?

This section highlights some key features of the present social context for ageing.

1. This is the first period in history when longevity is occurring 'en masse' that is, it is a normative experience.
2. There is evidence of increasing fear about and avoidance of the concept of death in those societies that we call 'developed' (but which might more accurately be described as technologically dependent). Segregation of, and distancing from, aged and/or dying people indicate processes of unconscious social control to limit this fear.
3. Such technologically dependent societies appear to foster the pursuit of personal and individual goals, in contrast to goals that represent the future of the community.
4. Older people tend to be seen as more closely aligned with disability and dying (no matter how positive they themselves may be in their experience and response) and as a result will be more likely to be viewed in a negative light for example, as a threat or an object of ridicule.
5. The lives of the people we currently call 'older' have spanned probably the greatest social, political and economic changes in history, all within a few decades – psychologically this is important because of the additional challenge to maintaining meaningful connections across the generations.

It is therefore timely that the new positive psychology be applied – so that we can turn the old frightening questions about old age (such as 'How many kinds of dementia are there?' and 'How would euthanasia work?') into more constructive enquiry such as 'What would it take to support the person with dementia, or the person with pain, to enable them to fulfil their life and to be pain-free – and in a way that maintains their connection with their community and supports their unique value?'

Who Are the People We Call Older People?

The older person is first and foremost a person who is living a part of the normal lifespan. But this is experienced in the context of other individuals and of the customs and practices of a given society. In the technologically dependent world, positive ideas about a 'successful later life' may make for a particularly difficult context for the ageing individual – perhaps hindered by lack of positive images and expectations about ageing (Featherstone and Hepworth, 1990) and having to construct a positive reality while surrounded by global negative ideas about ageing such as seeing it in terms of loss and decay, burden on others or economically unproductive.

In addition, changes in society over the lifespan of the present generation of older people mean generations having to learn new ways of relating in what is essentially a normative vacuum (Jerrome, 1990).

Modelling is generally acknowledged in social psychology as being a powerful mechanism by which social roles transfer from one individual to another and across groups and cohorts of individuals. Nevertheless, even when individuals are unwilling to accept such negative stereotypes, they can be hard to resist.

For example, most individuals find it easy to make ageist jokes about themselves in a society where this is the norm. The harm comes from the fact that these perpetuate the second and third levels of impairment in ageing and makes it more likely, ultimately, to be a negative personal experience.

High, or even ordinary, achievements in the life of the older person (e.g. to write, to travel, to work, to keep fit) are at risk of being perceived as 'extraordinary' – and may even be ridiculed.

Early life social and interpersonal experiences

The generations we now call older have typically experienced more limited educational opportunities in childhood than currently is the case, together with an early exposure to adulthood responsibilities.

The differences are particularly pronounced for those whose childhood was prior to the middle of the twentieth century. In the early part of the century it was not uncommon for a child to experience the death of a sibling, a peer-group member, a mother in childbirth, or either parent from accident or infection.

Childhood illnesses were commonly treated with long periods of isolation from other children and own family, and children were required to look after sick siblings or parents at home.

The World Wars brought evacuation and, for some, the experience of abuse or humiliation at the hands of the receiving families, the death of parents or close family, and separation from family. This is the generation which came out of World War II with a strong belief in justice and a given order of things. Smail (1984, 2001) has argued that this phenomenon was driven by the psychological need for belief in self-efficacy (that the actions of war had 'worked' and been worthwhile).

The notion of resilience formed a strong underpinning to the beliefs of those who had come through the chaos and pain of war; they now had to believe that order would ensue, and bring with it well-being and opportunity. In the earlier part of the twentieth century, childhood was a time of hope and aspiration but with a much more limited range of social roles available or expected. Saving, economizing, re-using, repairing and passing on to others are the values in which many people were socialized throughout the early and mid-twentieth century. There were no all-encompassing worldwide media and the child of the first part of the century was entirely likely to develop a world-view, and a view of self in it, formed and shaped by persons and events in a close physical proximity. They solved problems by using local resources, or learnt how to find a solvable problem instead.

Current social environmental influences

The effect of social environmental influences on the individual's experience of ageing can be understood at three levels, ranging from the societal level to the community and the immediate family (Table 1.1).

The *societal level* may be far removed from the awareness of the individual, but it is the level where the cumulative effects of denial and unconsciousness become embodied in practices and policies – where stereotypes and prejudiced practices become 'custom and practice'.

For example, older people are not referred for psychological services in the same proportions as younger people despite the similar prevalence and incidence rates of anxiety and depression (British Psychological Society, 2002). The fact that the first standard to be identified in the 2001 National Service Standards for Older People in the United Kingdom was 'rooting out age-ism' shows the reality of age inequities in access to health care resources. The question however is whether equity can be achieved by policing the behaviour of resource gatekeepers, or whether the responsibility and the opportunity to make such positive changes lies more truly in the surrounding social systems.

At the *community level* are groupings that have grown out of some common purpose, shared experience or value system amongst sub-groups of the society for example neighbourhood, leisure, occupation, and belief communities.

At the *family and immediate network level* are the core interdependency re-lationships in people's lives. For example, the parent–child relationship in later

Table 1.1 Three levels of social influence on the experience of ageing

Level	Potential negative social influences	Potential positive social influences
Societal	Little interest in ageing people. Medical perfection an ideal. Collective denial of death or disability. Relative deprivation in funding for older age groups. Seen as 'invisible', 'special needs', 'burdensome' or 'not worth it'.	Older people as 'holders' of valued traits for example, responsibility, citizenship, transcendence of material goals. Older people as altruistic – net givers to society. Older people valuing self-reliance and control.
Community	Islands of positive assertive action by older people, but no real older person's movement. Organizations sign up to anti-ageist policies, but still excluding people. Age separatist practices.	Experience self as happy, and satisfied with life. Experience self as having capacity for vocation, courage, aesthetic sensibilities, pro-social activities, future focus.
Family Immediate network	Role reversals. Power balance shifts to younger persons, as 'carers'. Reduced financial security. Perceived as 'a burden'. Perceived as 'not the same person'.	Experience self as having self-agency and autonomy. Capacity to re-process and move forward irrespective of early life difficulties or deprivations. Experience self with sense of continuity, and part of a 'whole' community. Experience of self as 'own person' – acknowledging constraints and maintaining hope.

life is often thought of clinically in terms of negative pressures such as role reversal (Knight, 1996) or the re-emergence of dysfunctional earlier relationship patterns such as insecure attachment (Bowlby, 1988; Hazan and Shaver, 1994). There are many ways in which longevity may provide opportunities for positive changes in adult relationships for example fulfilment of the parenting role and re-processing of relationships within the family. Positive psychologists argue that optimism, although clearly related to the beliefs and life experiences to which the person is exposed in earlier life (Snyder, 1994), can always be developed by further life experiences and particularly by changing negative beliefs and learning techniques of establishing attainable goals – similar to positive reframing and cognitive therapy techniques.

Summary points – who are 'older people'?

1. 'Old people' are persons of a certain generational context – who were born into, and had their earlier life socialization experiences in, cultures that were more likely to value the following:
   - non-reliance on technology
   - collective activities on basic life-support tasks, such as food production
   - sharing practical wisdom and experience
   - structuring of time by natural rhythms such as nightfall and the seasons
   - intergenerational expectancies about the roles that the older and younger generations would transact for each other (caregiving, teaching, transmission of skills, values and beliefs, etc.)

2. Collective effort, regenerativity and interpersonal reliance are the values likely to have been internalized by earlier generations. Individualism, consumerism and technological reliance are very recent values in the history of our societies.

3. At this time in history we therefore have generations living contiguously with probably the biggest gap in experiences ever encountered historically. In itself this is not the problem – that the experiences are *valued differently* in the current social context is the problem. It leads to:- the presumption that one set of values is 'right or good' while the other is 'wrong or bad'; the devaluing of the group of people associated with the rejected values; the socially engineered rejection of this group of people so associated and ultimately denial and defensive eugenic measures at a societal level.

4. Consequently, such cultures offer weak social roles for the rejected group, in this case for the older members of the society. The intergenerational sharing of practical wisdom and experience is devalued and reliance placed instead on technical solutions. The use and re-use of material resources are devalued and reliance placed instead on consumption and disposal. Regeneration as an integral part of harvesting nature, as in food and materials production, is devalued and replaced with reliance on continuous manufacture. Reliance on others is devalued and reliance placed instead on technology.

5. Nevertheless, positive ageing clearly does occur for many individuals in technologically dependent societies, and so it is not an inevitable 'fate' that every ageing person will become a 'victim' of social denial and role loss. What helps some 'resist' the powerful pressures of devaluation and role depletion within their society, and go on to achieve satisfying lives in old age? Clearly, there are contexts in which this is happening. Inner resiliency (the potential for positive development) is a recognized part of human development, including later life (Snyder and Lopez, 2005; Lemay and Ghazal, 2001; Seligman, 1991, 1998, 2002a, 2002b; Seligman and Csikszentmihalyi, 2001). Equally crucial to a sense of positive well-being for individuals is the 'health' of the

environment, social and physical, in which they exist. Recognition of positive roles for 'seniors' in our technologically dependent societies will challenge the denial, age cleansing and other defensive measures transacted against older people, and lead ultimately to more balanced, open and less death-anxious communities.

What are the needs of older people?

In the technologically dependent world, some powerful forces shape how aged people are responded to.

1. Older people are still dealt with in ways that would be unacceptable for other groups in society. For example, they continue to be deposited in institutions that would not be deemed suitable for other needs groups.
2. In a technological era ageing can be seen as the breakdown of the 'machine', and thereby ageing implies or symbolizes the failure of the technical fix. Technologically dependent societies find comfort in the paradigm of the 'body as machine' since it offers the illusory hope of eternity through technical fixes.
3. The illusion of physical perfection, perfect comfort, denial of death and eternal life is only maintained at a cost to society – by concealment of older people away from mainstream life, and particularly of frail or cognitively disabled older people.

The Old Paradigm for Understanding Ageing: How Beliefs About Ageing Historically Have Influenced Social Responses and Service Models

Table 1.2 traces how the various beliefs about the nature of ageing in technologically dependent societies have influenced societal responses to older individuals and groups, and consequently the service models deemed appropriate by the society. It includes the 'ecological' belief as a positive alternative.

'Biologically pre-programmed'. Seen as biologically programmed to age and die. The evidence now points instead to 'DNA repair' as the underlying mechanism for ageing (Kirkwood, 2004).

'Unable'. Being seen predominantly in terms of dependence, neediness and essentially deprived of a meaningful future. The reality is that the majority of older people live independent lives in their own communities.

'Unproductive'. Being perceived as an economic threat and blamed for using up society's diminishing financial resources. The reality is that older people are net 'givers' in society.

Table 1.2 How beliefs about ageing in technologically dependent societies have influenced societal responses and service models

Belief: definition of ageing	Image: person seen as	Society's response	Service model
Biologically pre-programmed	Reminder of mortality/death	Protect society: denial	Separation, detention
Disability, cumulative	No future	Containment for safety	Warehouse, all together
Unproductive	Limited value, economic burden	Protect society from economic 'dependence'	Separate services and benefits
Disease	Sick	Technical: find the cure	Hospital, disease, fund-raising
Second childhood	Child again	Protect, contain: for own safety	Caretaking, sitting, pretend living
Decay	Suffering, wanting to exit by choice	Pity, fear	Euthanasia, extermination, non-treatment
'Broken' machine	To be fixed	Technical: fix the machine	Therapies, accreditation of providers
Social oppression	'Geri'-activist	Political action	Expect all elders to be activists
No different	Just like younger people	Don't have to grow up; extended life	'Stay young', individualistic self-care
Ecological, continuity	*Part of a whole; unique purpose; part of a wider environmental context*	*Conscious about death; future focus; taking care of each other and the environment*	*Community development; promote humanitarian and pro-social competencies*

'*Disease*'. Ageing seen as a cumulation of disease processes in the body. It lends itself to the image of the old person as, predominantly, a sick person. The reality is that well-being exists alongside illness, and that people live more healthy years not just more years of ill health.

'*Second childhood*'. The older individual seen as child-like or returning to their first childhood.

'*Decay*'. Being seen in terms of a body that has already started to 'fall apart' even before death. It encourages the response of pity, and lends itself to ideas about 'exit' and 'euthanasia'. However, it has no objective basis as a theory of biological ageing.

'*Broken machine*'. Ageing seen in terms of damage to, or breakdown of, the machine (the body) has an appeal to the society that is technologically dependent and in the habit of responding with a technological 'fix' to all challenges that are moral, ethical and technical.

'*Social oppression*'. Ageing seen as predominantly the result of a negative social psychology. Lends itself to the idea of elders as a predominantly 'activist' group or movement, rather than as ordinary, individual, diverse members of a society. In this image of ageing, society might expect 'successful' ageing only of those elders who are political or community activists.

'*No different*'. The idea that older people are 'just like younger people' – conveys a static image of the life course. A society that accepted this belief would have a 'Peter Pan' expectation of the individual – expecting its members neither to grow up, nor to differ in their values from the younger generations.

'*Ecological*'. A contrast to the negative images/beliefs about loss, and pointing out the wider biopsychosocial context of ageing. This concept envisages ageing as a meaningful part within a meaningful system. In an ecological approach to understanding the natural world all parts (e.g. species, individuals, behaviours, habitats) are necessary and have an equal role in sustaining the whole system. All component parts contribute to the whole, derive meaning and status from it, and are constantly interactive to sustain the homeostasis and growth of the living system. A society that viewed ageing positively as a part of a homeostatic system would be conscious, but not fearful, of the processes of renewal and regeneration. Such a society might have less need for denial (of suffering), and thereby become a more stable and tolerant society. It might also have the human capacity to embrace what David Smail calls a 'taking care of one another' kind of society (Smail, 1987). In ecological terms this forms part of what is required for the survival of the earth's natural systems – that they be sustained by forms and patterns of human activity that are benign and tolerant, that can perceive individual gain in the pursuit of the long-term collective goal. Service models within this kind of societal system would focus on supporting the practical skills and wisdom already in individuals and communities. They would place the coping experience of persons living with distress, disability, loss or dying high in the values stakes, and would consider those individuals as being teachers and leaders of human experience.

The Vicious Circle of Ageing

Beliefs held in a society about ageing are of more than philosophical interest. They are powerful influences in shaping how that society sees the older person, how the society responds to the individual and to groups and what services are deemed to be appropriate for that group of people.

The old paradigm in 'western' cultures involves understanding ageing largely in mechanistic, medical and economic terms. There is little in the culture that encourages understanding in terms of social worth, personal fulfilment or socioeconomic value. This has not always been the case, and in earlier cultures, and other cultures worldwide this is still not the case. In the old paradigm, the second and third levels of impairment in the vicious circle, and the 'wounds' described in Chapter 2 are widespread human experiences.

When one thing is seen as different, and it need not be a significant difference (e.g. having a different colour of hair or skin of a different elasticity) this in itself need be no problem and cause no obstacle to living. It is when that feature, or difference, is *valued negatively* in the society that the person is drawn into the vicious circle – of *prejudice* (lowered expectancies and opportunities) and subsequently the *self-blame* (internalizing the lowered expectations and seeing self as worth less and responsible).

Figure 1.1 illustrates the processes that can be involved in the vicious circle of social devaluation and internalized devaluation that can happen for some people with ageing. The changes that come with ageing (such as a change in colour of hair, less elastic skin, a health problem, bereavement or a reduction in material income) may cause impairment, although not necessarily so; they may be challenging and may also promote positive adaptation and development. However, in societies where ageing is negatively viewed and people are likely to be socially devalued as they become older, the real problems arise with the second and third levels of 'impairment'. For example, loss of health can be coped with; but being viewed as 'a burden' causes damage to relationships and to self-worth. Feelings of disappointment can be coped with; but the belief that 'old people should be grateful for what they've got and such feelings are bad' is devaluing and damaging. When people are asked about what they most fear about 'old age' they identify such things as loss of dignity and loss of control. Yet these things have no necessary connection with old age. They result from the contextual and systemic responses to old age, but have no intrinsic relationship to the factor of age itself. In other words, the most feared and most damaging events that are seen

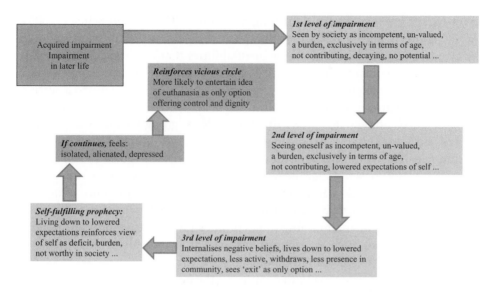

Figure 1.1 Vicious circle of ageing. Based on 'The Relevance of Role Expectancy and Role Circularity to Deviancy-Making and Deviancy-Unmaking' Wolfensberger, W and Thomas, S, 1983, Canadian NIMR. Reproduced by permission of Wolf Wolfensberger.

to accompany 'old age' are an artifice of the society in which the phenomenon of ageing occurs, and not a necessary part of ageing.

Which individuals are pushed into the circle, and which are not, is largely down to social valuations of particular 'level-one' afflictions. Societies that value speed and technological fixing may find mental disability less tolerable than physical disability – the latter may seem more amenable to technological solutions or prostheses and so require less adaptation on 'our' part. Persons who are slow or who have difficulty communicating may pose a greater challenge to 'business as normal' in their society and so be more likely to experience levels two and three difficulties. On the other hand, if a society held speed as a low priority, and alternatively found positive value in having challenging communicators in its midst, such individuals would have very different pathways of experience.

The approach of positive psychology is to identify factors that enable individuals to respond in a resilient way naturally in the face of deprivations or difficulties. This has two aspects, the first being the capacity to appraise and address realistically the true nature of the difficulties, and the second being the tendency to respond with actions to counter or prevent potential 'wounds'. The study of optimists, for example, shows that far from being simply people who stick their head in the sand, they attend to risks – but selectively – and so do not suffer from elevated levels of vigilance. Pessimists have been shown to be more likely to engage in behaviours that reflect a tendency to give up and accordingly show higher levels of health-damaging behaviours (Carver and Scheier, 2005). Applying this to ageing we can see that positive ageing is certainly not achieved by avoidance of the real limitations or disabilities that can and do accompany ageing – on the contrary the evidence would indicate that those who age well are individuals who can engage with adversity realistically and who tend to assertive, not avoidant, patterns of coping.

Positive psychology also views therapy goals as 'going beyond the baseline' (Keyes and Lopez, 2005). Accordingly, the emphasis is shifted from simply re-ducing negative symptoms to achieving positive desirable goals (irrespective). Positive therapy goals for later life would, for example, focus on: the experiences of well-being, satisfaction and happiness (irrespective of the presence of disabil-ity or illness symptoms); hope and future-mindedness (irrespective of time to live); and creating or maintaining opportunities for the expression of humani-tarian competencies, such as responsibility, nurturance, altruism and other civic virtues (irrespective of impaired physical competencies).

In Chapter Two, we look at both countering the negatives (the acquired second and third levels of damage) and prevention of such 'wounds'. Chapters Three and Four introduce and work through the positive principles (the 'new paradigm') as they apply to Assessment and Intervention with the Older Person. This is essentially a person-centred approach. In Chapters Five and Six, we look at the potential psychological impacts of cognitive disabilities acquired in later life, and emphasize the practical benefits of having person-centred goals at the heart of both clinical practice and care policies. Finally, Chapter Seven identifies and exemplifies aspects of selected psychological therapies, which particularly lend themselves to creating a positive understanding of later life experiences, challenges and goals.

2
Preventive Psychology in Later Life

Common Wounds and Ageing

Jean Vanier (1982) has called the devaluing life experiences of people with long-term disabilities 'wounds'. This concept sees it as essential for people to accumulate a predominance of positive experiences for them to build and maintain a sense of self-worth and to feel that their life is validated, meaningful and worth living.

More recently, resiliency theory (Bandura, 2001; Lemay and Ghazal, 2001) has made the point that most, or many, of either children or adults who experience potentially damaging trauma and deprivation develop into competent and able individuals leading happy and stable lives. The evidence indicates that resilience (normal development under difficult circumstances) is based on three important things. These provide the base from which individuals develop futures unmarked by earlier life traumas:

(a)   a sense of a secure base,
(b)   a sense of self-worth arising from relationships, and
(c)   a sense of self-efficacy (Gilligan, 2000).

In this sense, the two approaches are in agreement – adverse events have an impact, but this is strongly positively mediated by the presence of a social environment that supports secure and harmonious relationships. This explains why not all trauma-exposed persons have long-term, pervasive and enduring difficulties in their lives. However, where individual resilience makes no difference is where certain groups of people are subject to systematic devaluation and exclusion, and it is in these circumstances that 'wounding experiences' occur and need to be recognized:

> there are classes of individuals who, because of race, impairment and intelligence, are systematically excluded from opportunities to develop self-efficacy on the one hand, and where one might doubt the likelihood of self-efficacy being the necessary factor for change in their life courses. (Lemay, 2001, page 4)

Processes of systematic devaluation and socially engineered separation transacted against a group of people incur second and third level impairments, and further push the individual to a point on the vicious circle, which is beyond reach of the normal protective factors. This is relevant for understanding ageing as older people are more likely than others to encounter multiple difficulties, arising from loss of work and income, and changes in functioning, mental abilities and physical characteristics. These changes are usually attributed negative values within northern hemisphere technologically dependent and production-focused societies. They can be life-defining within these societies for example the person described as 'is retired' rather than 'has knowledge, experience and a perspective'.

Arguably, therefore the people we call 'old' people in so-called 'developed' societies do end up on the receiving end of systematic exclusion from the normal opportunities in life to a disproportionate extent compared to younger groups. The concept of 'wounds' is therefore helpful in unpacking what is happening in these contexts as individuals age. The following elaboration of wounds is based on that of Jo Osburn (1998) derived from social role valorization (SRV) theory (Wolfensberger and Thomas, 1983). Kitwood (1993, 1997) and Kitwood and Bredin (1992) extended this analysis specifically to the systematic processes of 'malignant social psychology', which contribute significantly to the disabling of persons with dementia.

Loss of Control, Autonomy and Individualism

There is a useful distinction to be made between autonomy and independence in relation to disability. Autonomy is being able to achieve our chosen state or goal – with whatever degree of support is required – that is, our choices are exerted irrespective of the level of instrumental help required to achieve these outcomes. For example, a person may rely on help to get dressed but in exerting their own choices about dress (and given respectful assistance) they can maintain a sense of autonomy. In contrast, 'independence' would involve carrying out the actions oneself. Individualism as a value system (which tends to focus on individual independence) is a relatively recent philosophy in human history and one which is not universal. It can be argued that many of the freedoms that individuals in 'the West' experience to function independently of other people (i.e. without having to negotiate with others to achieve their desired outcome) have only been achieved through dependence on technology instead. For example, instead of having to engage in cooperative effort to travel, or harvest food supplies, individuals can use machines – cars or combine harvesters, in these cases. However it is illusory to call this independence, since if these means are unavailable for any reason, individuals are exposed to severe disability and may lack the alternative skills to achieve their goals, such as, how to repair a car, or how to function without electricity, or how (in the case of children) to negotiate with other children. People of earlier generations may have the experience of having such competencies but they also have a challenging responsibility to try to pass on such competencies, or at least to raise awareness, at the same time avoiding the sentiment of 'everything in the past was rosy and better'. To strive towards open communication and understanding across generations is not a sentimental aspiration. Coming to terms with 'dependency' (and the limits of 'independence') is a positive survival skill – and much can be learnt from people in later life.

Being Seen As a Fiscal and Social Burden

In technologically dependent societies, many aspects of the human lifespan are treated as commodities. Not just the satisfaction of basic life needs, although these are primary concerns of the market-place economy, but also the satisfaction of 'higher' needs (our relationships and self-esteem, for example) is of considerable concern to the production economy. In such societies, people are surrounded by images and ideas that send out the message that there are 'good' and 'bad' possessions, lifestyles and relationships. People are enticed to spend money with the idea of 'improving' their lifestyle, obtaining 'good' relationships and having 'good' self-images.

Some groups become disenfranchized or marginalized from the production paradigm, either through feeling to have suffered from it themselves (e.g. don't have jobs or have poorly valued jobs), or through rejection of it at a personal level (e.g. so-called alternative lifestyles). Society may name such groups as 'odd', 'eccentric' or even 'threatening'.

This is a particularly relevant issue in the experience of older people. The most common public image and belief about old age is as a social problem and an economic burden (Victor, 1987). For example, through not being in traditional work roles, older people are at risk of being construed as bored, idle or dependent. The evidence points to the contrary – that most of the older people have contributed substantially to the economy, and continue to carry out productive social roles, such as organizing community activities and caregiving. However, the stereotype is powerful, and still results in older people being vulnerable to taking on the blame as a 'burden' in their own society. There is a challenging responsibility on the older person *not* to take on this particular self-belief – doing so effectively deprives others of owning their own distress or pain.

There are various life conditions or changes that are relevant here. In particular

1. retiring from paid occupation,
2. having a physical appearance which does not match the stereotype of the culture, and
3. having experiences and values that are different from those prevailing in the current culture.

Whilst retiral from paid occupation might be embraced and valued by the individual at a personal level, if it is not similarly valued by the culture, there will be conflicts for the individual. The discovery that what we value personally is not also valued by our native culture is at the very least a source of disappointment, and is at the worst a cause of personal stress and social marginalization.

However, population changes mean that older people now have more options open to them – volunteer work, part-time work, underpaid jobs that contribute much to the community, prestigious advisory roles, as well as continuing in work or retiring at the customary time. The positive psychology argument here would be that people who feel in control of choices about their work role (and other important factors in their life) are healthier and less depressed people (Seligman, 1975; Taylor and Brown, 1988). Rowe and Kahn (1998) propose that along with avoiding disease and maintaining high physical and mental function, 'engagement with life' is a core component of successful ageing. Williamson (2005) argues that this is virtually synonymous with continuing valued personal activities. However, the SRV argument is also relevant here; if what is personally valued is valued negatively by the culture (e.g. one's activities, beliefs, lifestyle) this conflict is a potential cause of impairment of well-being. And the potential damage from wounding stereotypes such as 'getting in the way of younger people' may have to be counterbalanced consciously in order that activity restriction is not the response of the older person.

In the context of the delivery of health care resources there are well-known inequalities (Department of Health, 2001), which may be at least partially related to this stereotype of the old as a financial burden. The fear of 'the rising tide' has acted as a brake on the development of some 'basic' forms of care for older people on a par with younger adult groups. For example, many deaths and extra disabilities are 'accepted' for older people after stroke, which are not accepted for younger people after stroke, simply as a result of older people being excluded from accessing the most effective forms of specialist stroke care (Department of Health, 2001; Knapp, 2000; Rudd et al., 1999). New forms of care in the community for older people with chronic health needs were routinely refused funding during the latter two decades on grounds of 'no evidence' for their efficacy. Yet traditional forms of care, such as hospital long-term care and residential home care, which are expensive, have not been subjected to comparable levels of scientific scrutiny and examination. As a result older people continue to be offered fewer choices about their futures. Paradoxically, they may also be 'blamed' for consuming expensive resources when in fact they are offered less.

Similar effects resulted from some kinds of health economic indicators. For example, the 'Quality Adjusted Life Years' (QALYS) measure was developed with the purpose of attaching to any potential treatment a value estimating the potential 'life years saved' (Kerridge, Glasziou and Hillman, 1995). Whilst this discriminated directly against older people, it also puts out the message that 'saving' productive output years is the ultimate goal of health treatments. The Layard report of 2005 perpetuates this same message – based as it is on the argument that psychological therapies should be provided not on the grounds that they are effective but on the grounds that they get people of the traditional working age back into the labour market. In the positive psychology approach, we would want to make a more radical argument such as the following: 'Psychological therapies should be provided on the grounds they are effective in supporting people's natural tendency to stay engaged in all kinds of activities (of value to the social enterprise) up to and including a point when they might encounter a disability'.

Rejection

Rejection can be recognized as happening to a group or individual in a society when it is deemed that the group or a person would be 'better off' away from the 'cruel world' – they are being cast as 'not one of us', who of course do want to be in the 'cruel world'. When older persons' own feelings about where they want to live their life are in some way ignored or minimized, for example labelled as 'not realistic' or 'lacking insight', this is in effect a rejection of their personhood.

Vacated hospitals and institutions 'in the community' are tolerated for older people where they are not considered appropriate for other special needs groupings, such as people with learning disabilities or people with mental health problems.

'Risk' may be offered as the rationale behind the tendency to take older people away from the mainstream society's facilities to have their needs met.

However, risk is often as perceived by other people rather than by the older person. The risk of falling at home, for example, may be presented as unacceptable and used as a reason for taking an older person into care; this is despite the evidence that the risk of falling at home is lower than the risk of having a fall in care. Despite a raft of legislation and guidelines (e.g. Scottish Executive 2000; Department of Health, 2005) risk assessment is not necessarily always undertaken with the purpose of obtaining maximal benefit for the older person. The rule may be to find the 'least intrusive option', but lack of resources or will to make it work results in practice and custom that is considerably at odds with that requirement.

All through the changes to services in the 1970s, 1980s and 1990s, which were called 'community care', institutional forms of care were being recognized as not acceptable for many groups in society, such as children and adults with learning disabilities and people with physical disabilities. Yet, society continued to be willing to place older people in the kinds of settings considered not acceptable for these other groups. Buildings where it always had been difficult to offer people individual care and support were handed over to services for older people. New buildings were allowed, which simply re-created the institutional living arrangements of the 'old' institutions – but this time 'within the community'. Why would this be the case? Are there social processes that make it more compelling to keep aged frail persons at a comfortable distance away from us, as compared to other needs groups? Since there are no differences in the types of disabilities that older and younger people have, the answer must be sought in how the society perceives its older members – and accordingly in what the society deems appropriate and acceptable for older people.

Treachery

Treachery was defined by Kitwood (1997) as the use of deception to manipulate a person or force them into compliance. One example that most of us will recognize happens when an older frail person is 'tricked' into attending a service when it is not primarily for their benefit but is for the benefit of another person or persons. The person may be asked to attend a day service in a residential facility with the hidden intent of moving them towards accepting residential care. There are also small treacheries: for example, the stacking up of evidence 'against' the person with the purpose of undermining their confidence or limiting the choices available to them (sometimes this is the role of the case conference); the person's concerns are not taken seriously or paid caregivers are asked to provide care for older person but are not given the necessary picture of the whole person.

Segregation and Congregation

In many areas of technologically dependent societies, older people are separated and relocated 'for their own safety' or 'for their own good'. They are expected to find contact with only other old (or frail) persons sufficient. Ultimately, they are subjects of 'age cleansing' and 'age apartheid', with the attendant, weakening effects that these processes have (in any of their forms) on both the society and the individuals.

Segregation

When a group in society is seen as, or regards it self as, needing to be separate from the mainstream society, the way is open for segregation to begin. It may begin with a perceived need for special activities (such as treatments) or the need for special environments (e.g. with orientation cues, or safe places to walk). When older citizens feel that their needs are inadequately provided for in the mainstream community (e.g. they feel unsafe as a result of the disproportionate reporting of violent crimes involving older people, or they fear they might suffer unattended pain at home) they may 'opt' for separatist 'solutions'. However this is not free choice in favour of segregation and separation, but simply a forced choice in the context of limited desirable options. History indicates that the segregation of groups within a society makes for destabilization and violence within the society in the long term. There is no evidence that apartheid in a society brings well-being to individuals. Although segregation might bring older people some freedoms in the short term (e.g. from noise, from excess demands), in the longer term it can bring a sense of isolation, and prevent people from pursuing essential of life goals – in particular those identified by positive psychology as the 'group level' goals of responsibility, nurturance, altruism, civility, civic virtues and citizenship (Seligman, 2002b).

Congregation

Bringing people together for reasons of meeting *special needs* is at one level a benign and instrumental activity – for example people learn from each other practical ways of coping and feel less alone in their experience. Historically, however, services also began to provide for people's *general needs* within the special needs groupings. The result has been that, inappropriately, services take on life-defining proportions when actually their business is to address one area of need. With this mission creep in services comes 'blanket' meeting of needs, loss of individuality, and barriers to assimilation in the wider community. As the separation between older people and the wider community is allowed to extend, so does the community lose an essential part of itself too. When older people are put together, and away, in groupings according to their disabilities (e.g. dementia) the remaining members of society are left without role models – either for coping with serious disability or for adaptive ageing. Models of positive adaptive behaviour in the transitions of later life are as important as at any other life stage.

Dehumanization

Kitwood (1997) describes this as 'objectification' – when a person is treated as if they were a piece of dead matter, to be pushed, lifted, filled, pumped or drained without proper reference to the fact that they are sentient beings. Highly likely to be denied, this particular form of harm may also be recognized in actions surrounding older persons that convey they are seen as less than human. An example of this form of harm is when older persons are seen in terms of proximity to death, and are given less rigorous, or even risky or experimental treatments. Examples would be basing a decision about a scarce medical treatment on a formula that includes the likely 'life-years' gained by the treatment (thus weighting the decision against the older person, and thereby allocating to them treatments not regarded as the first choice for others), or expecting older people to clean up after a nuclear contamination or accident or to take on some similar self-sacrificing role. In smaller, day-to-day ways dehumanization is enacted whenever people are talked about in front of them, when their existence as sexual beings is ignored or denied, or when conditions of living are accepted for them, which would not be tolerated for others (e.g. being expected to live in hospital wards when no other groups in a society are expected to do this and even when these same wards may have been recently vacated by other groups for whom more appropriate services were provided). Such 'second-choice' treatments are often cast as 'their choice', and the older person often internalizes the message of 'I am worth less than others and so should accept what others would not', hence entering into the third level of wounding.

Invalidation (Denial of True Feelings)

In its most insidious form this is a shift in the interpretations that are attributed to older persons' actions by other people, which differ from the attributions made about the same actions in younger people. To be independent if you are young may be seen as 'good', but if you are old with dementia or a stroke 'bad'. To express intense emotions and fears if you are young may be seen as 'good', but if you are old 'not good'. Sometimes expressions of feelings are belittled by being labelled as 'symptoms'. Or the person's psychological/spiritual concerns may not be taken seriously because their physical safety is the single issue seen as of overriding importance.

For the younger persons who face a bereavement, a loss of their home or a significant disability there is more likely to be an acknowledgement of the subjective reality of their suffering; anger, frustration, grief, magical or distorted thinking will more than probably be accommodated and such feelings and thoughts will be taken seriously. In contrast, if the person is aged, or has dementia, or both, the interpretation of the same actions in the exactly same situations is more likely to be a mechanical one for example 'have a changed personality', 'don't appreciate what is going on', 'not really aware'. There is a failure to acknowledge the subjective reality of the older person's experience, in particular their feelings. The implication is that 'these people don't feel as we do', and hence that such experiences as losing their home or life patterns may be seen as not having any meaning for them.

In fact, the conditions that damage higher cortical functions spare the brain areas associated with feeling and immediate apprehension (Holden and Woods, 1995), and the organic pathology is only one factor in a multifactor process in which social pathology is by far likely to be the most significant factor (Kitwood and Bredin, 1992). We are all exposed to the stereotypes of the older person as asexual, unloving, insensitive of others and self-centred. Such stereotyping may lead to real feelings of being dismissed or belittled as 'silly', 'attention seeking' or 'selfish'.

When older people are talked about in terms that reduce them to only pathology (e.g. 'does this person's degree of dementia warrant residential care or nursing home care?'), they are having their humanity denied. The question as asked is then not a question about the person but a matter of warehousing.

Another form in which invalidation appears is infantilization as Kitwood has discussed in relation to older people with dementia. People in distress appear to be seeking security. However, for how many distress groups are dolls considered an appropriate or enhancing means of providing a sense of security? Any comfort afforded by the physical contact with a doll is outweighed by the childlike image conveyed. The ends are only as good as the means – accordingly, any comfort achieved is at a cost of damage to the standing of the adult. Other people relate to these persons in narrower ways; the image of 'child' becomes the life-defining characteristic. When this continues over time, they are less and less likely to be drawn into adult-to-adult modes of interaction, and so are deprived of the very social transactions that would have enabled them to hold on to a sense of 'self'.

Discontinuity in the Physical Environment

To ensure even the ordinary things in life, such as a sense of safety or companion-ship, older people are commonly expected to move that is, to (serially) break up relationships, home and the social roles of a lifetime. Sometimes older people can appear at first to welcome the discontinuity; they may undertake it in the hope of securing a more meaningful environment in which to live. However, instead of finding companionship they may discover the loneliness of the aged ghetto, and simultaneously irrevocably lose the connections with their communities of interest.

This is in contrast with other groups in society who are increasingly being served by forms of assistance that mould around, and support, their normal lives in their own homes and communities. False beliefs that perpetuate this state of affairs include the following. 'Older people want to live in a retirement home; it's what old people do' – in reality, even in times when the idea of a 'retirement home' seemed to have positive connotations, it was neither attainable nor desirable for the majority of people and this remains so. 'Families don't, or don't want to, cope with providing assistance' is contradicted by the evidence that most families and friends do continue to provide assistance for their older relatives and friends. However, under pressure 'not to feel a burden' older people may often go along with life-changing discontinuities.

Positive psychology would take the approach of asking what would enable older disabled people to continue to pursue life in as ordinary a way as possible? Continuing to have a physical presence in the community is a necessary (though not a sufficient) factor for constructing and sustaining a valued (not just good enough) life.

Discontinuity in Relationships

Cultures and periods in history vary in their expectancies about what are typical valued relationships for older citizens. It is by no means universal, and in fact it is a relatively recent and restricted phenomenon to expect older persons to have and hold relationships primarily with other older people. It is certainly a phenomenon arising in the technologically oriented, rich countries in the post-Second World war era to expect persons who have a disability to share large parts of their lives with and to have relationships with other similarly disabled people. In other cultures and in other times, relationships across generations have been more diverse – perhaps as a result of less conflation of economic production with human worth, and greater emphasis on competency-enhancing and mutually efficacious cross-generational relationships.

The potential power of relationships to 'hold' the person with dementia is recognized now through theories of 'personhood' (Kitwood and Bredin, 1992; Sixsmith and Stillwell, 1993), which identify that personal growth can be retained within a favourable psychosocial environment irrespective of cognitive impairments.

Seen in Terms of Disability

For vulnerable people, such as those who have to rely on assistance (especially from services), the power of the language used about them can be life-defining. Even the use of a noun (e.g. 'the elderly', 'the functionals') instead of an adjective (e.g. 'older people', ' people with mental health needs') can have major effects on how the person is regarded by others, which in turn determines the opportunities that may be held open or closed off from the person. The simple choice of 'persons who are older' or 'persons who have disabilities related to dementia' communicates that the experience of old persons engaging with this service/society will encounter equal, non-coercive relationships with the people they meet, can expect to have their uniqueness as a person understood through becoming known as a person, and can expect assisting people to work in non-stereotyping and person-centred ways.

The challenge for positive psychology will be to understand how positive beliefs about ageing for example, belief in agency, and hope for the future (irrespective of disabilities) can change the course of a life.

Having One's Life 'Wasted'

A prevalent expectation about growing older is that life becomes empty of both achievements and satisfactions. Older people are expected to exist in the absence of challenges, stimulation, risks, demands and all the other things that make life a worthwhile experience. Waiting, filling time, sheltered activities, sheltered places, watered down or pretend occupation may be common experiences for many older people – it would not therefore be surprising if some expressed their experience through behavioural disturbance and show signs of emotional turmoil.

Phrases such as 'living on borrowed time', 'didn't expect to live this long', 'what else can I expect at this time of life', 'got to be grateful for what I've got' may suggest the extent to which empty time imposed on the older person becomes their internal view of the self. In addition, these negative evaluations are transmitted to staff and other caregivers for older people leaving them feeling demoralized about their role.

The challenge for positive psychology is to identify the ways in which many individuals manage to see their own ageing as transcending time, as having meaning that reaches beyond the self to the community and beyond the present to the future. If these beliefs relate to strong roles and 're-moralization' for ageing persons, they can be 'taught' to others and potentially prevent many negative experiences of growing older.

Blamed for the Problems, and Intimidated

Limited historical vision seems to result in a tendency for the preceding generation to be blamed for the 'evils' of the world inherited by the next generation. After all, 'they' created the values and the world of today, didn't they? To take this argument to its extreme, 'they' would also be blamed for the very 'ageism' in society from which they now suffer. In reality, there is no evidence that the individual has the power to change the attitudes of their society in the space of a few decades of life. Such changes historically take several generations, and even in response to the impact of a particularly influential individual there is a lag effect before change is incorporated into the culture and its beliefs.

In terms of health, older persons are likely to have the kinds of difficulties (e.g. long-term health problems, progressive conditions) for which technical solutions are not enough. This sets them up as threats to the 'cure' system and evidence of the failure of the technical 'fix'. The denial response is commonly to blame the older person, for example to describe them as 'unsuitable' for the treatment, or 'non-compliant' with the technology.

Picture the scene: a 75-year-old woman sits in a rehabilitation ward in a general hospital, after several months recovering from injuries following a mugging in the street. She is frail, and her entire hopes are around going home to her own home where she has lived for 40 years, and where she wants to feel safe again. She hopes that she has managed to hide from the doctors and nurses just how fragile her memory and other mental processes have become. She fears that they will use this as 'evidence against her' if she lets slip the front she is holding up. It is announced that there will be a 'home visit', with the OT and the family present, and that her performance on that visit will determine whether she can go home again or not. The person in this scene is living with the threat of the 'trial' home visit. Even if she 'passes' she will live under the shadow of

> *potential future failure; if she 'fails' and still insists on going home she risks being blamed. In these conditions a person is often intimidated into believing that they are to blame for 'failing' to be good enough for the system – then accepting a direction for their life, which is not desired and potentially damaging of self-esteem.*

A positive approach would be to ask 'What extra would it take to assist Mrs. X to stay at home and have a sense of security?' Instead the hospital service in this case was asking 'Can we use the discovery of more severe impairments of function as a lever to coerce her to accept a more secure option such as residential care'. The person who enters into a care home in such circumstances may be well on the way to becoming potentially the next 'problem behaviour' in care. When 'attention-seeking' is used as a description of behaviour, without concern to look for the need or message that lies behind it, the circle of blaming closes again.

'Outpacing' is another common mechanism by which the older person can be put under pressure, humiliated, threatened with failure and blamed for the problems. In a society where speed of processing is disproportionately highly valued, the person who is slow to respond is at risk of devaluation.

The positive approach is to identify in what ways a different and slower pace can be *advantageous*. For example, it might be conducive to good communication, supportive of nurturing and harmonious relationships, or valuable for enabling creativity.

The Cumulative Effects of Wounds

Wounds are essentially experiences of secondary and tertiary impairments. These experiences on a daily basis destroy people's self-esteem, confidence and hope. Having a stroke, fall or heart disease, for example, may precipitate experiences of 'secondary impairment'. No hope of escape from the initial problem, together with neglect of the rest of the person's life needs, which have been lost from sight behind the disability, can result in fear of being a 'burden' and at its worst in suicidal ideas.

The Role of the Unconscious

Technological advances have made the societies who hold them more able to be 'eugenic' in deciding who will be eligible for life-saving treatments, and more controlling in decisions about how those in pain will be treated. Wolfensberger has argued that the reality of wounding processes is 'death-making', and that this process is detoxified by euphemisms so that their true nature is not consciously seen (Wolfensberger, 1987, 1994). So, for example, the rhetoric surrounding care systems for older people may present the image of active, positive and life-enhancing (such as, 'rooting out ageism', 'dignified care', 'home for life', 'ageing in place', 'in the community'); however, it masks a reality where older disabled people are treated as different; required to use services that no other groups would tolerate as acceptable; have their biological needs met but without their personal and social needs being acknowledged; kept in institutional settings that would be rejected on behalf of other groups in society; and 'warehoused' away from mainstream life in a proliferation of institutions that are described (disingenuously) as 'in the community'. The concepts of 'care in the community' in social policy have become distorted and misconstrued, resulting in a situation of unchecked wounding of older people, particularly those made more vulnerable by having to rely on services (Hamarsnes, 2002).

However, older persons themselves are not the only ones to experience the wounding process. Those people who provide care for them (in particular those with very disabling conditions, such as dementia) also share the experience. It is common for such people to feel demoralized, hopeless and unable to find a positive meaning in what they do. They attend training courses, in search of 'answers', new technology and the 'fix' for the problems. If they are lucky they will find some sharing of experience and validation of ideas. They are 'containing' and carrying the same experiences and wounds as the older persons they serve. They are in the position to be aware of both the social policy rhetoric and the reality on the ground, and to see clearly the gap between the two. Morale is traditionally low, and training (because it is consciousness-raising) has the effect (opposite from that intended) of making it even more difficult in the long term to sustain morale.

There is frequently a contradiction between the goals which services say they have (such as, to support older persons in the community) and actually what they do. Observation of what services do, and how they deliver it, reveals the opposite of a 'community care' model –- they sort people into categories according to levels of disability, and then spend significant resources on the definitions of these categories and on the 'training' of staff to fit these different categories. They then expend further resources on moving people from one cat-egory of service to another as their needs increase or change. Take as example persons with dementia who begin to press the help-bell in their room repeat-edly. The behaviour is typically construed as a 'symptom' of the dementia, and the service manager seeks a further 'assessment' ostensibly to help cope with the behaviour. In fact, 'assessment' is commonly a euphemism for 'remove the nuisance behaviour, or person'. To preserve the 'rules', the 'misfit' individuals are moved on – euphemistically, to elsewhere, which 'will better meet their needs'.

Societies can only behave in such ways because of denial, and unwillingness to own the death-making potential of their customs and practices towards old people. In this context, the positive question to be asked in services concerns how such wounding might be prevented or the damage limited. This is where positive psychology offers real alternatives to the clinician, in place of the customary approach of symptom alleviation.

The New Paradigm of Ageing

Positive psychology does not ignore the reality of the wounding process, but it does indicate that much can be learnt from focussing on goals beyond mere symptom alleviation or disability management. There may be much greater proportional benefits to be gained by planning with the person around achieving 'beyond baseline' goals for example, supporting friendships and developing a healthy lifestyle (irrespective of co-existing disability).

Assisting people to define and pursue a desirable future requires commitment, an openness of mind, a highly developed empathic skill and a willingness to think outside of existing service policies. It requires the recognition that secondary impairments can be prevented, and that initial impairments can be used to work for us not against us in building relationships around older people with disabilities. Positive goals foster good morale for those providing care or support.

This model requires a willingness to abandon the denial and avoidance that surround death. It requires journeying alongside the older person, and open acknowledgement of the issues that they face. It requires the positive belief that such encounters are genuinely contributing to the foundations of a strong society and are paving the way for persons of the next generations to live their lives free from denial and dehumanization. It may require at the clinical or personal level enabling the older disabled person to give over responsibility for other people's pain. People who say they feel a 'burden' and want to die are taking responsibility (or being made to take responsibility) for other's distress. Being able to allow 'the other' to own their own pain can be a major achievement in later life, positive for both older individuals and their successors.

Maturing and communities

In global ecology terms, it is said that the presence of a vulnerable species is an indicator of a healthy local environment. The same can be said of the presence of vulnerable groups in a society as an index of 'community health'. We might consider such societies to be achieving maturity.

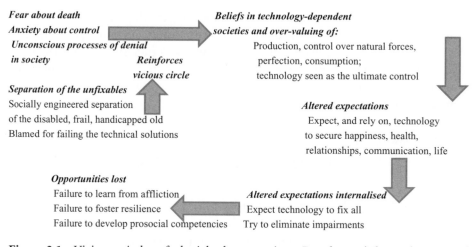

Fear about death
Anxiety about control
 Unconscious processes of denial
   in society

Separation of the unfixables
Socially engineered separation
of the disabled, frail, handicapped old
Blamed for failing the technical solutions

Reinforces
vicious circle

Beliefs in technology-dependent
societies and over-valuing of:
   Production, control over natural forces,
     perfection, consumption;
   technology seen as the ultimate control

Altered expectations
   Expect, and rely on, technology
   to secure happiness, health,
     relationships, communication, life

Opportunities lost
   Failure to learn from affliction
   Failure to foster resilience
   Failure to develop prosocial competencies

Altered expectations internalised
   Expect technology to fix all
   Try to eliminate impairments

Figure 2.1 Vicious circle of denial about ageing. Based on 'The Relevance of Role Expectancy and Role Circularity to Deviancy-Making and Deviancy-Unmaking' Wolfensberger, W and Thomas, S, 1983, Canadian NIMR. Reproduced by permission of Wolf Wolfensberger.

In contrast, there are societies within which individual 'perfection' serves as the overarching goal of life; here strong forces separate off the 'unfixables' and those who are too close to death for comfort. We might consider these societies to be underdeveloped and immature in respect of the kind of community strength referred to earlier. History has repeatedly shown that societies that are overly focused on a single, over-arching belief tend to require to be maintained by social structures whose purpose is the continued repression of what is incompatible with the beliefs of the society, and that apartheid or separation of social groups makes for intrinsically unstable and unsound societies. Figure 2.1 shows the potential connections between technology dependence (in pursuing individual perfection) and the destabilization of the society.

In a positive psychology context we would seek to answer such questions as 'What *competencies* are there in the society to cope with diverse forms of existence (such as disability, ageing and death) without the need for denial and repression?'

Maturing and individuals

Individuals can, of course, have a positive experience of ageing even within a relatively age-hostile social environment – arguably, technological advances have made 'developed' societies more able to eliminate their 'unfixables'. The positive experiences that come out of having to live with a disability are lost on many people who may think of themselves as 'able-bodied'. In reality, however, Smith (2003) has argued that each and every one of us is no more than temporarily able-bodied (i.e. all of us are 'TABs').

Taking every opportunity to support an older person in their choice to live in their own home in their own community, and to die there in dignity, is a straightforward but powerful way in which to build strength into communities. In this way everyone benefits, by learning how to deal openly with fears about death and anxieties about increased dependence. People learn through observing another human being encounter a difficulty and witnessing their responses. Open awareness contexts provide the opportunities for mutually supportive communication and for trusting relationships in the face of distress and death.

Smail has argued that 'growing up' is a process of developing the capacity to 'take care' of one another in a society, instead of developing reliance on artificial supports such as psychological or chemical therapies (Smail, 1987, 2001). Since that time the person-centred approach has developed in clinical use, bringing with it a new and positive definition of therapeutic goals that is more in keeping with Smail's challenge.

A person-centred framework for understanding needs

The frequency of the use of the word 'person-centred' in health and in personal and social services for older people, over the last decade of the twentieth and the first part of the twenty-first century, has risen significantly. Where once the term would have had use limited to services for people with learning disabilities, its range began to extend and now it is reasonably common to see the term appear in documentation relating to training programmes in services for older people and people with different disabilities. However, its use and meaning can vary, and can be susceptible to superficial use without full acceptance of the responsibility for the meaning of the word. For example, it has been increasingly common in the past several decades to find words such as 'dignity', 'choice' and 'person-centred' appear in the goals and mission statements of services for people with learning disabilities, when the reality on the ground has been that people do not have access to choices, dignity or person-centred life experiences in the same ways or to the same degree that ordinary persons in the mainstream of society have such experiences allocated to them. Accordingly, it is important to first understand in pragmatic terms what 'personhood' means, and what it would feel like and look like in real-life contexts.

The concept of 'personhood' was identified and formally introduced into the discourse on services for people with dementia largely by a psychologist, Tom

Kitwood (Kitwood, 1993, 1997; Kitwood and Bredin, 1992). The definition used by him emphasizes that personhood is interpersonal and arises from the dynamic process of the 'person in a social context':

> It is a standing or status bestowed upon one human being, by others, in the context of relationship and social being. It implies recognition, respect and trust. Both the according of personhood, and the failure to do so, have consequences that are empirically testable. (Kitwood, 1997, page 8)

This definition, applied to the understanding of dementia, is very powerful as an alternative to the medical model of dementia since it encourages and enables people to look to interpersonal 'solutions' instead of to technical fixes in 'the temple of biomedical science' (Kitwood, 1997, page 8).

The term 'person-focused' is used instead by Cheston and Bender (1999); this is to emphasize that the relationship between the person and the social context is active and interactive. Where 'bestowing' may imply a one-way street between the social context and the person, Cheston and Bender see the relationship in terms of active struggle to maintain identity (i.e. sense of personhood) and active problem-solving and coping. Their descriptions of the person-focused approach include the following:

> . . . this person-focused approach . . . describes how people with dementia struggle to maintain their identities and develop coping strategies that are formed from and by their diminished cognitive abilities.
>   . . . the need to focus on the feelings and beliefs of the person with dementia rather than the views of a relative or a professional. (Cheston and Bender, 1999, page 17)

As already represented in the definitions, it is clear that the first ground-breaking thinking about person-centred models in services for older people emanated from the world of 'dementia care'. This is likely to be for a combination of reasons. The experience of dementia is arguably the most painful of any of the disabilities encountered in later life; accordingly, it strikes a chord in the wider population. It has been relatively common for services, and community representation, surrounding people with dementia to have a separate identity. This kind of intense focus did not develop in relation to older people with arthritis or stroke disease, for example, leaving the discourse around these disabilities much more in the organic approach. In addition, psychologists have been working in mental health services for older people in sufficient numbers and for sufficient time to have developed alternative models of dementia, which were regarded broadly as more helpful and more appropriate than the mechanistic, organic models previously available.

The most highly developed and coherent applications of 'person-centred' principles remain, however, within services for people with learning disabilities and to some extent also in the world of adults with mental health problems or physical disabilities. Their presence there takes the form of community *action and service planning*, which is in contrast to the more conceptual or intellectual stage of raised awareness that we see in services for older people with dementia. The language in the learning disabilities world is of 'person-centred planning', and the definitions all clearly identify implementation and practical action. For example:

> The purpose of person-centered planning is learning through shared action. People who engage in person centered planning may produce documentation of their meetings, proposals, contract specifications, or budgets. These are only footprints: the path is made by people walking together.
>
> Person centered planning aims to change common patterns of community life. ... Person centered planning stimulates community hospitality and enlists community members in assisting focus people to define and work towards a desirable future. (O'Brien and Lovett, 1992, page 2).

The Implications of the Person-Centred Paradigm for the Relationships between Services and the Persons They Serve

The relationship between a service and the persons it serves is wholly shaped by the definition and understanding of 'need' that the service adopts. Paul Williams' (2003) definition is particularly clear as a definition of need on which we can base person-centred planning.

> The question to be asked about 'need' is:
>
> How do I need my community to respond to my experiences (of disablement, oppression, marginalisation, or other suffering) in my best interests *and* to create community competence? (Williams, 2003)

The features of 'person-centred planning', which take it beyond the concepts of 'personhood' and 'person focused' are listed below:

1. *It is action oriented that is, raising awareness is not enough.* It focuses on action through the social and physical environment, not on changing the person. It acknowledges that the objective for change is not the alleviation of symptoms (e.g., of dementia) but the environmental potential for retaining for the person meaningful relationships, roles and presence in the community of life.

2. *It is about building competent community.* The community is as much the focus and beneficiary as the individual concerned. The community and individuals in it become more competent as a result of having the opportunity to relate to and hold the presence of a person in their midst who is living with for example, mental health problems, physical disabilities or the cognitive disabilities of dementia or stroke. Their experiences, as human beings living with supremely challenging difficulties, add to the pool of community resource on which all members can then draw.

3. *Its goals are to improve people's chances for a desirable life experience.* The latter is easy to define since we are surrounded by evidence of what is desirable by the ordinary citizen in the ordinary mainstream community. *Desirable life experience* in later life is not something special – it is what is 'desirable' generally in the culture (such things as having one's own home, having a sense of one's life being connected to others who are meaningful to us, having a presence in our community and having roles that are reciprocated and respected in our community). The value of 'life' cannot be measured, either by years or by the spurious concept of 'quality of life'. The concept of 'maximizing a person's chances of a desirable future' is the antithesis of 'quality of life'. 'Quality of life' is hard to define while 'desirable life' is easy to define (it is observable in the person's history and in the culture). 'Quality of life' is arbitrary, and its definition and cut-offs are created by the particular culture or technology. 'Quality of life' is a concept that, if we once entertain it, takes us on the path to not only judging different as 'poor' but also on the risky road to eugenic measures to eliminate those judged as 'poor'. 'Desirable life' is a concept that values all life and does not judge some lives to be less worth living than others. It gives clear practical goals for interventions, namely, to secure arrangements by which the chances of retaining (or rebuilding) the 'good things in life' for the focus person are enhanced, maximized or otherwise protected – the 'good things' being social presence, meaningful relationships, unambiguous support, self identity – in other words all those things that cannot be measured but which support the people's natural resilience in the face of adverse experiences in life. 'Quality of life' panders to the compulsion of many materialistic, technologically dependent cultures to measure and, possibly, thereby to control things. Even those things that makes no sense to measure tend to be subjected to measurement in our materialistic technological ways of thinking – measuring becomes a form of obscuring and obfuscating from the real issue. 'Desirable life' is easy to see, as it is roughly the same, non-materialistic things that are held in high value by other citizens. It is amenable to open and transparent goal-setting with the person concerned. We must distinguish between what is the statistical norm for a group in society and what is desirable (valued) by the group. For example, racial apartheid within a country may result in a situation

where it is statistically normative for one group in the population to be, say, congregated together in large groups or unemployed. But this does not mean that this is a valued way of life – we must look to the wider culture, and to comparative cultures to discern what conditions of life are generally valued, and to see how some groups have simply been excluded by some process of social engineering from accessing these valued states. The same argument applies to older people, who may appear to live to a different (often reduced) set of life conditions compared to their fellow citizens, for example, living in residential care homes, having medical labels dominate their lives and being required to uproot themselves every time their needs for support change. However, this does not reflect a different set of life values; it is simply that these people have capitulated to their exclusion from 'the good things in life' in the name of seeking a lower order goal that is (commonly) to find help with personal and household care.

4. *It requires from those involved in it collaborative action and non-coercive relationships with the people they are planning with.* This will require a willingness to challenge the service practices that separate people and perpetuate controlling relationships; and a commitment to sustained search for effective ways to deal with difficult barriers and conflicting demands.

5. *It is not 'just another technique' but a pathway to personal growth for all of us.* To use Wesley Smith's term, those of us who may think ourselves 'able-bodied' are actually TABs. Our privilege is to be allowed to live alongside and work with people who are already living with a disability, and to learn with and plan with them. The ways they discover for living with their disability will be visible for others to witness. Through this the pressure to 'cope well' (and feeling a failure if we do not 'cope well') will be modified, and in its place will be the importance of discovering our own way to live with those things in life that stretch us all and come to us all.

In the context of the deeply rooted organic and medical models in services for older people (especially but not exclusively those with disabilities) the impact of 'personhood' and 'person focused' has been mainly at the level of the individual practitioner. There is no doubt that these approaches have made vast differences to significant numbers of people, both those with dementia and those who support them. However, what is crucial is to change practices and policies, not simply to change the language used to understand older people's painful experiences, nor to 'make things better' for older people in institutions.

If a society is serious about shifting to the person-centred paradigm in its transactions with its older members, the first step will be signing up to older people having their fair share of the 'desirable' things in life (i.e. the same things others regard as desirable). The services fit for such an enlightened society will be systematically different from those we are familiar with. The practical changes will include the following:

- to move beyond the institution
- to stop practices which segregate and congregate people because of age or because of disability
- to enlist the community in forming and sustaining meaningful relationships with older people in the knowledge that to fail to do so will little benefit those older people we seek to assist
- to define staff roles and responsibilities such that uncertainty or conflict about what is desirable or possible for the focus person is accepted, and becomes part of the work of planning
- to provide a forum for person centred planning in which those who plan with the focus person, the person themselves, and members enlisted from the community work towards a desirable future in a spirit of open acceptance
- to change the ways in which those who assist spend money, such that they are not in controlling relationships, but rather are able to act instrumentally to pursue the goals that have been planned together

The Myth of 'Evidence' in the New Paradigm and in Service Change

The concepts around person-centred care represent an entirely 'new paradigm' (Kitwood, 1997), which opens up new and sometimes startling implications for our understanding of how to deliver services that can support older people who have to live with impairments, disabilities and losses, without damaging those persons in the process. Certainly, this can be threatening to those who have a vested interest in maintaining the paradigms which prevail – in the main, the medical and the mechanistic/technological paradigms. The obstacles to developing services in the 'new' paradigm may be rooted in and maintained by the unconsciousness that prevails about the traditional services – an avoidance of awareness about their wounding impact on older people's lives, and about the fragility of the evidence on which they themselves are based.

The 'evaluation myth' is a powerful obstacle familiar to those who may have attempted to put in place a new paradigm programme in health or social services. Historically, traditional forms of services and their models of delivery, such as hospital long-term care, residential care, 'home helps' and 'home meals delivery' simply evolved – there was no evaluation, and no evidence base, although they came to consume all the mainstream resources allocated in a society for a given user group. To the extent that there is any evidence about the worth of traditional forms of service, it has been collected post hoc, and tends to be negative. For instance, the population in residential homes has a higher rate of depression (Copeland et al., 1992), hospitals have a higher risk of falls (Leipzig, Cummings and Tinetti, 1999) and the quality of life of our community-dwelling older citizens is damaged by social isolation and negative attitudes leading to poor self-esteem and self-blame (Coleman, Aubin, Robinson, Ivani-Chalian and Briggs, 1993). However, a practitioner or change agent wanting to re-arrange the form or delivery of service in the new paradigm is required to provide evidence that this form will be desired, effective and efficient for the purpose. Similar scrutiny is not, on the contrary, directed to the existing models of service or their delivery, which continue to swallow up the mainstream budgets of older people's services; they continue on the basis of historical inertia, but without evidence that they are achieving, or are even capable of achieving, the desired life goals of the older people they serve.

The *'evidence block'* is a second powerful obstacle familiar to those who have experience of attempting to lead change in non-acute human services (usually called long-term care, continuing care or such like). The 'evidence addiction' serves as a focussing mechanism, conveniently excluding values-based arguments from consideration, and doing so in an apparently justifiable way. It works like this. For most people, generally those who are not viewed as disabled or otherwise different, certain things in life are regarded as an 'ordinary' part of life and not requiring special justification – having one's own home, a range of friends, a variety of different places in which to spend the day or week, boundaries between work/leisure/home life, contacts with people we choose not just with people thrust upon us, and so on. For some people, in this case older people who have to rely on others for assistance, those same things in life are regarded as dispensable; the way services are arranged necessitates those older people who have to rely on them to give up one or several of these 'ordinary' things. The 'values-based' principle would say that there are some things in life for which evidence should not be asked that is, they are 'ordinary' basic things expected in the life of any citizen, without which human life would not thrive. Such things generally fall into those categories which the new paradigm recognizes to be as essential as air to breathe or water to drink, such as relationships, participation, a sense of being valued and part of the community. On the other hand, in the context of the predominance of the medical–mechanistic paradigm these same things are regarded as secondary to biomedical goals, and sometimes as even dispensable in their pursuit. This can be observed in instances where older people who need assistance are expected to be content with relationships exclusively with other older disabled people, in order that other goals (usually physical e.g., nutrition, sleep and personal care) can be fulfilled in the way that suits current service delivery models. If the change agent is intent on addressing these interpersonal needs within services, they are met with requests to 'provide evidence' that addressing such needs will be 'effective and efficient' in the delivery of the care for the persons concerned. What is normative and expected for some is perceived as extraordinary and in need of justification for others in a society. This usually reflects the *us–them* divide, where what is regarded as ordinary and necessary for *us*, is given a different status for *them*, and extra 'evidence' requested that for example *they* would be damaged by doing without it, or that by having it their health would be measurably improved. Having a home of our own, varied contacts and access to friends, is not justified in the mainstream world in terms of being good for health (although it may be!); it is seen as a natural part of living, just as eating and drinking is, and as such is not subjected to any question about evidence. For services to be delivered to a paradigm which is blind to such core aspects of living, results in some disabled older people having significant life goals denied, and consequently being forced to live with feelings of turmoil and a sense of deprivation. Exposed to this experience on a daily basis the vicious circle closes, and the person is pushed to make the false interpretation that they themselves must be the cause of their problems.

'*The effectiveness god*'. Deciding on effectiveness is not value-free. The outcome measures selected reflect underlying values. For example, a care environment that focuses on achieving a low 'number of falls per year' might seem to be 'effective' in caring for disabled older people; however, this may mask a failure to achieve other more important outcomes such as the promotion of mobility, citizenship, participation and freedom from restraint. The problem with the 'effectiveness god' is that it generally directs our attention (a) to things which are *easy to measure* and (b) to things that are *problems*. In the traditional paradigm services for older people are commonly focused on such effectiveness measures; for example, they may aim 'to reduce problem behaviours in dementia', 'to reduce the number of falls' or 'to minimize episodes of wandering'. In many instances however the most effective method of achieving the stated aim will not be the most valued – that is, will risk doing damage to other aspects of the person's life. The most 'effective' method for getting rid of 'problem behaviours' with dementia might be to use medication (as measured by the number of incidents of problem behaviour) – but this is not the same as the most valued way. The most 'effective' method for getting rid of the anxiety of neighbours and of eliminating episodes of 'wandering' might be to admit the person with dementia to hospital (as measured by the number of phone calls from neighbours or the number of episodes of walking outside the home) – but this is not the same as the most valued method or the one which, in the long term, would increase the overall capacity of the community and services to support people with dementia.

Making Choices – A Valued Life Versus Effectiveness of Technology

If a method is available that would effectively eliminate or control a problem (e.g. drugs or locked accommodation) but it would damage the person's valued roles, status and place in the community, new paradigm services would not choose that approach, no matter how effective it is, and would always seek an alternative approach to address the problems. For example, even if the technology existed to effectively treat behaviour 'problems' in persons with dementia or stroke by means of say admission to special care units, the new paradigm would always choose a course of intervention that before all else protected the person's social and personal presence (relationships, and so on), would respond to the behaviour problems with methods effective within this environment and would actively choose *not* to use the *special care* option (no matter how effective on the single issue of behaviour) on the grounds that the ensuing intrusion on and destruction of important human dimensions of life would be unjustifiable. Although primarily protecting the community roles, respect and self-respect of the person the new paradigm service will give serious consideration to alleviating the 'problems'; however it would not resort to intrusive methods even if it takes longer to, or does not at all, eliminate the 'problem behaviour'. It may ultimately require other persons to change their behaviour, for example by increasing their tolerance of 'problem behaviours' in the community, and it will usually mean enlisting other persons from the community in a practical way. Hence, new paradigm services give greater emphasis to the outcomes of 'community life' and 'desired life', and regard 'effectiveness' as only properly measured if it focuses on achievements in these dimensions. Clearly the new paradigm approach will utilize technologies, in relation to say 'problem behaviour' in dementia, but will never use them if they will create a major obstacle to maintaining community and social presence, and will always put energy into creating alternatives whether 'solutions' or increased tolerance of the behaviour.

In services for person-centred care, the priorities are fundamentally re-arranged. The demand for evidence will require to be seen as a separate, and not always entirely relevant, issue. Where it is valued in a society to live in one's own home (ordinary members of the society who are free to express their choices, choose this for themselves), it is not necessary to 'prove that home care is better than hospital care'. This is a distraction, and a false comparison. Rather than 'Is home care better than hospital care?' the question should be "Knowing that living in one's own home in one's own community is a valued and desirable condition of life in our society, how can more robust forms of non-intrusive support and care be designed so that we can become more competent as a society and in our local communities in supporting older people with particular needs or disabilities in achieving the good side of life?' Where the service mission is to support the older person in 'an ordinary life', the business of the service is to get to know the previous patterns of life for that individual, which will be evident from their previous life, and this will set the goals for their personal support. Chasing 'evidence' about the comparative 'effectiveness' of Institution Type 1 versus Institution Type 2 is a meaningless question from the user perspective; it is so badly missing the point as to forget the *person* whose needs generated the building of these temples of care in the first place. It has, of course, generated series of research undertakings, only because much research is allowed to take place in a so-called values free context. It generates the kinds of questions on which the research institutions depend.

In the new paradigm, the particular forms in which the assistance is delivered will follow the principle of least intrusion and least damage to the person's previous patterns of life. Thus forms of assistance will be expected which will not deny, and in fact will primarily address, person-centred needs as against biological needs; the latter will be regarded as important because of supporting and being essential to person-centred needs, but not as predominant. The demand for evidence will need to be removed where it is used as a discriminatory instrument i.e. where it is used as a reason for perpetuating forms of service and of delivery which deny or do not address the most important life needs of the older person.

It is crucial to make distinctions between the following very different kinds of issues (Wolfensberger, 2003).

Ethical issues

Questions that are about ethical or values matters should not and cannot be answered by empirical (scientific) means, although people may mistakenly attempt to take this route in an era where science is the dominant mode of thought. Ethical issues are matters of morality, and may be debated at a level that is trans-cultural. An ethical question might be, for example, 'Is retribution or reform the purpose of prisons?' or 'Is the right of the individual or the right of the community more important?'

Values issues

Values are associated with the culture and are not absolute, but are related to the particular culture. They can be deciphered by observation of the mainstream life of communities within the culture and by discerning what are the desirable conditions for life within that culture for citizens who themselves are valued. Examples of values questions might be:- 'For the ordinary (valued) person within the society what are the desirable conditions of life? – regarding who we live with (to have our own home is valued), regarding our choice of who we regard as friends (to choose our own, usually not all the same age or disability condition as ourselves, is valued) or regarding routine and habits (to practice our own is valued and not the routines that suit an institution) and so on'; 'What group in the society is deemed to have lower value, that it might be expected to clear up after a nuclear accident, or give up its rights to the good side of life (home, family, friends, meaningful occupation, money)?'

Empirical issues

Empirical questions are answered by scientific means, and will usually be in a quantifiable form. They are never morality-free or values-free, and this is of course a cause of major debate in the case of some controversial technological 'advances'. In contrast to the values question earlier, for example, an empirical question would be 'What groups or individuals are likely to survive longest after exposure to nuclear fallout?' 'Do losses in relation to 'the good side of life' have the same or different impact on the mental health of older as compared to younger adults?'

The 'sanctity of life' issue

To follow Smith (2003) we need to ask the question:

'Does every life have value?' (i.e. intrinsically, and irrespective of any other considerations.)

If the answer is YES, then we follow the path to 'How can we become better at making and protecting a desirable life for our fellows including those who are different from us, who are older, more ill or disabled, and who as a result are at risk of devaluation and/or exclusion from the good side of life?' (a new paradigm approach).

If the answer is NO, then we follow the path to a narrow obsession with measuring and defining 'quality of life', to redefining those less worthwhile lives in negative ways (e.g. 'too much suffering', 'wouldn't want to be like that') and ultimately to justifying the elimination of the 'less worthwhile' lives. Euthanasia is a concept that is more popular with the able-bodied and those who have not themselves experienced significant and perhaps life-threatening states. It is virtually absent among those who know what it is like to live with impairment, or who have a child who is seriously disabled. On the occasions when individuals have directed that they do not wish resuscitation in the event of acquiring brain damage (for example after an accident), there is almost always a change of mind in the event of this actually happening (Smith, 2003a, 2003b). Life becomes valued for itself, and disability is seen as something that can be lived with.

The experience of disability (our own and others') teaches us to live fully; the experience of dying teaches us to live. These are values statements, and are also confirmed by empirical scrutiny (de Hennezel, 1997).

One: Person Centred planning for quality interventions requires four steps interlinked.

1. Identify key people in key roles
E.g. family, neighbours,
friends, people who are having a
good experience in ageing

2. Decide what "quality" means
Not only desirable personal future
(e.g. person surrounded by people
they trust) but also desirable
community future (e.g. community
will acquire more competence
and experience less denial)

3. Constructive actions
A real change in the quality of at least
one person's experience ... *and* ...
a significant improvement in the
competence and understanding of
other important people

4. Learn from constructive actions
Widen the circle of people involved,
who see value in the experience of
ageing and opportunity for growth

STRATEGY The role of services is to support the older person and their friends/family in such a way as to achieve:

☐ valued connections between people irrespective of generation or age
☐ new connections between people such as will focus on the person not the disability in later life
☐ more open competent communities, able to see later life as desirable and meaningful to the community and competent to live in an integrated way with older people with disabilities.

Support not supplant: The service focus is on increasing opportunities in the particular community to value and to live *with* ageing persons, and disabled older persons, not to take the place of that support. Services that miss the COMMUNITY out of the loop are likely to institutionalise care, whether in the community or in special buildings. The triangle below identifies this vision of the process of support.

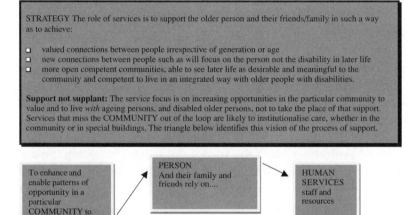

Two: Identifying and measuring desired outcomes for service users

With reference to the four life areas overleaf:
1. What are desirable outcomes for the older person and for the particular community under each of the four life areas?
2. What are the consequences of *not* accomplishing these – for the person and for the community?

Figure 2.2   Person-centred planning with an older person who relies on services. Based on O'Brien, J and Lyle, C, *Framework,* 1986. Reproduced with permission of Responsive Systems Associates, Decatur, Georgia.

Relating PEOPLE to PLACES
Does the service serve people in natural settings and in the use of ordinary community resources? E.g. Disabled older person attends social club in village hall along with everyone else.

Relating PEOPLE to other PEOPLE
Does the service support the person's relationships with their family, friends, and other generations, including past relationships and those that may outlive the person? E.g. Disabled older person meets and mixes with successfully ageing people with support as necessary.

Relating PEOPLE to ACTIVITIES and TIME
Does the service support people in the same sorts of activities, for the same purposes, and at the same time as non-disabled or other older adults E.g. Disabled older person takes part in local whist drive with support as necessary not at 'special' time or on 'special' activities.

Relating PEOPLE to IMAGES and SYMBOLS
What messages are put out by the language, surroundings, staff and others that the service involves (see Tables 1.2, 5.2 and 5.7) E.g. Disabled older person is invited to make a presentation to local Rotary Club on experience of business with support as necessary.

Three: An example with an older person with significant cognitive disabilities

1. Reframe the PROBLEM ⟶ as a NEED
E.g. Saying 'No' repeatedly may indicate *I need to feel Ican trust the people around me*

2. Who is the PERSON?
- use Getting To Know You
- use ordinary interactions in natural settings
- use friends, network, peers
Summarise your sense of WHO the person is

5. If means not available or community not competent enough
WHAT WOULD IT TAKE TO BUILD COMMUNITY CONFIDENCE AND COMPETENCE? E.g. involve families who have good experiences of caring for someone with dementia in planning services

4. Even if technologies are available to 'fix the problems' in effective efficient ways (e.g. drugs, institutions, special care) WHAT WOULD IT TAKE TO HOLD THIS PERSON IN THE COMMUNITY?
in the belief that having an ordinary life, in ordinary places, mixing with different other people is essential for life
The *least intrusive* principle says these would not be used.

3. WHAT WOULD IT TAKE TO WORK TOWARDS A DESIRABLE EXPERIENCE AND MAKE THE COMMUNITY MORE COMPETENT?
1. What is currently happening?
2. What are the 2nd and 3rd levels of damage that are happening for this person? E.g. isolation technologies
3. What would it take to prevent or reverse the 2nd and 3rd levels of damage? E.g. involve people who have a good experience of ageing
4. Summarise what a *desirable experience* for this person's later life would be and how we might work towards it. E.g. plan support such that the person can achieve life goals/share in ordinary places, people, activities and times.

Figure 2.2   (*Continued*)

General Principles of Psychological Interventions with Older People

1. Ask the question '*What are the second and third levels of impairment that are happening for this person in this situation?*' Almost always these will outweigh the first level of impairment (the original problem) whether it be mental, physical or social in nature. These may include ageism, but will likely also involve rejection, distancing, denial, self-blame and alienation/loss of identity. Focus on these second and third levels as they *can be* changed and meaning restored to life.
2. *Focus on supporting 'the person' in their 'own' experience of their life*, and this will assist them in living with the loss or disabilities they have encountered.
3. If I am being asked to do something by a service or by the community in relation to an older person, ask '*Is this for the benefit of the person?*' that is, will it support or enhance their valued social roles, social status, connections with others who are meaningful in their life or the competence of the community to provide the same? *If not – do not do it!*
4. Particularly with changes in life status that historically in the culture have been life-changing, such as in dementia, use the *Person-Centred Planning Map* to help formulate and design your plan for intervention. Keep referring to this plan to monitor and to keep track. Figure 2.2 illustrates the steps and questions by which to monitor what is being achieved for the older person concerned.

3
Assessment in the New Paradigm

An Ecological Framework for the New Paradigm

Historically in societies, many of the institutions of law and medicine have been built up from individual cases. Cases of similar kinds tend to aggregate and thereby enable patterns of response, which become incorporated in the laws or medical categories of societies. Clearly, there is a benefit in this system of classificatory approach for the society and for the institutions of law and medicine, as it can be tied to principles for responding to individuals' behaviours. Without it, societies would lack the means for behaving systematically and would no doubt respond more slowly and less effectively. Without a classificatory approach, no case law and no diagnostic categories of illness would be built; consequently there would be no way to proceed systematically in treating individuals – there would be no means for the implementation of 'fairness' or the distribution of 'public assistance' in a society.

The Legacy of the Classificatory Approach

Classification has enabled societies to progress and to develop laws that are 'fair' and medical treatments that are effective in combating disease and illness. However, classification is intrinsically a subjective procedure, and there have been many examples historically in societies where classification has been used to convey, or impose, the ideas of the time rather than to reflect the aggregated facts. For example, weeping and wailing as a behaviour might have been classified as 'evil' at one time in history, then at a later time classified as 'morally weak', 'deviant', or 'illness' – and later again classified as 'normal coping'. Classifications 'fit' the prevailing concepts of the time. The classification and naming of the behaviour would have been viewed in these different lights depending on the era and culture in which they were expressed. In a culture whose constructs are dominated by religious belief or church institution, the expression of distress would be likely to be 'explained' in terms of 'evil' or 'spirits'. In a culture where the dominant constructs of the time are medical, then the same behaviour patterns are likely to be 'explained' as illness. Hence, many diverse and different patterns of behaviour, which would once have been deemed 'evil' or 'illness', are now seen pragmatically as a human coping response to stress or a reaction to trauma. Stark examples exist. Before the turn of the twentieth century, conscientious objection (the refusal to fight or go to war) was a behaviour categorized as 'criminal'; the associated societal response was that those expressing such behaviours were executed, or at different times imprisoned and humiliated. In the earlier part of the twentieth century, around the end of World War I, the same behaviours were categorized as 'illness'; the associated societal response was to place those expressing such behaviours in hospital-style buildings with treatment from medical personnel. By the second half of the twentieth century societal concepts had again changed so that these same behaviours could be portrayed in the popular culture as 'comically sane'. The 'catch 22' situation in the Joseph Heller novel of the same name is that behaviour that shows unwillingness to fight is evidence of sanity (and hence of fitness to fight). Hence the same behaviour that was once treated as criminal is seen a few decades on as intelligent and inspirational.

Dementia is accompanied by what are seen as 'odd' behaviours and it is unsurprising therefore that the medical approach has been used to classify these behaviours as if they are symptoms of the illness. This helps to match behaviour categories with management options and treatments, although arguably it misses the point that behaviour in illness is many other things, such coping responses, problem solving, and communication about the experience of the illness.

In recent years, for example, practitioners have argued that dementia is better understood as a disability. This paradigm shift enables those who work with people with dementia to ask questions that can be answered. Instead of asking 'What is the diagnosis?' people can ask 'What skills are compromised?' and 'What would it take to make the most of the skills there are, to assist adaptation, reduce stress and support valued social roles and relationships?'

Classifications are Historically Expedient and can Change

Definitions can change according to current pressures in the society. For example, the definition of Alzheimer's disease in the *Diagnostic and Statistical Manual of*

Mental Disorders, Fourth Edition (DSM IV) (American Psychiatric Association, 2000) has changed and broadened from the DSM of the 1970s. It is suggested that the reasons for this shift are as much to do with increasing the possibilities of securing funding for medical research as to do with the understanding or treatment of the condition (Cheston and Bender, 1999). The classificatory approach has been a vehicle for extending medical territory. An example was the use of classifications of learning/developmental disabilities in the past (e.g. 'moron', 'imbecile', 'low grade', 'high grade') as means of medicalizing the understanding, the research and the services.

The classificatory approach can also result in avoidance of undesirable territory – as seen in the dispute about 'personality disorder'. Although recognized as a category, there is the argument that it is not treatable medically and therefore should not be a medical/health responsibility. In this way people who are potentially costly to support and therefore undesirable as a group are diverted elsewhere.

Although dementia is as importantly a psychosocial problem and a disability as it is an illness it has been taken into the medical paradigm. This can draw attention away from understanding that challenging behaviours in dementia are often either communicating the person's experience (needs, feelings, intent, aspirations, etc.) or problem solving in reaction to the limitations the person now faces. The traditional medical paradigm construction of these behaviours as symptoms can limit our thinking. At one extreme it can result in overprescribing and inappropriate use of psychotropic medications (McGrath and Jackson, 1996). At the other it can blinker our everyday sensitivities, so that we fail to receive the messages being sent by the person with dementia, and add to their sense of isolation and invalidation.

Classificatory Creep

Classificatory creep happens when the classificatory approach is used on *people* rather than on the patterns of behaviours or symptoms. So, whenever we witness the use of category names such as 'the middle class', 'townie', 'refugee', 'asylum seeker', 'Jew', 'Christian', 'Muslim', 'dement', 'patient' or 'the elderly', we are witnessing the process by which one aspect, or dimension, of a person's life is used to classify or categorize important things about them as a person – to the extent that there is a serious risk of *the person* being entirely subsumed by the descriptor label, or classification. It follows that classificatory creep is most likely to be harmful when it is denied or there is failure to recognize its existence. The difference between 'the elderly' and 'a person in later life' is significant. The 'elderly' conveys a notion of people all carrying the same, or very similar, attributes, experiences and status. It implies that their similarities in respect of being 'elderly' are more important than their individual differences. It draws attention away from individual characteristics and uniqueness, and distorts the expectations that others form about the individuals so categorized. The 'person in later life' focuses on the person first, and conveys that the qualifier ('in later life') refers to one aspect only out of a potential range of other equally or more important dimensions of the person's existence.

The Sanitization of the Traditional Medical Paradigm

The new 'person-centred' paradigm is not simply the 'old paradigm' dressed up in person-centred language. The 'old paradigm' works by categorization of problems and needs and matching to existing services. In the new paradigm, the person-centred approach is partnership work between the service user and the service providers towards important and valued life goals. There is a shared sense of direction and of cooperation in an orderly process for organizing resources towards a desirable future for the individual with disabilities. This phenomenon has become evident in relation to other groups of disabled people, such as in services for people with learning disabilities and younger adults with physical disabilities. For example personal futures planning does genuinely happen in some services for people with learning disabilities.

However, it is common for services to have service plans and goals written in 'person-centred' language yet at the same time they inherit the old patterns of service practices. In such services strain is created for staff who are required to aspire to outcomes which the system itself prevents. For example, they are asked to enhance people's dignity and personhood but are caring for people in large groupings, in institutions that are not valued community places and the people they care for have already been taken from the valued social roles that previously defined their personhood. Services have been 'window dressed' with mission statements framed in apparently person-centred language ('dignity', 'choice', personal care plans' and so on) but they continue to deny the people who rely on the service any real role in the decisions and choices which govern their lives. 'Window dressing' may have various causes – the pressure to meet inspection standards, or to make the service eligible for resources, for example. In some cases it is may be due to a lack of understanding of 'person centred' or 'personal futures planning'. The process of 'window dressing' (sanitization with new paradigm language) results in muddled thinking and uncertainty about service goals and whether the service is successful or not. Services that group disabled older people together away from valued places, people, activities and routines by definition cannot achieve new paradigm goals. A change in rhetoric for example 'home-like' or 'community-based' is not sufficient for change to be realized in people's lives, and it can lead to muddled thinking over outcome measures and a sense of failure in those delivering the service. For example, when serving the needs of people with ongoing and deteriorating disabilities it makes no sense to count how many 'improve' or 'get better' (an old paradigm outcome measure) and indeed such measures convey messages of implicit failure. People involved in delivering such services experience directly the stress of impossible goals and the pain of the individuals they try to serve. Such circumstances typically result in low morale and high staff turnover.

What is assessment in the new paradigm?

The distinction between short-term/acute needs assessment and assessment for futures planning
The models of assessment that are needed for short-term needs (as in acute physical illness, or psychosocial crisis) will be different from those needed in relation to long-term or continuing life needs (such as arise in association with physical or mental disability). One of the major problems with the predominance of the medical model is the tendency for assessment technologies that are designed for short-term needs to be applied in the effort to deal with continuing life needs. This has resulted in the pattern of needs assessment we see commonly in relation to older people who come in contact with services. They are seen as 'outgrowing' the service (i.e. 'our service no longer can meet your needs') are assessed by a different service from the point of view of acceptability by that service (i.e. 'do you fit the service?') and are only likely to have their needs met in the future by a repeat replay of the same rejection and reassessment cycle. In the 'old paradigm', the person has to 'fit' the service model and move on when needs change. This is traumatic for both the person moved and for those caregivers whose sense of doing a worthwhile job is undermined. For society, it is wasteful of resources and catastrophic for the people and their families who are exposed to repeated relocation. The morale of staff is notoriously poor in the nursing and residential homes care sector (Allen-Burge, Stevens and Burgio, 1998) to the point where it is difficult to recruit and retain staff to work in such services for older people. As regards the person concerned, discontinuity and exposure to rejection are threatening experiences and contrary to any older person's desired future. They would be evaluated as extremely negative on quality of experiences measures, and there is evidence is that forced relocation can be damaging to health or even may be lethal (Baglioni, 1990).

A separate and different assessment process is needed to address and engage with the person's long-term needs for a desirable future.

Assessment for what?
Services that support people with disability have potentially a greater influence on the person's quality of experiences and on their aspirations about what is

possible – and this influence increases in proportion to the degree of disability and to their reliance on service assistance. For people whose impairment is severe and enduring, and particularly where the disability affects the person's capabilities to communicate, as in dementia, the importance of assessment cannot be overstated; there it is the cornerstone of everything else, determining who will be involved, what needs will be included, what kinds of resources will be required and what outcome measures will be valid for measuring 'success'.

The possible purposes of assessment in the new paradigm include the following:

- creating a better idea of quality outcomes for that person,
- identifying the social context within which the person's life has meaning – now and prior to the onset of the disability,
- identifying where the person's development was going had the disability not intervened,
- identifying the extra dimensions ('special needs') which are related to the impairment,
- focussing on the existing dimensions of the person's life ('general needs') which make the person who they are (the social relationships and roles that create the meaningful context of the person's life).

Because it is common for older people with disabilities to have first contact with a service at a time of crisis, it is appropriate in these situations to have two forms, and two models, of assessment. The first will address the acute needs and will identify what needs to happen to reduce or resolve the immediate threat. For example, in a situation where a person with dementia is leaving their home late at night, the acute need might be for overnight care. Once the immediate care-plan is in place to meet the crisis need, the assessment process can begin in relation to personal futures planning. It is likely then that a different strategy for action will be identified because different needs in different people drive the same behaviour. For example, one person may be identified as having a need to walk their dog, another may be feeling lonely at home. (See 4.1.1).

Such responses emerge from getting to know the person, not from diagnostic information about the type of illness or degree of disability.

The scene is a psychiatric hospital assessment ward for older people. The patient, a tell slender man in his seventies, struts up and down the corridor pulling at his arms and saying over and over in anguished tones 'I can't do anything. I've given up.' He has been there for a year now. He feels he is an utter failure; he dreads anyone from 'the outside world' seeing him in this state; he blames himself for failing to get better after all the treatments and investigations that the staff have organized for him. The nurses meet again; they have consulted with psychiatrists, neurologists, other nurses, the pharmacist and the clinical psychologist in the past. The look of despair and frustration is on their faces. They feel desperate. They have done so many assessments, and arranged more; they have tried so many treatments and none have 'worked'. They want to be nurses and to have a sense of getting people better, but they feel like gaolers. The man feels that gaolers, not nurses, would be indeed be more suitable – because then he would not have to feel that he is letting them all down, he would be accepted for what he feels himself to be, a failed husband, father and community member. The nurses ask, again, 'Do you think he will get better?' The psychologist asks 'Do you think we can travel with him on his journey, not knowing where that may be going, but holding to it just the same?' This question sounds discomforting and unsettling; where does it fit in the daily routine of hospital activities – measures of depression, charts of activities of daily living, care-planning and patient discharges? This patient has 'failed the system' on all these outcome measures, and his awareness of this intensifies his pain.

In such situations, where the person is chronically disabled (whether by dementia or by depression) the effect of services can often be to add to their struggle by imposing unrealistic expectations about 'getting better'. By the same token, the people who are employed in the health care system develop a deep sense of failing and can slide into self-blame by making the mistaken assumption that they are somehow applying their skills poorly or inadequately. In fact they are trapped, just as much as the patient in this example, in an impossible deception. The concept of 'treatment' is stretched to cover all sorts of activities. Art becomes art therapy, music becomes music therapy, fun becomes social therapy.

In the new paradigm what was known as 'challenging behaviour' is seen as a person communicating their experience; what was previously deemed to be broken down behaviour is now viewed as problem-solving behaviour in a challenging situation. In the new paradigm, 'getting better' is held open as a welcome possibility on the journey, but it is not the only waypoint to be included in the journey.

Hopes, aspirations, relationships and citizenship values might be asides in the acute model, but they are central planks in the person-centred paradigm for assessment.

"We can see the world only in the ways that human beings, with their own particular ways of sensing and experiencing (and interpreting sensation and experience) can see it. Whatever reality there may be beyond the 'reality' which filters to us through our individual, historical and cultural ways of seeing, we shall never be able to see what it 'is'. We have, of course, a naïve belief in a scientifically establishable objective reality, but subscribing to that belief is in truth doing no more than taking, in a very grandiose way, what is merely our best guess so far about the nature of things as the nature of things" "... our naïve belief in a scientifically establishable objective reality renders us dangerously blind to the influence of our dreaming". (Smail, 2001)

The purpose of a successful assessment, therefore, is at least to ascertain the nature of the way the person constructs meaning in their life – that is, their own individual subjective reality. There is no given reality in some sense beyond the perceived reality of the individual. A bad assessment ignores the subjective filters. And there is danger in attempting to impose one's own subjective version of reality, no matter how much training or professionalism has informed that view of reality, because it is just as much filtered and likely to mismatch the other person's version. A foundation principle of assessment must be to acknowledge that all reality is created, that this happens through subjective constructs which are shaped by historical, cultural and personal filters, and accordingly that it is crucial to get to know the personal constructs (meaning) of the other life we seek to assist. The assessment process will be successful in proportion to the success we have in getting to know the features of the other's subjective reality.

It is not uncommon to find an older person is assessed as 'needing company and stimulation', the recommended action is to attend the local day centre, and the person either refuses the 'help' or undermines it by failing to engage with it. In the traditional model, this behaviour is usually labelled as 'non-compliance' and money and staff time are spent on 'researching' how to improve 'compliance'. The problem lies in the assessment itself. It has been dangerously blinkered and failed to see the person's subjective reality. The possible reasons for not wanting to engage with outside groups, or to have people enter your personal space, are extensive and varied. Some people may be reminded of a painful childhood humiliation in a peer group, of a previous time they have felt manipulated and have experienced loss of trust or of deep-seated doubts about self and about coping in new situations. Unless the individual's way of seeing new experiences and of coping with past experiences has been explored and understood, the assessed 'need' cannot be developed into a successful 'intervention' for that person. Even worse, it carries the danger of harm to that person, by exposing them to insurmountable challenges, by denying their emotional pain and ultimately by blaming the victim ('non-compliant' is a descriptor that carries connotations of wilful 'bad behaviour').

When the service model is life-planning, the meaning of interactions with the focus person is 'travelling with', not 'doing to'; hence there are no failures in assessment, and only a possibility of discovering more, or more accurately, the subjective world of that person. In the traditional paradigm, where the expert advises and decides on the 'best' forms of assistance the wastage rate in services is considerable; it is common for older people to be reluctant to accept services or to 'fail to comply' or in other unconscious ways to reject the services offered.

In the new paradigm there is no 'us' and 'them', all individuals are seen as having a disability or potential disability, and accordingly the way forward is building community that is strong for all of us. Assessment is for everyone's future not just the focus person. Where a person's disability is significant, it becomes paramount to ensure that special needs do not outweigh general life needs.

The new paradigm

The medical paradigm sees long-term disability and death as the ultimate failures. In reality these are dimensions that lend meaning to life; their existence brings people into connection with each other, emphasizing the reality that none of us exists alone, and that we share the same environment depending on each other.

The medical paradigm implies the view that being able-bodied is better than being disabled and that being illness-free is a better state than illness. It fails to acknowledge that people experience purpose and quality in life through life-with-disability and life-before-death. It robs people with disability and those who are dying of the *meaning*, which they experience in their lives. Through this the paradigm saps morale and is wasteful of resources. The hospice movement offers an alternative paradigm for the support of people with cancer. A similar understanding is required for the support of people with dementia so that life can be understood in terms of hope and the future.

The new paradigm of futures planning is particularly appropriate for assisting people living with such life-defining conditions. More competent communities can be built by the following:

1. Creating a compelling image of a desirable future with an older person with serious disabilities (this requires asking the question, 'What would the valued older citizens consider worthwhile for themselves, who do not have identified disabilities and who are not in vulnerable circumstances?')
2. Inviting people whose cooperation is important to join with the focus older person to make it happen (i.e. involving and strengthening the social network that gives meaning to the life in question).
3. Strengthening personal relationships.
4. Helping people plan, act and learn by reflecting on their successes.

The emphasis here is that the environment must change first, providing supports and creating meaningful purpose for the older disabled persons in the community, and then the persons respond to the positive situation.

"This sequence contradicts the tradition that people with disabilities must change themselves as a condition of entry to new opportunities: environments effect change more powerfully than training can". (O'Brien and Lovett, 1992, page 3)

Mary sits by her bed in the hospital ward. The staff have placed a commode by her bed in the hope that she will be able to develop toilet habits again, and so be eligible to be discharged to a residential home rather than have to stay in hospital or nursing home care. Mary is only aware that she is frightened to go to the toilets at the end of the ward (they seem strange, and public, and don't smell pleasant to her). She senses the object by her bed is like a toilet, but it is discomforting to think about soiling next to your own bed and with only a flimsy curtain between yourself and strangers. She has no choice; she uses the object that looks like a toilet, but immediately feels so embarrassed that she grasps the box of tissues and successfully buries the offending soil in lots of clean white tissue paper. The only problem is where to hide it so no one will see her shame.

The assessment of Mary in the hospital placed her in a category of 'needs nursing home or hospital' because of her identified 'incontinence of faeces'.

Mary is visited by someone who (unusually) doesn't talk to her about the toilet. She is pleased to be asked about how she lived at home, and what she liked best about her home and her life. The person seems to understand that Mary always was shy in public places and very concerned about her own personal hygiene. She remembered how she aired and freshened her whole house every day, and how she liked her home, as well as herself, to be clean and neat.

The assessment of the new visitor is that Mary likes above all to be clean and perfumed in all aspects of her home and personal life, and that there is a familiar favourite scent that she associates with a clean bathroom. The assessment emphasized the importance to Mary of the freshening scent she used in her own home, of privacy in the bathroom area, and of the avoidance of shame and humiliation about personal hygiene (i.e. the use of words such as 'bathroom' and 'clean' when talking with Mary avoided the shame she felt at words like 'toilet', 'commode' and 'dirty').

George lives in a residential home for older people. He lived at home alone for a year after Rachel died. Rachel, his wife, used to love the meals they ate together – she was a talented cook but also looked forward to the weekends when George and she went out together for a meal. George recalls how they said he neglected himself in that year; he didn't think so himself, but there was no point in eating meals any more after Rachel had gone. He ate enough, of snacks, and this also meant he didn't have to eat a meal alone and think of the pain of Rachel not being with him now.

> The assessment of the care manager had been that George needed assistance with eating, and this was one of the reasons he had come to live in the home. And indeed he had needed assistance with eating ever since he had moved in. Someone even had to sit beside him, and 'remind' him how to use the fork and the spoon at every meal; he seemed not to know otherwise, and just used his fingers.
>
> After much persuasion George joins a group on their next outing from the home. They go to a pub restaurant for a meal. It is winter, and the room is cosy and welcoming. There are others at tables already enjoying hearty helpings of hot food. George takes his place at the table with his friends. When the plates are served, and steaming trays of vegetables arrive to accompany the meal, George picks up his knife and fork without thinking, helps himself to vegetables, and finds himself quietly pleased that no one has drawn attention to what has happened. It has been a surprise to him that he has not thought of Rachel until now, and even then his memory is a pleasant companion.
>
> The assessment of the group of friends is that George likes to be able to eat in a sociable environment, likes the company of others who enjoy good food, and enjoys entertaining with stories about wonderful places he has eaten in the past.

Out of the new paradigm comes the person-centred approach to interventions with people with cognitive disabilities. Chapter Four examines the person-centred principles for interventions with older people. Chapter Five focuses on the needs of older people with cognitive disabilities including memory disability. Chapter Six lays out the implications of new paradigm (person-centred) principles that can help us in the design and re-design of our services. Finally, Chapter Seven selects and outlines those psychological therapy approaches that particularly emphasize a whole person approach, illustrating these with formulations and interventions with older individuals.

4
New Paradigm Principles for Intervention

The person-centred approach is complex and demanding, and of course it will not be appropriate for every situation. The following will help in decision-making about whether it is going to be worthwhile and suitable for the persons concerned.

Levels of Need

To understand vulnerability, or risk, in relation to an individual there are two dimensions to be understood – both d*ependency* and perceived *differentness* can place a person at risk.

Dependency can be ascertained by the question: '*How much does the person rely on services (or others) for carrying out everyday instrumental activities?*'

Consider the following:

- How much of their day, and week, is structured by the ways they depend on assistance?
- How much in their future life is the person likely to depend on assistance?
- For which kinds of life areas does the person rely on assistance – that is, is it limited to some areas of life only, is it time-limited or does it affect home, social and community life?

The more dependent a person is on the assistance of others, especially of services, the more that the person-centred 'new' paradigm applies.

Differentness can be ascertained by the question: '*Is the person likely to be seen as 'different' by others in important and negative ways?*'
Consider the following:

- Are others in the community likely to have stereotyped ideas about people 'with that condition'? – for example, 'People with dementia don't appreciate where they are anyway' or 'Old people all get like that' or 'I would want to be put down if I had that.
- Are there commonly accepted negative labels that attach to the condition or situation with which the person lives? – for example, 'had a good innings', 'burden', 'childlike' (very late life); 'confused', 'poor soul', 'away' (dementia); 'crumbles', 'a danger', 'no hope', 'better dead' (terminal illness or significant frailty).
- Is there a history of unequal treatment, which has followed from these labels in times gone by – for example, older persons treated as children; very old persons given lower priority when there is competition for medical treatment; people with dementia treated as objects of pity; people with terminal illness avoided and kept from sight?

The dependency and differentness dimensions can be understood as acting together in an interactive way, as represented in the Table 4.1.

The more a person is seen as different the more the risk to their quality of life. Even with low dependency (e.g. mild or moderate difficulties with competencies), if the person is seen as *different* because of their age or condition or other label, they are at risk of limited access to things that determine quality of life. For example, a person with even mild dementia may be perceived as hugely different from other people of a similar age, and may have reduced chances of access to scarce health technologies such as cardiac surgery. A person is at highest risk of damage to their quality of life experiences if they are in box 4 (see Table 4.1), since they are not only highly dependent on others for important aspects of their life but they are also seen as different in a negative way. For example, prior to the hospice movement people with cancer would frequently

Table 4.1 When is the new paradigm person-centred approach appropriate?

	Dependency	
Difference	*Low*	*High*
High	3	4
Low	1	2

Source: O'Brien and Lyle (1986).

find themselves in box 4, both in need and also feared as objects of dread. A sea-change in attitudes about cancer came with the hospice movement from the 1970s onwards. The Hospice movement succeeded not only in advancing the technical assistance available for people with cancer (such as improved pain control), but by conscious effort it also succeeded in reducing the public demonization of the disease and showing communities a positive way to cope and live with cancer.

The old choices (hospitalization versus pain alone at home), which used to haunt cancer care are now replaced by hope – transformed by positive hospice care, in partnership with families and communities. Even in end of life care, hope is the overriding goal and achievement.

In contrast, the person with dementia may still live in fear that they will lose the life they know as their dementia progresses. In the new paradigm, the opposite would happen. 'Not managing' would be an indicator that the support package was failing, not that the person was failing. It would trigger a change in the forms and level of assistance required to enable the individual to live successfully and free of fear despite their dementia, including as the disabilities progress.

In itself technology (e.g. dementia delaying medication) is not *sufficient* to ensure quality in the person's life experiences although it may contribute positively. Quality in the person's life experiences is only achieved by a conscious philosophy of valuing all life irrespective of disability and acknowledging the reality of interdependency. The hospice movement, for example, focuses on hope, meaning and value in each moment of each life lived, and as such aims at supporting not supplanting the relationships that surround each person.

Hence the third question is '*Are available technologies likely to reduce the older person's dependency or differentness enough to move them out of box 4 in a reasonably short time?*'

If not, the person-centred 'new' paradigm seems most to apply. The emphasis will be to change the stereotyped perceptions, and to build stronger communities around the person such that they can achieve quality of life irrespective of impairments or disabilities.

In the past it was customary to think in terms of 'matching' older persons to services, by gauging level of dependency against the 'level' of available services. An example of this kind of technology is the CAPE (Clifton Assessment Procedures for the Elderly) (Pattie and Gilliard, 1979).

This situation of 'fitting' the person to the service available was challenged in the United Kingdom by the National Health Service and Community Care Act of 1990, which said services should be tailored and packaged to 'fit' the needs of the individual instead. Unmet needs in individuals would be identified and aggregated, and this would drive the re-design of services. What has evolved has been a mixed model (Stirling, 1996) where traditional practices of 'matching people to services' persist but dressed with person-centred rhetoric.

Immediate versus long-term needs

Most services will have first contact with a person with dementia when a crisis occurs, such as when a family member becomes ill, dies or no longer feels able to tolerate some aspect of the person's behaviour. The needs to be met at the point of contact with the service will reflect the immediate crisis needs, but they are not necessarily the same as the long-term future needs of the person.

The scene is a sheltered housing complex. A woman walks with her small dog on a lead towards the door marked 'Exit'; she feels confident about her route as she has done it before. In fact she is beginning to feel positive about living here, despite the fact she was reluctant, having been persuaded to move here by her son. She recalls the shock the day she first came here; she had believed it was for a visit – and then they told her this was going to be her home. People said she had been a danger to herself where she was before; but she'd lived there all her life and couldn't remember ever feeling anything other than safe there. They said they were worried and insisted she was going to be robbed or attacked because of her habit of not locking the front door in the daytime. Certainly there had been times when people she did not seem to know came in the house; and she was aware she missed the neighbours from times gone by, who'd all moved away or died. As she proceeds through the exit looking forward to happier times a horrifying noise starts up; bells scream and eventually people are running towards her and shouting. The warden is one of them – she is deciding that this must be the last time; this lady seems to be unable to learn that this door is alarmed after 5pm despite the notice on it and several explanations. The warden calls in the woman's son and explains that the other tenants are complaining about his mother's behaviour. He feels despairing and embarrassed; he concludes that his only way out is to contact the social services office to say his mother needs to be in a care home – after all, she has been tried in sheltered housing, it has failed, so now she must see that she needs residential care.

As it happens, a new service has just started up locally, whose purpose is to enable people with dementia to live in their own homes where that is their choice. Although the woman cannot return to her original home, since that has been given up, the service assists her and her son to make a plan concerning the neighbourhood she would like to return to. The woman is introduced to several other women who are in a similar position, and who come from the same neighbourhood. They spend time together each week at a local day centre and have the opportunity to get to know each other. Some of them she doesn't particularly like, including one woman she knew from school and didn't like much then; but one or two of the ladies she likes. When a house is identified the

> *friends are each invited to view it, and to consider moving in to it together. She feels this is next best to her own home; she has her own tenancy, and knows that this will be her home for life as long as that is what she wants. She is aware that the women who visit her each morning and evening are formally paid to help her, but she likes them and knows they will continue in the same way when she moves to her new house. She feels on the threshold of a new start, and sure about the friends who will be there when they are needed.*

In this story, the 'solution' that was chosen in the face of the crisis was sheltered housing – to meet needs for security. However, this resulted in other needs not being met for example, for previously familiar routines such as walking her dog. In addition, the new environment was ill-matched to her new learning capability; she was unable to learn the time restrictions on the use of the exit door. This exposed her to failure and rejection.

Arguably, the long-term need for 'Home' is frequently overlooked in the focus on addressing crisis needs. This begs the question 'What is the definition of home'? A definition of home would include having a place in the community, which provides a physical and social base for life; having a place from which relationships can be established and sustained; having a place that enables the separation of the different parts of one's life (e.g. occupation, leisure, social), domestic and personal and having a place in one's community, which is unique to the individual. 'Hospital' is understood to be a particular building in or from which high levels of expertise and technical assistance for clearly defined, limited-term medical problems can be dispensed. When hospitals drift into use *as if* they are people's homes this is a form of 'mission creep' – making hospitals 'homely' is a common sign.

Mission creep. Services evolve to meet the demands and expectations deemed important by a society at a given time – there is no imperative for the ordinary citizen to take stock of the general drift in which they are being drawn until perhaps a personal experience or scandal stimulates questioning. When large groupings of older people are placed in hospital-like buildings staffed with nurses and 'treated' on a medical model, that is primarily for the disease symptoms rather than for personal well-being and fulfilment, we have the recipe for stress, strain, low morale and emotional disturbance. This has been demonstrated over three or four decades in the form of care scandals and poor staff morale. The unpopularity of such a way of organizing care for older people grew, yet society continues to struggle to make a paradigm shift. Instead there has been 'creep' towards smaller groupings, but without the necessary change in the underpinning philosophy. The results are that staff feel demoralized, families continue to feel guilty about placing someone in care, and rates of depression and challenging behaviour are high in many older people's services.

Staff experience strain arising from the gap between what they see the older person most in need of (such as valued company, stimulation) and what the service requires them to do (such as cleaning or shopping tasks in a fixed time). Persons with significant disabilities, and particularly cognitive disabilities, are not in a position to 'shop around' or self-advocate. Neither are vulnerable people in a position to question or challenge what is available to them, for fear of losing all help and being labelled 'non-compliant'.

Special versus general needs

Historically, services evolved to provide a response to special needs. Health services evolved into specialist areas to provide better for the very specialist needs of people with diseases such as cancer, circulatory disease, chest and lung disease, neurological disorders and mental health problems, for example. Their responses involve specialist assessment technologies, special treatments and specific training for the staff who deliver these treatments. However, staff have to find ways to respond to the needs of the people for whom the specialist treatments are not a sufficient solution. (Most of the patients attending clinics are unlike the subjects admitted to scientific trials, having co-morbidities and psychosocial variables that have to be taken into account.) As a result services that were originally established to cater for special needs (related to the condition e.g. dementia, or circulatory disease) found themselves having to respond to people's general life needs as well. Staff, who have been recruited into medical services for example, as nurses or nursing assistants, and whose training has prepared them to deal with symptoms and to manage disease with skill and care, find themselves in a position of having to act as hairdressers, good neighbours, friends, guardians, family substitutes and counsellors. They find themselves expected to fill the gaps in life, which are ordinarily met within the fabric of the wider community. The specialist services are neither designed nor resourced to do carry out these activities. Similarly, social services originally were established to provide specific forms of help for example, housework, shopping, or 'hotel' services, but soon they were having to respond to the other, *general*, needs of their users as well – the need for friends and social contacts, for example.

Those people involved in providing home care, residential care, nursing home care and hospital care *inevitably* experience the emotional strain of having roles projected on to them, which are out-with the boundaries of the job. Staff may experience ordinary pride or pleasure that a person can place trust in them, yet at the same time be fearful of censure for stepping out of role. As human beings we recognize a person's need for valued friends and activities, but as workers in services we often witness the person relinquishing such human needs to secure more basic biological needs.

The situation is a bedroom in an ordinary house in a small town. A man lies in bed, waiting for the nurse to arrive on her next visit. He is relieved to be free of the pain, which the cancer causes, but is always reassured to know that his pain control is attended to by someone experienced and knowledgeable. When her visit is over, he can prepare himself for the afternoon and a neighbour's visit. He and his neighbour will go through some church papers that require decisions to be made. The nurse knows that her visit gives him reassurance and she is happy to leave as soon as her tasks are done, knowing that both her patient and his family have valued company and activities to look forward to.

Another situation is a bedroom in a nursing home in a small town. A man lies in bed, anxious for the nurse to arrive on her next visit. He is relieved to be free of the pain that the cancer causes, but is always reassured to know that his pain control is attended to by someone experienced and knowledgeable. He enjoys a conversation with her too; she knows his family, and his wife's family, and the church of which he has been a member all his life. She thinks, how much I enjoy these conversations with this gentleman, but there are so many other patients to attend to and I must not be seen to be giving more time to some than to others. He thinks, I am disappointed the nurse cannot stay and talk some more, as it makes me feel in touch again with things.

The difference between the two experiences for the person paid to be involved is vast. In the first scenario the nurse leaves, feeling she has done her job well and that other persons, who are unpaid, are quite appropriately sharing a part in the support he requires. In the second, the nurse leaves with a feeling that despite doing her job well, she will never be able to give or do enough for her patients. Such awareness weighs heavily and can result in a chronic sense of failure and 'burn-out'. Surprisingly, staff do not often complain about such impossible expectations; instead denial come into play and blame is projected on to other factors, such as shortage of funds. Demands are expressed for more large-scale care such as residential and nursing homes, blinding us to the fact that what we crave for ourselves is the opposite – the opportunity to be in our own community, in our own home, and surrounded by as much 'risk' as any other person, with our lives populated by ordinary people as far as possible. The use of such vocabulary as 'personal care plans', 'dignity', 'choice' and 'community' are easy window dressing; and are increasingly incorporated into service statements but without the paradigm shift to go with it. Since resources will always be limited, it is presumably better to have a little of what supports a thriving life, than a little (or a lot) of what suffocates life. A person-centred paradigm would place with the individual or their advocate, the decision-making power over how

Table 4.2   Matching services to acute and long-term needs

Service match for acute needs	Service match for long-term needs
Focus on therapy	Life planning approach
Episodes (beginning and end)	Peaks and troughs (life support)
Focus on the person ('fixing' model)	Focus on the environment ('adaptive' model)
Delivers a product (e.g. prescribed treatment)	Delivers a range of activities
Usually requires specialist personnel, equipment or buildings	Usually requires blend of specialist technology delivered in ordinary environments
Draws on one part of a range of skills and knowledge	Draws on a range of skills and knowledge

the limited resource there is can best support a life lived in ordinary settings, among typical people and engaging in ordinary activities that people of this culture regard as worthwhile (Table 4.2).

Services have most commonly evolved to respond to acute, illness-related episodes of need. The Acute Service Model is a good match when there is a dysfunction, which is amenable to a technical intervention and capable of restoring the individual to a level of functioning close to that which prevailed pre-morbidly. The service model of 'admission', 'treatment' and 'discharge' arises from this concept.

Long-term needs on the other hand may be episodic, cyclical and progressive. They may be characterized by peaks and troughs of need – the peaks arising from changes in the ongoing condition (e.g. dementia, cardiovascular disease or arthritis) or from acute problems superimposed on the condition (e.g. an accident or acute illness). These peaks and troughs are transient, and interventions do not necessarily end in a restoration of the previous level of functioning. Such needs are not best served by the acute services model. Crisis or acute levels of service input can make the situation worse by inducing dependency, supplanting natural supports and then exposing the person to failure when the service is withdrawn.

> *The scene is a hospital medical ward in a general hospital. A woman lies on a bed recovering from a fractured hip. She is burning in her mind with the memory of home, and wants nothing more in the world than for she and her daughter to pick up the threads of life again where they left off. The heaviness in her heart comes when she tries to think clearly about how she will manage to achieve this. Hope*

arrives when she sees a doctor is at the bedside; perhaps they will spot that she needs help to plan this. She hears the voice tell her she is going to need two nurses to help her to move about in the future, and an image of home surges reassuringly back into her mind. But, no, the voice goes on to talk about a hospital or nursing home. If only they would recognize that whether she spent the rest of her life in bed, or became able to walk again, it wouldn't matter to her – all that matters is that familiar heart-warming place, with familiar faces and people who seem to enjoy her company. They used to be with her when Joan was out at work or for an evening. Why can't they do that again?

Now Joan appears by her side; she has stories of a District Nurse who will help, and some people who will give extra help for as long as it is needed. It feels as if her world has been put back in place, the terrors abate and the future again lies ahead beckoning and inviting her forward.

The tale from the Care Manager's perspective is that the hospital prognosis for this patient, with severe dementia and having sustained a hip fracture, was that she was not expected to walk again. Community services, it was said, would not be able to supply the numbers of helpers needed in her own home. However, in that locality a new service had started and this woman was already receiving her assistance through them. The service had been established particularly to address the dilemma that the woman was now facing; she had already been introduced to some people other than her own assistants, so that if a time like this came along further help could be offered by known persons and at short notice. Only the task of winning over the support of the woman's GP remained to be done. The hospital had predicted the woman would not walk again, and probably would not live long consequent on the trauma of the fracture. In reality, she went home to be assisted by two helpers for as long as would be needed, the higher cost being met from the service's flexible, no-ceiling policy of budgets. After six weeks it was possible to tailor down her level of assistance and ultimately she lived on at home with her daughter, only occasionally needing higher levels of assistance, for another three years before she died.

Incidental to the woman's story, a financial manager from the local health agency worked out that the average weekly cost, and the total cost, of this way of arranging her assistance was cheaper over a year than a year in hospital or nursing home – even though during the weeks of high-intensity support following discharge from hospital the weekly cost approached twice that of nursing home care. In the next year the health agency purchased a number of 'places' from the service, and in this way was able to provide successfully an alternative form of supported living for a number of very frail older people who were in similar circumstances.

A crucial aspect of the success of a service is its match or mismatch to the actual needs of the persons who rely on it – as distinct from the needs as perceived by others, or from the needs of the service itself. This is the question of 'service model coherency' in the SRV framework (Wolfensberger and Glenn, 1975; Wolfensberger and Thomas, 1983). It is addressed by asking what does the service actually do for its users (this can be ascertained by observation and evidence), comparing this to what it says it does (the written service goals). Positive service change can be guided by improving the match between users' important life needs and what the service achieves.

Where people rely on services for long-term needs the service model coherency is more likely to have large impact and carries more danger of incurring life-defining damage, if poor.

Core Life Areas and Needs

The foundation of the new paradigm approach is the person-centred assessment. This is not an easy option. It involves painstaking and systematic work, deter-mination and single mindedness. It is the idea that knowing the person, and the context of their life, holds the key to assisting them successfully with special needs and disability. To understand a person's life goals and needs we need to ask about the aspirations that valued persons of a similar age in life have, as well as the unique memories and experiences of that individual.

The person-centred assessment is achieved through time spent with the person and with others who know the person well in the context of their life. Another person of course only knows a limited amount about another. There may be a need to guard against the tendency for older people's own children to claim they know all there is to know. Peer-group friends know different things, related to common socialization experiences and values. Even among same generation persons there are different perspectives. Friends from childhood, for example, share different memories of us and with us compared to a marriage partner. For some older people who outlive friends and family there may be no one to help us get to know the person; then we rely more on social history and sensitive communication with the person to build a picture

Getting To Know You

Getting To Know You (GTKY) was developed in relation to services for people with learning disabilities; it has been used widely in work assisting children, young people and younger adults (O'Brien and Lovett, 1992; O'Brien and Lyle, 1986; Brost and Johnson, 1982). It has more recently been recognized as a process for bringing meaning to the lives of older people who are disabled (Stirling,

1990), and particularly people with communication difficulties, such as those with dementia (Bailey and Kavanagh, 1998).

The philosophy can be understood by reading the 'I AM' statements below. Notice that nothing changes if it is read as 'I as an older person' as compared to I now'.

'I AM a member of a community'
'I AM connected with people in my community, both living and in living memory'
'I AM an individual, although I also have particular roles, and status, and I have rights in common with others'
'I AM a person who needs dignity accorded to me in public, for example in how others refer to me and address me. I also need privacy when I choose'
'I AM a person with a future. My present and past are bound up in my future and will continue to grow and develop until I die. I will develop as a person irrespective of a disability or illness – even if severe'

However, there are some special considerations in GTKY with an older person, which may have a powerful effect on some older people's life experiences in some situations. The pitfalls include the following:

- Other people's phobias and prejudiced beliefs about growing old
- Lack of sensory stimulation or sensory deprivation
- Overstimulation and outpacing
- Physical discomfort of fear, recurring pain or discomfort
- Missing someone or something and then feeling insecure
- Feeling stressed because old habits 'don't fit'
- Feeling isolated (even amidst lots of people)

The aim of GTKY is to build a picture of meaningful life experiences with one person. An older person's life may have spanned eight or nine decades; the period and culture in which their earlier life socialization took place will be important in understanding their values and expectations. *Public (shared)* life experiences can be accessed through local and national history records; they can help succeeding generations to understand the cultural and trans-generational context of the older person's life. *Personal* life experiences can be explored through communicating with the person themselves during ordinary daily activities – rather than as a formal interview. Where the person has communication difficulties there is nevertheless much to be learnt about a person's likes, dislikes, fears and hopes from spending time with them and observing non-verbal signals. Finally, talking to the person's family, friends and others can fill out the picture, though this information is, by definition, selective.

Important areas of a person's life: relationships. Relationships provide opportunities to develop a sense of self and to contribute to another person's sense of self. They provide the context for everything else – learning, competencies, occupation, leisure, reputation, respect and autonomy. All relationships, fulfilled or lost (through separation or death), continue to have significance in later life.

Important areas of a person's life: roles. The roles that a person takes on, or is given, have a significant influence on the reputation and respect with which the person is regarded. In current technologically dependent societies the highest value tends to be attributed to roles related to work, production of wealth or commercial outputs. Of course, individuals may value their roles (say as a volunteer or in social business); however, personal and cultural values can be in conflict, and that can result in distress or pressure to conform.

Important areas of a person's life: sharing places in the natural world. Physical sharing of places in the community is necessary, though not sufficient, for people to develop social competencies and to have the opportunity to have the high regard of valued others. Artificial 'communities', such as retirement communities, commonly exist for negative reasons, such as to *avoid* crime or ageism. They foster congregation (of similar needs) and stifle integration and interdependency (of different needs and strengths). As in all forms of institutional apartheid, a sense of safety may be achieved by the 'persecuted' group but at a cost to the diversity and health of society as a whole.

What then if the 'norm' in a society is age separation and the congregation of aged disabled persons away from the mainstream? The statistical 'norm' is not the same as what is valued in that society; what is 'good enough' for the disabled aged group is commonly not 'good enough' for 'us' (valued members of society). If valued citizens prefer to mix with a variety of persons and groupings, then this is an indicator of what is valued across the society.

Important areas of a person's life: the experience of competence. A person can have the experience of competently performing functional activities, irrespective of the assistance required to carry out that activity. One role of technology is to assist people to accomplish extraordinary things that they would otherwise not be able to accomplish for example, to travel at high speed or to fly. Another role, however, is to take over things that people can quite well do by themselves, but may choose not to do – for example, household chores or repetitive jobs in factories. In yet other areas it can assist people to accomplish ordinary things, where those people have no choice about doing them by themselves – for example, assist a person to move around who is not able to walk.

Competencies, however, carry values attributed to them by the society in which they are developed. For example, it was once highly valued to put community needs above individual needs and pool labour to achieve things that could not be done alone. Similarly, the use of technology is not values-free; some technologies are more highly valued than others, and this relates to the period in history, the culture and the purpose to which it is applied. For example, the pocket watch was a highly valued piece of technology at one time in history, but its use now would be regarded as odd, or even of low status, even though it still carried out the task of telling the time competently. Older persons are more likely to use technologies that were mainstream at an earlier point in their lives and which they have had no need or desire to update for example, records of music, manual record-keeping, paying accounts by cash, etc.

The competencies a person acquires are dependent on the places, people and activities and values to which they have been exposed in their earlier life.

Important areas of a person's life: making choices. To have the experience of autonomy over everyday and over life-defining matters is a core component of self-identity. To have the experience of not being listened to, of not having concerns taken seriously, and of being regarded as lesser priority relative to other people are all damaging to the person. These are experiences to which older people are exposed with relative frequency, particularly as competencies decline and the person is forced to rely on others, and on services, for assistance.

The applied psychologist's toolkit

GTKY is the foundation, with strengths/needs and goal planning to follow up. Goal planning has been of particular value in that it enables caregivers to reframe problems in terms of needs and then positive goals when other approaches seem to point only to the impairments. In working with older people with disabilities, it has been helpful in teaching caregivers the importance of identifying goals that are personally meaningful for the individual and of breaking goals into small steps so that each step is achievable and results in success. It also helps caregivers learn the principle that no outcome is a failure, but is a lesson learnt. The approach guides us to discover the goal or goal-step that is meaningful and achievable for the individual.

A GTKY guide and an outline strengths/needs assessment are included here – these can be reproduced for use. They are followed by an example of how GTKY, strengths/needs and goal planning were used in the support of an older person, 'Nancy'.

Getting to know you and Strengths/needs

GTKY is essential, not an optional extra. For a person who is living with cognitive disabilities, as a result of dementia or stroke, getting to know the person is the key to successful support and assistance. For those people who aspire to be the assistants of the person living with dementia or stroke, knowing the person and their needs is crucial.

People with dementia have general human needs, just as before their illness started, and just like everyone else. It is often these unmet human needs that express themselves as 'problems' in the person's behaviour. In getting to know these human needs we are able to build a sure foundation for positive support in dementia.

For example, 'walking' is not a 'symptom' of neurological damage, it is an expression of an unmet need, which has come to the fore at a particular time, perhaps because opportunities have been lost, or separation has occurred from those relationships that previously had met the need. The walking may be an expression of the need to find personal comfort – security, closeness, validation, contact with a known other person. Or it may be the result of an unmet need to reclaim, or find, a 'lost one'. Perhaps a core attachment relationship has become unavailable through death or separation. Or because the dementia disables the person from remembering, they cannot 'remind' themselves about the last contacts with the valued other. Of course, walking may have the purpose of meeting a straightforward physical need for exercise. Biological needs (such as to walk, to sleep, to eat) co-exist with psychological needs (for comfort, attachment, inclusion, occupation, identity, love) (Kitwood, 1997).

Social roles, status, relationships, occupations, typical routines and places in which we spend our lives – all contribute to *our identity*.

Knowing the physical and social context of the person's life, including early life socialization and the values of their generation, maximizes our chances of successfully understanding the message they are communicating.

The grid indicates how the five areas of a person's life needs interact with the physical and social opportunities available to them throughout their life, to produce 'the identity' of the person. Accordingly, to begin to 'get to know' a person late in their life, and after a great change has taken place for them (such as being disabled by dementia or stroke), we must unpack the concept of 'identity' into the particular opportunities and the specific life areas which have interacted to culminate in this unique person.

Table 4.3 Important areas of a person's life – necessary to get to know the person

Life area	What opportunities has the person had? For example:
1. Personal	Places I've spent time; where I've lived; my physical appearance and dress; the support I've had in these choices?
2. Social	The range of people I've met and mix with; my attachments, relationships, status; people who have respect for me.
3. Vocational	Activities I've carried out that I feel are worthwhile and people who acknowledge these competencies.
4. Home Life	Where I've been able to have privacy and choose who to spend time with.
5. Leisure/ Community Life	Opportunities I've had to be a neighbour, colleague, playmate, volunteer, contributor, leader, member, citizen, etc.

Kitwood (1997) helpfully compared psychological needs in people with dementia with the experience of any person when they are 'under great pressure, or facing severe deprivation, or when some hidden wound from earlier life is painfully reopened' (Kitwood, 1997, page 81). The person who is experiencing the disabilities of memory and processing that accompany dementia or stroke is more likely than other people to experience intense loss. In addition, people with such disabilities may face the stress of enforced relocation and loss of the normal social and civic life patterns they once knew – possibly fuelling attempts to re-establish the previous life patterns that once provided security, identity and comfort.

The GTKY headline questions below are useful in the process of building up a picture of a person's life. They are not intended for use as a questionnaire. However they can be thought of as a guide to enriching interactions and to optimizing the communication flow between the person, a relative or friend who knows them and the communication partner who wishes to get to know the person.

GETTING TO KNOW YOU

A GUIDE TO UNDERSTANDING LIFE NEEDS WITH THE OLDER PERSON

The answers to these questions will enable you to build up a profile of a person's past life; they will highlight important areas of that person's life and their present needs.

It should be remembered that any information contained within this document will be covered by rules of confidentiality.

NAME OF PERSON ....

DATE OF BIRTH ....

COMPLETED WITH THE ASSISTANCE OF ....

DATE STARTED ....

IMPORTANT AREAS OF A PERSON'S LIFE

1.   PERSONAL

Q.   How does he/she like to be addressed? _____

Q.   How have other people addressed him/her during his/her life?

_____

Q.   What have been his/her preferences in clothes, appearance, and so on?

_____

Q.   What have been his/her preferences in
what to eat and drink? _____

Q.   How would he/she have described themselves:
as a child?
as a teenager?
as an adult?
- and -
How would other people have described him/her?

_____

Q.   When, and where, was he/she a child? _____

Q.   What was typically going on for individuals of his/her age at that time in
that culture? _____

Q.   What choices did he/she make for themselves in their life? (for example over
smaller things like what to wear, or bigger things like work and marriage)

_____

2.   SOCIAL

Q.   Who have been the people close to him/her?

_____

Q.   Who have been the people he/she had other, less close connections with?

_____

Q.   Where are the places that he/she met those people? (for example at work,
home, school, in the forces, church, dances …..)

_____

Q.   In what ways did he/she keep up friendships and relationships?

_____

Q.   What have been the best aspects of his/her relationships?

_____

Q.   What have been the hardest aspects of his/her relationships?

_____

Q.   What have other people appreciated most about him/her in their contacts
with him/her? _____

3.   VOCATIONAL

Q.   What sorts of work has he/she carried out to earn a living (or work for the
benefit of others or himself/herself)? _____

Q.   What skills and abilities has he/she developed through their work?

_____

Q.   Are there any things he/she would like to have had more assistance and
       opportunities to develop? _____

Q.   What things does he/she still regard themselves as competent in now (given
       assistance if necessary)? _____

Q.   What productive or gainful activities does he/she have access to now?
       _____

Q.   What knowledge and experience does he/she have access to now?
       _____

Q.   What would have been a typical schedule for his/her working day
       (or week)? _____

4.   HOME LIFE

Q.   What parts of the home have he/she usually preferred to be private?
       _____

Q.   What parts of their home have they usually preferred to share?
       _____

Q.   How has he/she exerted choice over these things?
       _____

Q.   What personal possessions have been of most importance to him/her?
       _____

Q.   What other things are of importance to him/her about his/her home?
       _____

       include preferences and memories about …
       colours, light and shade, visual aspect,
       peace and quiet, kinds of music,
       radio stations or programmes,
       TV channels or programmes,
       smells and scents around the home,
       plants and gardens, keeping pets,
       furnishings, community spirit.

5.   LEISURE

Q.   What connections has he/she developed in his/her lifetime with
       organisations? _____
       For example: church groups, community groups, educational organizations,
       clubs (for sports, politics, hobbies), reminiscence groups (e.g. reunions).

Q.   What sorts of leisure interests has he/she enjoyed in his/her lifetime?
       _____
       For example: the arts (cinema, theatre, dance, music), reading (books,
       newspapers, magazines), education (of self, of others), activities, sports,
       hobbies, politics, special interests.

Q.   What sort of neighbourhood activities has he/she been most interested in
       during his/her lifetime? _____

STRENGTHS – NEEDS LIST

Person: **Date:**

Strengths What the individual can do, what she/he likes to do, and other people who are willing to help	**Needs** State these as positive, specific and meaningful to the individual you are planning with

USING STRENGTHS TO DEVELOP A LIST OF APPROACHES TO ASSIST THE PERSON	
Person: **Date:**	
Priority need	
Strengths (from Strengths – Needs list)	**Approaches**

An Example of a 'Getting To Know You' and Strengths/Needs Used in Support of a Person with Cognitive Disabilities in Later Life – Nancy

Who is the person?

I am Nancy, I'm always on the go, taking care of the house, planning the next visit of the grandchildren. I like snooker, walking, my family and I love my home. I am now learning to have someone with me when I walk because they say I can 'easily topple over, put things in the wrong place, and upset people because I cry'. I have a lot to learn about this new situation of relying on other people. My husband takes care of me, and says I like to have my own way.

What are the person's needs? — and strengths/gifts?

I need most of all to live in my own home because I love my family and my memories. I find it hard to accept the help of my husband as I'm particularly fussy about my appearance. I need to learn to have help to get to the bathroom, and to get dressed — in my own way! I know how to control this tremor I've got now, and I am very happy to choose my own entertainment and activities for the day. I like my grandchildren in small doses!

Desired relationships; people who can assist.

Adam (my husband) lives here. Avril (daughter one) (and her husband) I see every day. Susan (daughter two) I hear from weekly. George and Sandy (my grandchildren) every weekend. Winn at the post office. Pat (neighbour from ten years ago and my friend). Lyn, Diane, Debbie and Yvonne (from the Health Centre) I see one of them every day. Physio (from the hospital) I see monthly. Dr M. (my local physician) I see once a month at home. Sandra (at the Day Centre) I see weekly.

Desired roles; barriers to respect.

Important to me is being a friend, a mum, a wife, a grandma, providing hospitality for my visitors and being sure I'll be here for them all. My biggest threat is that someone else will make a judgement that might take all this away from me; some tell me my 'quality of life' isn't so good here at home, but when they ask me I tell them in my eyes it is very good and precious to me.

Desired places; places which could be involved.

My home is my secure and happy place. I love it when it has my friends and family in it, but I love it too when it's late at night and peaceful on my own. I am learning to enjoy the day centre, and will learn to go outside with the help I need to see Winn. The snooker club will still be there when I can get back again. The doctors said I should move out of my house to a home or a sheltered house

Choices which could be supported.

A stable home life with a loving family. An opportunity to be with my grandchildren growing up at home. No disruption.

1. *GTKY*

   The process of GTKY was begun with Nancy at a point in her life when she had been discharged to home from hospital. She had disabilities that included disturbance of perceptual–motor functions that prevented her from being able to dress, wash and groom herself independently. She also required help to find her way from the bedroom to the toilet if she awoke during the night. These disabilities caused her great anxiety, which further interfered with her capabilities. She and her husband were living in a negative downward emotional spiral since her discharge; his taking over her daily self-care and routines provoked distress, put severe pressure on the relationship and added to her sense of loss of self-worth.

   GTKY is a continuous process. When it is started it is not known what keys it might hold and what byways these might unlock. It is essential that it is undertaken with an open mind, because even the smallest point could potentially light the way forward.

2. *Strengths List*

   Information learned from the GTKY process can be the basis for drawing up a strengths list. This is the first step in devising an appropriately tailored Personal Goal Plan. Because crisis needs may overshadow life needs when a person is first in contact with a service it is necessary to know and understand the particular strengths the person brings to their situation. In identifying strengths we are entering into a partnership with the person, making an alliance and optimizing resources. To discover about the relationships, activities and places that have hitherto supported this person's resilience is of value in a crisis. The list below provides a valuable 'checklist' for good practice in assessment. By systematically including strengths and virtues in our assessment work we are breaking the negative roles that are commonly imposed on older clients of services. Not everyone will have the same personal strengths but there will be evidence from the person's life history to indicate their particular positive characteristics. The following is based on Seligman's (2004) classification of character:

   Fairness
   Citizenship (social responsibility loyalty, teamwork)
   Social intelligence (emotional intelligence, personal intelligence)
   Kindness (generosity, nurturance, care, compassion, altruistic love, niceness)
   Love and self-regulation (self-control)
   Prudence
   Humility and modesty
   Forgiveness and mercy
   Leadership
   Spirituality

Humour (playfulness)
Hope (optimism, future-mindedness, future orientation)
Gratitude
Appreciation of beauty and excellence (awe, wonder, elevation)
Vitality (zest, enthusiasm, vigor, energy)
Integrity (authenticity, honesty)
Persistence (perseverance, industriousness)
Bravery (valor)
Open-mindedness (judgement, critical thinking)
Curiosity (interest, novelty-seeking, openness to experience)
Creativity (originality, ingenuity)

3. *Needs List*
    Needs, both immediate/acute and longer term/lifespan, can be listed without prioritizing. The GTKY will inform the prioritisation process. For example, in Nancy's story, the Need 'To be able to dress myself in the morning' later emerged as the important Need for the reason that other core needs depended on it – including her ability to maintain a good personal appearance, her role as grandmother and 'head of the household', and her autonomy.

4. *Approaches List*
    This is a vehicle to assist us, as helpers of the person, to bring out into the open specifically how we can build with strengths rather than focus on problems with the person. For example, we use the strength 'Nancy likes to look neat and have a good appearance' to shape our language positively for example 'That looks smart', 'The grandchildren will enjoy seeing you in that', and to avoid a problem focus (all too commonly the negative, or problem is used as a focus, as in 'You can't wear a dressing-gown for the grandchildren's visit').

Summary Picture of Nancy's GTKY

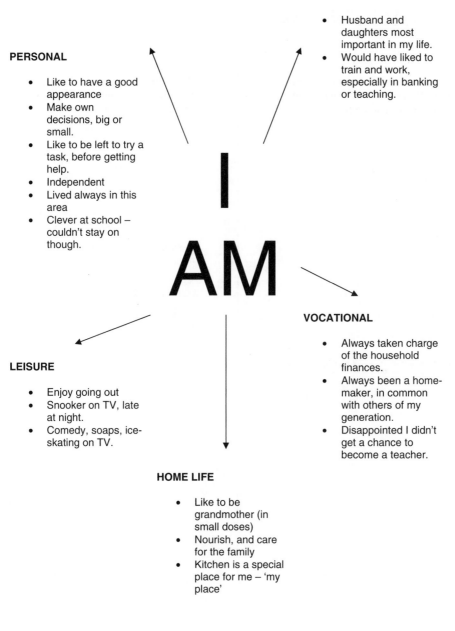

SOCIAL

- Husband and daughters most important in my life.
- Would have liked to train and work, especially in banking or teaching.

PERSONAL

- Like to have a good appearance
- Make own decisions, big or small.
- Like to be left to try a task, before getting help.
- Independent
- Lived always in this area
- Clever at school – couldn't stay on though.

I AM

VOCATIONAL

- Always taken charge of the household finances.
- Always been a home-maker, in common with others of my generation.
- Disappointed I didn't get a chance to become a teacher.

LEISURE

- Enjoy going out
- Snooker on TV, late at night.
- Comedy, soaps, ice-skating on TV.

HOME LIFE

- Like to be grandmother (in small doses)
- Nourish, and care for the family
- Kitchen is a special place for me – 'my place'

STRENGTHS – NEEDS LIST

Person : NANCY   Date: 2 August.

Strengths	Needs
What the individual can do, what she/he likes to do, and other people who are willing to help.	**State these as positive, specific and meaningful to the individual you are planning with.**
Controls her tremor by using special techniques.	Needs to have a daily routine
Used to do all the finances.	Needs to be able to use the toilet on her own.
Reads two words.	Needs to be able to pull on her own tights and underwear after using the toilet.
Wants to go out.	Needs to be able to dress herself in the morning.
Uses a calendar.	Needs to be able to wash face and hands, and clean teeth in the morning.
Likes to have good appearance.	Needs to be able to walk from the bedroom to the toilet at night.
Likes the kitchen to be neat and tidy.	
Likes to bake.	
Likes to be left to try a task by herself before getting help,	
Likes soaps, snooker, comedy, ice-skating on TV.	
Likes making things for the home.	
2 grandchildren (in small doses)	
Day Centre	

USING STRENGTHS TO DEVELOP A LIST OF APPROACHES TO ASSIST THE PERSON

Person: NANCY   Date: 14 August.

Priority Need

To be able to dress self in the morning, to own usual standards (with whatever assistance this takes).

Strength (from strengths-needs list)	Approaches (strengths can provide more than one approach)
Nancy likes to look neat and have a good appearance.	This will help in talking her through dressing, and reassuring her
Likes to be left to try a task by herself before getting help.	This will help in pacing her progress – she can feel good about what she successfully accomplishes for herself, making it easier for her to accept help with some aspects.
Likes her two grandchildren (in small doses)	When she begins to succeed with her goal it will be natural for her to enjoy the children's visits and this will encourage her.

Goal Planning with a person with disabilities in later life – an example – Nancy

GOAL PLANNING SHEET

Client's Name   Mrs Nancy B.   Date 14 August

Present client behaviour

Shouts, hits and cries when getting dressed in the morning.

Client's goal

> Mrs Nancy B. will put on her clothes by herself each morning after breakfast and after washing in the bathroom. She will sit in the sitting-room to dress.

Goal Plan Steps	Date achieved
1. Nancy will get dressed in the morning, assisted by her helper, in the sitting-room. The helper will give *physical help with laying the clothes in order and with tights*, and *verbal* prompting otherwise.	
2. Nancy will get dressed in the morning, assisted by her helper, in the sitting-room. The helper will give *physical prompting with laying the clothes in order*, and *verbal* prompting otherwise.	
3. Nancy will get dressed in the morning, assisted by her helper, in the sitting-room. The helper will lay the clothes in order and give no other prompts.	
4. Nancy will get dressed in the morning, in the sitting-room. Her husband will lay the clothes in order and give no other prompts.	

	GOAL PLAN PROGRESS CHART
OUTCOME	**Name of client** Mrs Nancy B.
Successful √ Continued √ Changed and continued Abandoned	**Goal planner's name** Yvonne, Debbie, Lyn, Diane
	Week beginning 21st August

Final Goal

Mrs Nancy B. will dress herself, with verbal prompting from her husband and her clothes handed to her in the correct order.

This week's step in GOAL PLAN

Step 1 – Nancy will get dressed in the morning assisted by her helper, in the sitting-room. The helper will give *physical* help with laying the clothes in order and with tights, and *verbal* prompting otherwise.

Instructions

1. One of the helpers (Yvonne, Debbie, Lyn, Diane) will arrive at 8.30 AM on pre-arranged morning, to meet Nancy in her living-room.

2. Invite Mr B. to sit across the room and observe (only).

3. Congratulate Mrs Nancy B. on getting up and having breakfast.

4. Lay clothes in a pile in this order – (at the bottom) brush and comb, cardigan, skirt, blouse, slip, tights, pants, bra (at the top).

5. Verbally prompt Nancy to put on each item from the top of the pile down. If she asks about stockings, acknowledge and then refer back to her tights. Point out label at the back of each garment. If she asks for Mr B.'s help, explain we'd like her to ask us instead, in the meantime. Give her time, and only step in when she is failing – with a minimum of help. Prompt for tights:- for left leg first put fist in tights leg; roll up tights leg, pull over foot & heel; repeat for right leg.

6. Comb and brush hair and congratulate Nancy on her appearance.

7. Note time taken to dress, in her diary. Place a tick if achieved.

8. Together, write in her diary visitors and events for today.

Date	24.8	25.8	26.8	27.8	28.8	29.8	30.8			
Outcome **Time in minutes**	√ 24	√ 22	√ 22	X	√ 21	√ 18	√ 20			

Goal Planning Charts based on **Barrowclough, C and Fleming, I (1985). Goal Planning with Elderly People. Making Plans to Meet Individual Needs. Manchester University Press, Manchester, UK.**

5
Older People with Cognitive Disabilities

To understand dementia, we need to understand a great deal more than the factual account of the impairment to neurological processes. It seems to be different from other disabilities in that it affects those functions that are seen as the basis of who we are – our memory and communication in particular. The concept of 'dementia' can trigger deeply concealed fears particularly in those who have difficulty conceiving of interdependency as a normal and valued aspect of life. In a social context that values individualism and independence, dementia is likely to be regarded as catastrophic. On the other hand, in a social context where pro-social behaviours and community are the epitome of achievement, a person with dementia is likely to be regarded as a person like any other but with progressive dependency needs. It is a mistake to view dementia as 'depersonalizing'; we are all at risk of loss of personhood in a pathological social context and the person with cognitive disabilities is merely more vulnerable to the effects of such social pathology.

The Standard Paradigm

When dementia is construed predominantly in terms of the medical paradigm behaviours such as walking, repeated questioning, hitting or shouting are re-garded as symptoms. However, an alternative way of looking at it, and one that opens up more positive interpersonal opportunities, is to consider all behaviour as communication. In this paradigm, such behaviours as walking, searching, repeated questioning, hitting, shouting or shunning contact are considered as

(1) the expression of unmet needs, not necessarily to do with the dementia or (2) attempts to problem-solve perhaps by using repertoires that have succeeded before or (3) the expression of emotions and hence a normal way of coping with new or bewildering challenges.

The disease model lends itself to the idea of dementia having a predictable course and progressive stages but this has the effect of conjuring the idea of 'no hope' and 'end of the line' – particularly demoralizing for caregivers. This does not mean we should give up assertively and positively investigating the cognitive disabilities and neurological patterning that present with dementia. It simply means that a diagnosis or neuropsychological profile is a key to understanding strengths and meaning in behaviour and is not an end in itself. Where good practices have evolved the medical model in dementia is now applied in a sophisticated way and in a new paradigm context. However, there continue to be difficulties associated with an oversimplistic interpretation of the medical model. One legacy of the 'old' paradigm for example is in the widespread difficulty that care homes have in expecting medical services to 'fix' behaviours that challenge – seeing them as symptoms and not as opportunities to communicate or promote understanding.

Others have questioned the adequacy of the disease model as an 'explanation' of dementia (Kirkwood, 1999; Dening, 1994). There is the need to account for the fact that different individuals with the same degree of neurological damage can show very different levels of functioning and behaviour. Some people with significant levels of serious neurological damage continue to have well-preserved functioning and can continue to fulfil roles in daily life. Others, with little detectable neurological damage, may show signs of very poor functioning and of stress in maintaining equilibrium with their environment. Shaping factors include the person's opportunities to hold on to roles in the community and to customary routines and patterns of ordinary life. We can deduce that *resilience* in older people living with long-term and progressive conditions or stress must account for some of this variance. Resilience of course is not simply construed as an internal capacity but in terms of the environmental factors that enable and enhance development and adaptation. Attitudes to dementia and to ageing themselves have a significant impact on the extent to which the environment may be toxic or benign for the person in coping with their dementia.

In addition, dementia progresses at different rates in different individuals and there is no universal course. This can be challenging for those charged with predicting levels of need for a given population. If variability between individuals outweighs the common features of the 'disease', as seems likely (Cheston and Bender, 1999), then service support packages for people with dementia would need to reflect this same variance instead of the 'one model fits all' contruct.

There is evidence of a similar effect in the impact of drug treatments. Systematic review of the research on the effects of the 'dementia-delaying' generation of drugs reveals that variation between individuals exceeds the drug effects in the trials, and that the use of average results conceals a range of outcomes and a number of other important factors. The quotes below are from the meta-review of Legg, Bryant, de Broe, Nicholson, Waugh and Gerard (2000) following which the licences were granted:

- The population was highly selected – 'patients with co-existing illness or concurrent treatment were often excluded from trials, providing a healthier patient population than might be seen in practice'.
- The individual variation is very high – 'average results conceal a range of outcomes, with some patients doing much better, but it should be noted that some patients in the placebo groups also showed good improvement'.
- There is possibly overestimation of the effects due to reasonably high dropout rates.
- 'The long-term effects of treatment with these drugs remain unknown' – typical trials were over a matter of weeks and yet the progression of *Alzheimer's disease* (AD) is likely to be beyond 5 years
- Other interventions may also be effective, but have not been subjected to trials in a comparable way.
- The outcome measures used 'may not reflect outcomes important to people with dementia or their carers'.
- There is possible increased distress as revealed by the few studies that used quality of life measures (though most did not collect quality of life evidence) – 'it could be that the drug slows progression but maintains the patient in a condition which may be distressing to the patient and their carer.'
- There is incomplete reporting of the adverse effects of these drugs – mild and transient adverse effects tend to be reported but not, for example, death rates possibly related to the short-term period of the trials.

The attraction of the standard paradigm

The medical/biological paradigm of dementia care persists in the public mind. Why is this, when some of its worst consequences, of warehousing and nihilism, appear to terrify the ordinary person? One attraction is that it unlocks funding for researchers and clinicians. However there is another dynamic – and this is rooted in unconscious needs in society.

Contrary to the idea their name implies, so-called 'developed' societies are in reality technologically dependent societies. Such societies have developed technologies to meet basic biological needs, for example to support food production and clean water supplies. They have also created large-scale technologies that control the natural environment, for example for energy production, flood control, land 'reclamation' and building. Dependence on these technologies results in populations who are de-skilled and unable to maintain even the basic requirements for life such as growing food, cooking, ensuring clean water or constructing shelter. The day the electricity is switched off is the day the 'developed' society becomes the disabled society, with probable chaotic and catastrophic results.

Although these technologies are largely benign in purpose (e.g. heating, water purification, surgery, antibiotics) at the same time they meet a deeper need to defend ourselves against the dark, or chaos, side of life. They help us to buffer ourselves against feared and overpowering natural forces, such as disease, hunger, flood and even death. (Similar principles are illustrated in the arguments about energy procurement – where the case for nuclear power places its faith in technology that exerts control over the forces of the environment versus the case for natural power sources such as wind and wave which places its faith in going with, not against, these forces.)

However, benign though the intentions may be, these technologies have fostered mass delusion and dependency. They are delusory in the sense that some individuals and societies behave *as if* disease and death will always be held at bay – for example, will blame someone or something else, or a lack of technology, for incidents of disease or death. They are dependency making in the sense that individuals' dependency on technology disables them from learning other survival skills that may be more sustainable and enduring in the long term – for example, people who learn biological 'pest' and 'weed' control methods are more likely to be able to feed themselves in a future short of energy and oil for the manufacture of chemical poisons and weed-killers.

As part of the dependency on technology to support physical health, there has grown an idea of achieving physical perfection. It is easy to see how the pursuit of the perfect body and material well-being through technology (from make-up to surgery) fuels the protective delusion against the reality of disability and death. It has become a major motivator of human behaviour and supports a large money-generating industry. However, the most powerful and possibly most disabling long-term effect of this is the fear and devaluation that it fosters of other states of being. Physical difference or disability, 'normal' distress and emotions, rejection of money or technology dependence and proximity to death tend to be shunned, 'fixed', made little of, and otherwise devalued in the technology-dependent societies.

Physical or psychological discomfort is regarded as undesirable and remedies are expected to be sought. 'Quick fixes' for normal transient episodes of distress or pain are demanded. The society that relies on technology has no time for the processing of discomfort or distress; it expects the individual to use some 'effective' technology to get back into working order as quickly as possible. The societal purpose of anti-depressant treatments, for example, is to get people back to work as quickly as possible. It is likely to be regarded as 'odd' in such a society to choose any other outcome measure than return to the production economy. To construe an episode of psychological disturbance as an opportunity for the individual to learn, to strengthen their coping capacity and to demonstrate resilience is likely to be considered 'odd'. Yet, the latter are those outcomes most valued by people themselves; they are also more likely to add to the capacity of the society and groups within it to endure loss and pain, to survive despite deprivation and to be enriched as a result.

A form of magical thinking develops within a technology-dependent culture. If a life can be extended by 5 years by treatments that 'conquer' cancer then it seems only an extension of this to think that a life could be indefinitely extended by other treatments of a similar order. Similarly, the rest of the natural world is to be exploited or 'managed' – to be brought within the power of the human species to serve their needs. The attraction of the standard paradigm in medicine is the belief (delusory, but comforting) that technology will conquer nature – with its associated de-skilling and undermining of individuals' own health care competencies.

Dementia poses extra challenges for this delusory schema of thinking, first by disabling the higher cortical centres on which denial and rationalization depend. Second, it introduces a possibility of experiencing one's world largely through emotions and developing emotional intelligence, in contrast to the cognition-based defences that are needed in a production society. By association dementia may conjure up unconscious fears about our own late life and mortality, which are likely to be unprocessed and exaggerated in a technologically dependent society. Dementia has defied the 'technological fix', with the consequence that the presence of people with dementia commonly embarrasses society and results in them being separated away from mainstream community life under the guise of 'care'. In this way society transacts against them patterns of control such as institutional containment and socially engineered separation that are deemed inappropriate now for other groups.

People with dementia may carry society's projected fears about ageing and the end of life to a disproportionate level compared to other 'sick' groups. They carry the double stereotypes of 'cognitive disability' (irreversible worthlessness to the production economy) and ageing (evidence of the failure of the ultimate technological goal – to gain control over life and death).

We now understand that emotional processes and the drive to problem-solve when in new and challenging circumstances lie behind many of the actions of the person with dementia, where previously in the 'standard paradigm' these would have been of no interest or been classified as 'behavioural symptoms' (Kitwood, 1997). This 'new paradigm' helps those who assist the person with dementia to understand how to provide meaningful and effective care.

The New Paradigm – Dementia as an Information Processing Disability

The model of mind in dementia developed by clinical psychologists represents a new paradigm in the technologically developed world for thinking about and understanding the nature of dementia (Bender, 1998; Bender and Wainwright, 1998). It is an information processing model of mind – it takes into account that human cognitive functions have the fundamental purpose of processing information so that it is meaningful for the individual and that it produces an equilibrium or dynamic between the individual and their environment. It offers insights into the emotional and problem-solving experience of persons with dementia. It views them as actively striving to engage in valued social roles – which give identity and purpose.

> . . .what is most centrally damaged in dementia is the ability to process information. Moreover, the loss of this ability further threatens a person's capacity to engage in socially valued roles. Both information processing and psychosocial changes act to threaten a person's sense of identity and self-worth. (Cheston and Bender, 1999, page 132)

The Meaning System and Safety System Model of Mind in Dementia

Bender and Wainwright's (1998) model of mind proposes that information is processed at two levels. The Meaning System is a verbal conceptual system, through which incoming information is evaluated. The Safety System, in contrast, is non-conceptual, non-evaluative, non-verbal and directly concerned with survival. The safety system picks up signals of danger and it makes the individual respond in particular ways. Safety system behaviours (a) are rapid, (b) override other responses and (c) are either fight, flight or freeze.

The natural human response is to escape from an uncomfortable state such as prolonged high arousal (the Safety System) to seek the familiar Meaning System. The searching, questioning and attachment behaviours expressed by persons with dementia can be understood as these seeking behaviours. However, as neurological damage progresses it may take longer and be more difficult for the person to regain their familiar Meaning System. As a result the individual spends increasing amounts of time in the Safety System probably experiencing uncomfortable levels of arousal.

> *The setting is a pleasant bungalow in a leafy suburb. The man with the worried eyes sits in his living room, asking his wife 'Is the insurance paid?' and 'I have done terrible things – I'm frightened I've not saved enough money – what will we do?' A friend visits and he begs him 'But how can I be sure that there's enough money to live on?' and 'I just know that something terrible could happen – all this could be taken away'. His final and ultimate despair is then expressed 'I know I'm causing you all such a problem, but I'm really a wicked person and I can't believe you when you tell me not to worry'.*
>
> *Through understanding that this behaviour is a result of a deep-seated feeling of general anxiety and loss, the man's wife was able to change her concept of how to help him. She stopped trying change his beliefs (she used to try to reassure him about money, to no avail) and began to think about things that might validate his feelings. 'It's a very frightening place for you to be' 'It would be awful if there were no money or no home, but we have thanks to you'. She stopped trying to rationalize, she accepted his worries, which allowed her to relax and return to their more usual lifestyle, which in turn helped the man to feel more secure.*

A person experiencing prolonged high levels of panic or arousal may associate this with previous fear experiences, such as having been a prisoner of war or having been abused.

> *'You are keeping me prisoner', 'Someone has stolen my keys', 'I am being threatened' – such statements may mirror earlier life experiences. Understanding that these are genuine communications, and that the person is responding with anxiety to a traumatising situation, helps us to respond. The carers for the woman who made these statements agreed that trying to 'reassure' was only denying her feelings and pushing her deeper into terror. Instead they tried to put themselves in her shoes; this made them stop arguing and rationalizing with her, and instead they asked her more about her mother, her home and the way these made her feel. The woman still on occasions became distressed but for less time and she was much more trusting of the carers.*

In a predominantly biological paradigm, the behaviour is seen as entirely a result of neurological impairment. Consequently, the behaviour is viewed as a symptom, to be classified and managed by chemical or other technical means. In a behavioural paradigm, the function of each behaviour is sought out and through this shaping of behaviour. A behavioural functional analysis follows the antecedents–behaviour–consequence (ABC) model for assessment (Stokes, 1990). The concept of 'challenging behaviour' indicates an understanding that the person's behaviour challenges others – it is not a 'problem' but the communication of an unmet need or emotion. This challenges us to identify and respond appropriately to that unmet need (Stokes, 2000). The person-centred paradigm, however, goes beyond behavioural technologies and places on 'the other' the responsibility to use their highest level of consciousness, to regard all behaviour as communication and to hold people with dementia in valuing relationships in the heart of our communities (Kitwood, 1997).

The information-processing model of mind helps us to approach and understand the behaviour of the person with dementia in this 'enlightened' way. We can 'see' behaviour such as hitting in terms of 'expressing feelings of desperation' or 'searching for a loved one', for example. Knowledge of each individual context and the unique person will help us to tune in to the 'best' understanding.

The setting is a spacious room which is light and airy, with large windows and very pale pink painted walls. The floors gleam in the light, stretching into the distance to further spacious rooms and uncluttered corridors. Figures in white, and some in blue, appear to glide effortlessly over the floors, purposefully and silently. The roof above is high and vaulted and painted in white. The woman with the tired eyes walks slowly across the floor, asking 'Where is this?' and 'Is this a space ship?'

The place is actually a ward within a psychiatric hospital; it is housed in a prefabricated building whose interior décor is indeed pale and shining with few features by which it could be identified. The woman has made an interpretation based on the failure to recognize as familiar any feature of her present environment. She has probably not reassured herself with this interpretation, since it is not necessarily a comforting prospect to consider oneself to be inhabiting a spaceship, but forming the construct has allowed her to remove some of the uncertainty about her environment and she can feel less worried and less bewildered.

Knowing that her communications were full of information that would help them to help her, the woman's carers started to listen to her, and so found it much easier to offer her comfort through validation of her feelings of anxiety. They could say with confidence, 'It looks a bit like a spaceship here, and that can be frightening' while creating opportunities for her to do purposeful walks, such as outdoors for exercise, and indoors for looking after her room and clothes.

Understanding Memory in the Person-Centred Paradigm

The machine versus the person

Cognitive psychologists and cognitive neuroscientists typically have described memory in terms of different memory systems. Various models have evolved.

One schema distinguishes memory stages as sensory, short term and long term (Atkinson and Shiffrin, 1968). An extended version of this scheme identifies five major systems; they are procedural, perceptual representational, primary, episodic and semantic memory (Schacter and Tulving, 1994). Evidence supports the concept of separate memory systems – for example that brain damage affects the separate systems differently (Craik, 2000). However, memory is not fully or sufficiently explained by even the most sophisticated cognitive science. As well as its sophisticated mechanics, we have to understand how memory supports key psychological functions such as personal identity and social relationships. The essential characteristics of memory are

- it exists in a context of *interactive* awareness
- other persons carry 'our' memories and we carry 'theirs'
- it is not in fixed form but is continually *reconstructed*
- the meaning of a memory may change as life goes on – some memories become less troubling, others more uncomfortable
- meaning is changed and extended whenever a memory is reviewed
- *shared or public memories are individually filtered.* People who have had similar experiences (e.g. of life in war time) do not have identical memories, and these memories change with perspective and further experience.

With impairment to memory, the trauma experienced by the person is not simply related to the reduced capacity to register and retain new information; the grief felt is because of the loss to their identity and difficulties in sustaining valued roles and relationships. For other people in the person's life the loss may be also keenly felt, since they have lost the part of their identity that resided in the memory of the other and is not now accessible.

Memory as a vehicle of existence in a social and cultural dimension

Whilst neuropsychological profiling provides uniquely valuable information in the clinical and rehabilitation arena (e.g. for diagnosis and understanding strengths and needs), the social dimension is a completely different analysis. Smail (2001) makes the point that human experience is 'alienated existence' if it has no connections between self and social worth. When memory is not fully functional then these connections are at risk. This demonstrates how problematical it can be to 'lose one's memory' – it not just a matter of 'forgetting' information, but the individual's sense of self may be placed under threat. Also, in close relationships each person's memories support the partner's memories and sense of self, so that loss of one's effective memory results in distress for both. For this reason maintaining ties with known places, people and routines holds in place the connections that prevent the state of 'alienation'. When others act positively to compensate for memory losses, the sense of self-worth that is the antithesis of 'alienation' can be protected.

Logically, therefore, there should be a person-centred dimension in all memory assessments and interventions. This can be addressed by asking such questions as 'What does this memory disability *mean* to this individual?' and 'How does it impact on their *life and sense of self*?' (as well as the more usual questions that help to quantify and describe the memory pathology.)

For example, damaged memory processing may interfere with the 'life review' process. Although previously laid down memories are preserved, if they cannot be linked to new experiences and memories then the person will have difficulty in updating their model of the world and of the self in it. Hence, the present reality may seem challenging or the person may feel alienated and increasingly retreat into their past memories.

For another example, some traumatic memories remain dormant through adult life, but can push through to demand conscious processing in very late life. Childhood abuse or severe war experiences are known examples of such memories being disclosed for the first time in later life. Such painful remembered experiences may trigger a reprocessing of intervening memories and can result in a negative re-evaluation of a lifetime's work, family and relationships. Without current strong memory processes the person may become trapped in a past of demon memories unable to benefit from the support of people around them.

The Place of Behavioural Assessment in the New Paradigm

The traditional paradigm takes the classificatory approach to challenging behaviour in dementia in the same way as it deals with symptoms. The rationale of this is that by classifying, defining and measuring these events we will arrive at some means by which they can be reduced by treatments and interventions. The new paradigm is based on the premise that *all behaviour is communication* and hence that it can be understood and potentially alleviated (or not) by detecting the message that is being communicated. Challenging behaviour can then be understood as the following:

- *Emotions* experienced by the person in reaction to the strange situation in which they find themselves for example, fear, grief and other distress.
- *Attempts to meet unmet needs* (commonly, needs *not* related to cognitive disability). When there is cognitive disability the person is often placed in a restricted environment. Then they are unable to meet ordinary needs for example, to exercise freely, or to socialize with others who value them.

- *Problem-solving* in the face of an apparently hostile, rejecting, annihilating, bewildering or demanding environment. Each of us seeks social roles in which we can experience success and being valued by others – and in the absence of this we may enact social roles from another part of our life in which we were appreciated for example, as a worker, neighbour, carer, mother or child.
- *Enacting patterns of previous relationships* for example, the person tries to make sense of, and relate to, the apparent strangers around them using previous patterns of social behaviour.

In the new paradigm therefore, the behaviour which is 'challenging' resides as much in the actions and problem-solving responses of 'the other' as in the actions and problem-solving attempts of the person with the disability. (See 5.9)

The scene is a nursing home for older people. A woman who does not see well sits in an armchair at one end of the sitting room. She shouts out 'nurse' and when nothing happens she shouts it again. This continues until eventually something happens – another resident speaks back to her, or a member of staff comes up to her and speaks. After this has happened she pauses, looking ahead but apparently not seeing much, for she shouts again within a few minutes. The observer in the corner charts her behaviour; it is marked under the column 'very frequent'. The chart from 6 months ago, when she first came here was marked mostly in the 'occasional' column. The observer thinks, 'The behaviour is increasing in frequency and there are other worsening symptoms as evidenced on the "agitation" column.' It is likely that questions will be raised about treating her behaviour possibly with medication or snoezelen therapy; alternatively staff might consider whether her needs would be better met by a move to a different service such as a long-term care ward in a hospital. The woman thinks how difficult it is to be sure what she is seeing in the fog of the distance; shapes drift in and out of the fog but none seem to be to do with her. She wonders indeed who she is now, as she used to know this when things were different and she lived in the place she acknowledges as home; but here no one seems to know her as her self. The only way to regain that sense of being seems to involve getting away from here to the familiar and friendly place of home. She tried telling people, for a long time, how she felt lost and couldn't see to know who was there; and when it was always strangers who came, and some of them were not too friendly, she began to feel abandoned, as she does right now and this feeling becomes overwhelming and the only relief is to cry out and hope that this time something she understands will result.

In the new paradigm it is acknowledged that behaviours that are difficult to tolerate may never 'go away'; that a person living with a severe disability is in need of people who will *cooperate* in making sense of the challenges, and who will not judge the other for their actions and feelings about the journey they are travelling and the hurdles they must surmount or find a way around. The focus is not on getting rid of the problems, behavioural or otherwise, but on cooperating in the ways the person must develop for coping with their disabilities. Through sincere cooperation the person comes to be made to feel less of a burden, and consequently behaves differently, that is in a less panic-stricken and alienated way. For some, the neuropathy may be so severe that their behaviour will always be affected, and for this person helping others in their community to continue to value them may be the overarching goal (not the removal of the behaviour). Here the issue is not cure – it is belief in the human benefit which comes from being 'known' as the person one is, and being understood and accepted in certain roles and relationships with one's peers and community. Receiving person-centred therapy involves receiving the genuine unclouded effort of another human being to understand our experience of the world and our disability.

How Society's Responses and Service Models are Influenced by Beliefs About the Nature of Dementia and Its Problems

Historically, beliefs about the nature of dementia and its problems have varied dramatically (Rottenberg and Hoffberg, 1977). At different times it has been thought of as torture of the soul, loss of mind, insanity, chronic brain failure, contamination from the physical environment, genetic error, malignant social psychology and an opportunity for enhanced personal growth. However, as our understanding of dementia has progressed it has become apparent that the social context and social roles have an important influence on the person's resilience and how they live with their cognitive disabilities, rather than thinking of it as simply something within the individual.

The Three Levels of Disability

The first level of disability is that arising from the neuropathy itself, and commonly includes impairment in three main areas of neuropsychological processing – registration into memory, visual–spatial processing and execution of complex sequences of responses. These difficulties can fade into relative insignificance, however, compared to the disabilities incurred at the second and third levels. People find ways to tolerate and live with impaired memory but find it much more difficult to survive loss of valued roles, separation from significant others and loss of the normal patterns of daily living that give life its meaning and structure. Individual disability is not separable from its social context and it is necessary to understand how a person's sense of identity may be threatened by the neuropathy that interferes with normal memory and planning – however, their connection to their community can be the 'holding' influence that is capable of limiting or even stabilizing the first level of disabilities. For example, others who have known us in life 'hold' our identity in their memories; and being valued by our neighbours and fellow citizens can survive losses in cognitive competence because others remember our worth even if we cannot (see Table 5.1).

Table 5.1   The three levels of disability

First level of disability	Neurological damage/cognitive impairments
Second level of disability	Roles and relationships stolen away/anxiety
Third level of disability	Seen by others as not having the full range of human needs and internalizing this view

The second level of disability arises from the responses of other persons in the environment to the person with dementia and their difficulties; others' responses are shaped by the beliefs that are held in the culture about the nature of dementia and the service models that come with this paradigm. If the institutionalized responses to dementia are to 'take care of', 'to protect' and to 'separate away' the individual is at increasing risk of being seen by others as 'different'. This continuum can lead to being seen as not needing the same as other people. Third, when experienced over a considerable period of time these beliefs are internalized and the person experiences themselves as not fully human.

Beliefs About Dementia

Table 5.2 follows Wolfensberger's method of analysis of how beliefs about a group influence: (a) image and society's responses towards that group, (b) the service models which the society deems appropriate for that group and (c) behaviours transacted by services on behalf of the society in relation to the members of the group.

'*Not there*'. This is the belief that goes with a reductionist biological conceptualization of psychological functioning. In this belief, there is an identification of brain with mind and of organic functioning with personal identity. With neuropathy as the dominant image the person is seen as 'damaged' or 'not there'. We

Table 5.2 How beliefs about dementia in technologically dependent societies have influenced societal responses and service models

Belief: definition of dementia	Image: person seen as	Society's response	Service model
'Not there'/distressed	Not a person but a problem; challenging behaviour	Fear, dementia as 'death of the person'; embarrassment; protect society	Separation; detention; eradication of the behaviour
'Not there'/content	Not a person; not able to appreciate	Pity; distance; 'us–them'	Separation; no futures; living in limbo; no good to the community
Simple/closer to god	Not a person; detached	Shut away from the world	Pretend living; ordinary life not expected
Disease	'The Dementia's'; victims of neurological cell death	Technical: find the cure; objectification e.g. 'conquer the disease'	Medical; vast resources to pharmacological and technical research
Machine with error	DNA error	Pursuit of perfection; genetic control	Genetic engineering
Part of 'normal' continuum	Part of 'old age'; different from younger people	Loss of mental faculties inevitable	Receiving social care/terminal care; not giving to the community
Malignant social pathology	Personhood: the person first; the disease second	Confused; communities lacking strength to support people	Mixed models; making the institution 'more person-centred'
Information processing impairment	*Engaged in process of holding on to the meaning level of processing; holding on to sense of 'self'*	*Conscious of the person first, the disability second; able to learn from this*	*Focus on personal futures planning, strengths, relationships, reputation, value as a person*
Ecological	*Part of range of natural events*	*Conscious of value of taking care of each other Conscious of well-being irrespective of dementia*	*Community strengthening; building people's competencies to live with disability*

hear such phrases as 'This is not the person I married'. The medical model links into this by regarding 'behaviours' as symptoms to be classified and placed in a taxonomy of pathological features.

Behaviour that is seen as out-of-control is perceived as threatening, and society's response has often been to see people with dementia whose behaviour is odd as at best an embarrassment, and at worst a cause for fear. In either case, the impact has been to encourage a service model which separates the people so perceived away from mainstream places and services, detains them indefinitely and sets up programmes of activity to eradicate the behaviours.

Another version of 'the person is not there' occurs when the person with dementia is perceived as in a state of blissful unawareness. Then they are more responded to as objects of pity rather than of fear. With pity goes a distancing of 'us' from 'them' – allowing society to view itself as compassionate whilst really perpetrating social exclusion against the pitied persons. As a consequence, people who are pitied are often allowed to live in limbo, with few or no expectations about their future as different, and without any sense that they can contribute to their wider community.

'*Simple/closer to god*'. This is the idea that the person with dementia has slipped away from the complexities of the material world to inhabit a much simpler world. The association of simple with pure occurs throughout human thinking. It was reflected in the holy orders who considered children with learning disabilities as in a state closer to god. It can be recognized in such language as 'poor soul' or 'living in another world', when used to describe the person with dementia. Through this image the person is being cast as detached from 'our' world, and their disconnection from current real-world concerns is being presented as a virtue. The associated service model is likely to emphasize spiritual needs rather than the full range of human needs (de-emphasizing, for example, needs for relationships, roles and risks in the mainstream world).

'*Disease*'. Dementia itself is not a disease but a name for a constellation of signs and changes. In standard medical terms, these are understood to be attributable to underlying disease processes of one kind or another, either structural changes in the neuronal cell system or circulatory system changes. This requires that there be a distinct separation between the concept of 'dementia' and that of 'normal ageing'. Some have argued, however, that the evidence indicates the opposite and that a continuum is the case (Dening, 1994). For example, clinical postmortem evidence is that the plaques and neurofibrillary tangles that are said to be the characteristic features of AD also occur in the brains of people who have not shown clinical signs of AD during life. Further evidence against the category model is that people's scores on memory and other tests form a normal distribution curve, and people with dementia do not fall into a distinct group separate from the 'normal' range.

One implication of the continuum concept is that it dissolves the boundary between 'them' and 'us', and in so doing highlights the wide variance in the ways people age naturally.

The disease model, on the other hand, makes a separation between 'them' and 'us' and so eases the way to certain responses being enacted towards 'them', which would not be acceptable to other members of the community, such as detention in places deemed as 'safe' or 'for care'.

Frailty and ageing pose difficulties for societies that value physical perfection and eternal youth. In current western societies the elimination of faulty genes and cloning are often seen as scientific 'advances', which could eliminate imperfection and, by implication, frailty and ageing. The compelling need these values create in people is the pursuit of comfort and 'happiness' in an impossible process of denial of pain and death.

The disease model suits the technological society since it supports and fuels the existing social structures, including the medical, drugs and research businesses. At the same time it hinders the raising of awareness about the reality and variety of ageing, by 'pretending' all negative ageing experiences are disease processes and fostering the illusion of ageing simply as a linear extension of the earlier part of the lifespan. As a result, when individuals encounter the real difficulties that come with ageing, they are made to feel that this is 'wrong' – that they (or someone else) must have failed to create the perfect 'old age'. Feelings of inadequacy and isolation result, which only make more difficult the process of coping with adversities that occur in late life.

Instead of seeing 'odd behaviour' as simply the effects of neuropathy combined with coping behaviours, the issue is complicated by seeing it as a symptom of mental illness. This steers the individual to be dealt with by medically credentialed personnel that is, doctors and nurses, who in turn may experience demoralization about their expected role in 'curing' this behaviour.

'*Machine with error*'. There is a clear example of this in the idea that dementia is associated with a fault in the DNA. In a commemorative interview with the BBC, James Watson (2003) revealed his beliefs about the value of the celebrated discovery of the coding of DNA, which he and Francis Crick had published 50 years earlier (Watson and Crick, 1953a, 1953b). His motivation for carrying out the research was that eugenics as a technology would be capable of ensuring 'intelligence' by genetic replication. Watson gave the example: 'If I marry, I want to marry an intelligent woman with whom I can have a conversation'. Eugenic selection and de-selection would enable conservation of those traits Watson deemed desirable. This may sound naïve to scientific minds half a century later, in a time when science and culture acknowledge the diversity of human qualities and celebrate the fact that 'intelligence' is a constellation of abilities rather than a single 'trait'. However, science is values-blind; it will yield evidence about the effectiveness of a particular method but will not examine its ethical or moral implications. Euthanasia, for example, would be 100 per cent effective in eliminating challenging behaviours and distress in dementia! And drugs can be highly effective in limiting the overt expression of distress! This does not, however, mean that euthanasia and drugs are the most effective 'treatments' in dementia – merely that they eradicate specified effects deemed to be undesirable. The values base with which euthanasia is in conflict is that which values all experience, views disability as being a universal experience, and recognises that taking care of each other is the ground from which competencies and happiness grow irrespective of (and because of) our various disabilities and abilities. The persons with dementia and their behaviour, therefore, might be more usefully understood as something we can all learn from, than as a broken machine in need of rewiring. Indeed for many the blocking off of intellectual processes such as memory and language can be a prerequisite for aesthetic appreciation or creative expression. Where Watson might have seen only 'lack of intelligence in need of fixing' in his uni-dimensional view of human worth, we now recognize diversity and rich potential. For example, emotional intelligence, and communication through poetry or music, may be facilitated in dementia (Killick and Allan, 2001). Dementia may result in people acting differently but this is not sufficient reason to put forward eugenics as 'the solution'.

If it is possible to control length of life why not aim for greater longevity or even eliminate death? If it is possible to control size of memory, why not aim for encyclopaedic memory? If it is possible to manipulate speed of thinking, why not aim at every person having a fast brain? The 'machine with error' belief seems to encourage an unimaginative view of the future of life. Genetic interventions that could make 'perfect' individuals and make them live forever conjure images of a sterile society, with disproportionate resources going into the maintenance of selected individuals at the expense of community and diversity. Communities do not develop competence by becoming dependent on technologies; on the contrary, the competent community is the sum of its members' resilience and capacity to benefit from all forms of experience including adversity and distress.

'*Part of a normal continuum*'. Research in the last 10 years (Park and Schwarz, 2000) has indicated that specific changes in higher cognitive functions are identifiable with ageing and particularly in the seventh and eighth decades. These changes, however, are distinguishable from the neuropsychological profiles associated with the conditions that cause dementia. Intrinsic brain changes such as those associated with AD have distinctive hallmarks. Extrinsic causes of brain changes, such as vascular or systemic pathologies, have other different hallmarks. Therefore, age-related changes neither herald nor are synonymous with dementia, even though some areas, such as new learning and planning may be implicated in both. In conclusion, ageing may bring cognitive changes such as a slower response time and a shift of memory focus from the present to previous memories – however, these are not necessarily negative changes. Trading speed for effort, and present detail for past memories, may be an opportunity for the development of new positive abilities, such as the capacity for reflection, trust, civic responsibility, altruism, pro-social behaviours, humanitarian aspirations and new roles and relationships that are values-based rather than instrumentally functional.

One challenge of an ageing population is the need to embrace the cognitive changes that accompany ageing as positive opportunities to be valued. Another is to 'hold' those with the most challenging disabilities of later life – namely dementia – in the heart of the community and so build stronger communities and pro-social competencies.

'*Malignant social psychology (MSP)*'. This was the phrase coined by Kitwood (1993, 1997). His work is rooted in social role valorization (SRV) and represents a 'social model of disablement'. In particular, the psychosocial environment is understood to have an effect on the well-being of the individual that far outweighs the underlying neuropathy. When cultural beliefs are such that a characteristic, condition, or behaviour are valued negatively then patterns of behaviour damaging to personhood are likely to occur and this is termed 'malignant'. (The term 'malignant' does not signify intent on the part of the perpetrators, but simply describes the impact on the lives of the persons concerned.) Useful devices for spotting such 'malignancies' are the following: (a) they happen disproportionately frequently and cumulatively in relation to the group of persons concerned (in this case people with dementia) and (b) they would not be tolerated by other groups in society. A description of the more common elements of malignant social psychology affecting persons with dementia were identified by Kitwood (1997) as treachery, disempowerment, infantilization, intimidation, labelling, stigmatization, outpacing, invalidation, banishment, objectification, ignoring, imposition, withholding, accusation, disruption, mockery, disparagement. (These are defined in the 'Wounds' section in Chapter 2.)

The concept of 'malignant social psychology' focuses attention on the potential power of a positive (or 'benign') psychosocial environment, in particular to valuing relationships, to enable an individual to live fully irrespective of adversity. It indicates that society (and not just services) has a unique part to play, which is to protect the roles and relationships of the person with dementia within their natural community. To prevent MSP, society and services would find ways of addressing the special needs of people with dementia that do not damage their status, roles or relationships in their communities.

Dementia Care Mapping (Kitwood and Bredin, 1992; Kitwood, 1997) was devised to operationalize the detection of such 'malignancies' through the systematic application of observational methods in care settings. However, changing institutional practices to make them more person-centred misses the point. It is not caregivers in services who are 'dehumanizing' – the malignancy flows from society when it deems that people with dementia can, and should, be taken out of the normal patterns of daily life, and their roles and relationships sacrificed to become patients and to live with similarly disabled people. Making the institution 'person-centred' or 'homely' was never the intent of SRV or Tom Kitwood. The real goals are to build community capacity and to enable the growth of pro-social attitudes and behaviours throughout the community. The hallmarks of a robustly 'person-centred' society would include (a) the most vulnerable community members endure the least threat to their position in society, while (b) the more able members of the community change their patterns of response and so extend their behavioural repertoire and increase their complexity of thinking.

'Information processing impairment'. In this model the individual is understood as being a sub-system of the wider system – the physical and social environment. The business of the brain is to process information in such a way that the organism remains adaptive and capable of successful survival in their environment. Accordingly, dementia is understood as causing alterations to the ways information is processed; behaviour in dementia is therefore understood in terms of the individual attempting to respond optimally to their environment, albeit with altered or limited information. Each behaviour is then meaningful. It is not 'wrong' or 'pathological', but the 'right' behaviour given the subjective experience that has resulted from altered processing.

This model changes the questions about cognitive disabilities from 'What is wrong with this person?' to 'What needs to be arranged and what responses do assistants of this person and the community need to make, so that they can continue to transact the important dimensions of their life (e.g. relationships and roles)?' It is akin to providing skilled and respectful interpreters for people whose language is different, instead of excluding or blaming them for their different mode of communication.

From this perspective to place the individual in a new environment would be most likely to be counterproductive, given that this would add to the overload on a stressed neurological processing system.

'Ecological'. Human psychological and economic systems are merely sub-systems of the wider systems, including ecosystems and the physical environment – and are entirely dependent on these. Without respect for physical systems in all their varieties, there is no environment to support life. Similarly, without the capacity to see value in all forms and varieties of life – plant, insect, bird, animal and human (including individual differences and disabilities) – there is little chance of survival of these complex systems. In this model the image of the person with dementia is as a contributing part of a whole living and evolving system, necessary to the balance of the whole and as necessary as every other element in the system. Individuals with cognitive disabilities would be valued as contributors in an organic and evolving society. The service model is community development (rather than 'repairing' individuals).

Understanding the Person and Their Experience of Living with Dementia

A person will tend to deal with the changes that dementia brings by using the patterns of coping they have developed earlier in adult life. Each individual has a unique constellation of ways of processing emotions and expressing their needs. Accordingly, the most powerful approach for us as assistants or friends of the person with dementia is to understand who the person is and what are these unique patterns? This principle underpins both the 'person-centred' (Kitwood, 1997) and 'person-focused' (Cheston and Bender, 1999) approaches. Through this we can learn how to respond therapeutically and meaningfully to the behaviours of the individual through detecting what lies behind them. SRV goes further and indicates how the values of the culture (not just individual values) determine what it is to be a person. The opportunity to be 'held' in valued social roles, relationships and images are as important for creating personhood as personal goals, aspirations, hopes and instrumental attainments.

We can think of what is commonly called 'challenging behaviour' in dementia as a veil – behind it we might detect one or more of the following:

- The expression of an emotion
- The expression of an unmet need
- An attempt to problem-solve
- The transaction of a familiar role or relationship
- Neurological impairment (NI) itself.

In all cases, if we look behind the person's behaviour we will learn what the underlying factors or causes are. We will discover that most probably it is not 'deliberately obstructive' or 'attention seeking', but explained by some combination of the above-mentioned factors.

Expression of an emotion

A person with cognitive disabilities does not stop experiencing the emotions associated with ordinary life – hope, fear, joy, disappointment, belonging, alienation and a sense of flow or complete absorption in activities (Nakamura and Csikszentmihalyi, 2005). Although there are emotional responses specific to the impact of a disability, a person's emotional life does not become restricted to a tunnel of disability.

Emotions commonly associated with later life in technology-dependent societies include feelings of alienation and loss of status and value as a member of society. Just like their peer group the person with dementia is dealing with these experiences and emotions. However, because of communication difficulties persons with dementia may be less able to describe and share their experiences of age-related change, and as a consequence become more vulnerable to misinterpretation.

Emma had lived all her life with her two brothers in the family home, and had now outlived all her family. She had been a schoolteacher and a well-respected member of her community. However, at 90 years of age, frail, unable to see or hear very well, and now also having difficulties with remembering and with communicating herself, she was in a hospital ward for 'assessment' of her future needs for care. If she could have written about what she felt she might have written the following:

'*This place echoes with strangers' voices, people who don't know me or what my life was like before. It's not possible to see as far as the end of the ward where the nurses' office is, and I'm so terrified I'll not get to the toilet on time. I need two of them to help me now, and it's preying on my mind all the time if I can't see someone. What shame it would cause me if I couldn't get help in time; so there is never a moment I feel safe. I feel so constantly ashamed that my life has come to this. The only reassuring moments I have are when I recall being at home with the boys and my mother and father, and all felt good and the world felt safe. Now I hardly know what is going to happen next, far less be able to control it; I feel like a lump of flesh, abandoned for the crows, not a person worth keeping alive. There's no shame to lose now, it's too late for all that. When I start to feel there's no one in sight, and I panic, I cry out for a nurse. That makes someone come, and I don't care if they scold me, because it's unbearable when they disappear into the haze that begins just at the next bed.*'

There are many possible emotions behind an individual behaviour, and Table 5.3 illustrates only some examples. To identify an individual's emotions, it requires knowing the person well, knowing about their past ways of processing feelings and coping with adversities, and the imagination to picture the emotional terrain they inhabit behind the 'veil' of behaviours.

Expression of an unmet need

When previous lifelong ways of meeting a need are made inaccessible for the person as a result of their disability or removal from their usual environment, the person may seek to meet the need through other means. Needs for security and attachment (Bowlby, 1973) are highly likely to emerge and be expressed in

Table 5.3 Possible emotions behind behaviours

Behaviour	Possible emotion behind	Objective of behaviour
'Hitting'	Fear of an apparent stranger and their intentions	To keep threat at a distance and so lower fear levels
	Fear of being hurt	To make self feel safe
	Frustration e.g. feeling kept away from one's familiar life	To get closer to one's familiar life as remembered
	Shame	Make other take away the shame
	Desperate to be listened to	To feel I am taken seriously
'Wandering'	Panic/feeling lost	To find familiar cues, feel calm
	Need for attachment figure/security such as a parent	To find lost attachment object and to feel secure
	Happiness, enjoyment of socializing	To maintain source of enjoyment
	Sadness, looking for a lost person	To find person and peace of mind
'Shouting'	Fear of being alone	To make human contact
	Fear of the unknown	To evoke a familiar response
	Feeling alone	To feel part of something
	Feeling rejected	Evidence I'm not abandoned
'Crying'	Loss of what is familiar in life	To express grief, seek validation
	Feeling as if no one knows who I really am	To find someone who knows who I really am
	Feeling as if I have lost my self	To find someone to 'hold' my identity
	Need for security	To remember the sense of childhood security

unfamiliar guises. The need to be related to as a mother, partner, sibling, friend, colleague or neighbour will outweigh the 'need' to be a good patient.

The challenge to those in face to face contact with people with dementia is to 'read behind' the surface behaviour, to see through to the person's ordinary general human needs (as well as any special needs) and to take those needs seriously.

'Challenging behaviour' is not the person with dementia challenging others but the result of others and the environment around challenging the person – often through our poor listening skills and our failure to see the needs being communicated. When a need is unacknowledged or unmet and when the person's previous ways of meeting that need are not now available to them (e.g. through frailty) then the person's repeated attempts to meet that need are likely to be labelled as a 'problem' behaviour. For example, the need for exercise may go unacknowledged

Table 5.4 General versus special needs in dementia

Definition of general needs	Examples of special needs in dementia
Ask the question 'How do I need my community to respond to me as a person whose life is worthy of living (and irrespective of any current adverse life conditions)?'	Ask the question 'How do I need my community to respond to my disablement in my best interests and in a way that increases community competence?'
Respect: To have opportunities to hold and be held in worthwhile roles in the community; to be regarded with respect and with good reputation	Cognitive functions: To have support from my community with memory, including people who know me and can hold our memories; assistance with perceptual, executive or any other functions to whatever level needed, and using means that are typical and valued
Relationships: To have opportunities to sustain and grow in relationships, and to take up new relationships (that may outlive me)	Motor functions: To have assistance from my community with carrying out sequences of actions e.g. for self care, for activities of daily living and for community life, and using means that are typical and valued
Places: To have a presence in the community; to share places that typical, valued people use for occupation, leisure, learning, socializing	Communication: To have assistance from my community with successful communication, including people who know me and can read my non-verbal behaviour, and using means that are typical and valued
Choices: To have the experience of autonomy in every day matters and in life-defining matters	Physical mobility: To have assistance from my community with accessing places and people, and in exerting choices commensurate with my living a worthy and valued life, and using means that are typical and valued
Contributing: To have the experience of carrying out functional and meaningful activities competently; to have the sense of self as developing, not static	

All of these remain general human needs whatever level of assistance is required to accomplish the need

or a restricted environment or frailty prevents exercise; then attempts to walk may be seen mistakenly as 'wandering' or 'interference'. Table 5.4 shows examples of general and disability-related needs (based on the Framework for Accomplishment of O'Brien and Lyle, 1986). To the extent that these go unacknowledged in dementia, the environment around the person is experienced as challenging and hostile, with a commensurate effect on behaviour.

Table 5.5 Possible unmet needs behind behaviours

Behaviour	Possible unmet need	Objective of behaviour
Searching for keys *Asking to go home*	Need to have the experience of self as valued, contributing meaningfully	To rediscover places and opportunities in which the self was valued and contributed competently
Repeated shouting e.g. 'Help', 'Nurse'	Need to be recognised by others as a unique person	To locate people who might reflect the unique 'me' and so provide comfort
Resisting *Not cooperating*	Need to experience autonomy in everyday and in life-defining matters	To avoid feeling overcome by others' choices; to rediscover own choices
Repeatedly asking for the toilet	Need for sense of control and security (in the absence of physical control)	To feel safe and out of danger of soiling oneself
Refusal to get out of bed	Need to prevent feeling shame	To prevent others seeing me; to hide

> *Nancy's life was centred on her home and her family – and vice versa. She was the one who looked after the household finances, and on whom her daughters relied in times of personal need. Her personal appearance and the welcoming atmosphere of her home were important to her always, in her role as centre of the family. Now disabled by a neurological condition, she felt trapped at home, helpless to maintain it, unable to exert choices over her own personal dress and grooming, and wary of every visit by her daughters and grandchildren. Each and every day was marred from the start by Nancy's distress; she would shout and weep inconsolably, and reject comfort from husband, family or professionals.*
>
> *'I feel so frustrated that I can't look decent for my grandchildren to visit me; I have bedsocks put on me in the morning, and Jim says it doesn't matter as I don't go out now anyway. I have a sense that he isn't doing the accounts and keeping up the house – I so long to be able to welcome my family here and all I do is cry. I don't want them to visit, because I can't manage to get the conversation round to them – it's always me and my illness. My sense of despair increases as there is already talk of a move to a care home because the family can't cope. I need to be able to be their grandma and mum again – and everything seems to be going against it'.*

Nancy is sinking under the pressure of attention to her 'special needs', and is suffering as a result of others' blindness to her general human needs. In the vicious circle, her behaviour becomes more 'challenging' the more she is expected to comply as a patient and her other needs go unattended and dismissed. Table 5.5

provides some examples of possible unmet needs behind common behaviours that 'challenge' others around the person with dementia.

Problem-solving

When a person experiences themselves as being in problem situation, the natural human response is to attempt to solve the problem. The person with cognitive disabilities tries to find ways out of, or to resolve, their dilemma. However, they have to do this in an environment that is no longer easy to make sense of. As a result they may express behaviours that seem unusual to others but are a logical response to their perception of the situation.

'*Stress*' is an imbalance between the demands of the environment and the resources available to the individual to respond. Under conditions of stress, human beings respond by attempting to reduce the level of environmental demand or to increase resourcesto restore equilibrium that is they problem-solve. People living with dementia are often obliged to be creative in finding ways to restore equilibrium – although their solutions are not always given this interpretation.

> '*I am Flora and I now live in a residential home in a city. I don't know the people who live here. I'm fitter than most of them, and I like to walk about a lot. I know my way around well enough now though I haven't got used to it – there are coverings on the floors, walls and staircases that seem shiny, echoing and brilliantly bright. Everything I see around me is rectangular and enclosed and nothing like the places I've lived all my life. I used to walk miles, for days on end, on grass and rough tracks; I slept out on the fells, sometimes in a bothy, often in the open in the summers. My job was to tend the sheep, and only bring them in for lambing and tupping. Only occasionally now do I see the trees and feel the freshness of the open air on my face. Inside this home there are tall plants in plant pots, and that is the closest to my old life I get. I pass by the stair well where the plants in pots are the tallest and the windows on to the sky the largest, and there I have the strong sensation of being back where I belong, where things are as they were when I was free and strong. I sometimes stay around the stairwell and relive the long days on the fells and the nights under the hedgerows or in the bothy. One day my bladder was 'bursting' as I walked around – it seemed like the most natural thing to use the bushes to hide behind. But people became upset with me, and said it was dirty, and there was no need to go there. They don't seem to notice the smell in the toilets here – strong artificial scents and strange chemical smells that make me want to escape!*'

Table 5.6 Possible problem-solving behind behaviours

Behaviour	Possible problem-solving	Objective of behaviour
Wandering	I do not recognise where I am, and when this has happened to me in the past searching has succeeded	To find clues as to where I am and what to do next
Hiding faeces	I fear I will fail to find the toilets; I am embarrassed to use communal toilets; or I am embarrassed to use a commode	To avoid the dilemma; to keep clean; to hide the evidence of my failure; to avoid shame; to avoid public humiliation
Urinating in inappropriate places e.g. sink, or plant pot	I need to empty my bladder but don't recognise a toilet amongst the furniture around me, so I try to identify something that looks suitable	To find a similar receptacle or a place I have used in the past (such as under a bush, a sink, or a bucket)
Repeatedly telephoning a family member or friend	I panic when I cannot work out what is to be done next; in the past telephoning my family/friend has been successful in reducing this panic and resolving my dilemma	To reduce the feeling of panic, which I know only makes things worse, and to feel secure from having the correct information

Table 5.6 provides some examples of possible problem-solving behaviours.

Functioning in a familiar role or relationship

The roles and relationships of a lifetime are often made inaccessible or hard to sustain in the context of cognitive disabilities. To some extent this is a result of the impairments themselves; for example, when a person has failures of communication or memory. However, the person may also disengage to avoid embarrassment. In addition, people in the community commonly lack the competencies to communicate with the person with dementia; as a result people with dementia find their opportunities to continue in known roles and relationships progressively stripped away. The natural human response is to seek out these roles and relationships. Perhaps the person concerned has been the physical centre of the household and the emotional hub of the family; they may respond to the loss of these roles by behaving in a mothering way in relation to people in their environment. Such behaviour would be deemed inappropriate if the person transacts it towards staff or other residents in a care setting. It could make the person resist accepting care, since they see their role as the caregiver. The person might express (apparently inappropriate) familiarity in relation to a caregiver or fellow resident. To label it 'uncooperative' does not point towards a solution. If there is a relationship vacancy that is being transposed on to someone else this insight can be used to create a resolution and ease the way to a more successful relationship.

Tony had to retire early from his work as a successful senior salesman for a technology company because of dementia. The living room at home had been turned into his 'bed-sit' so that family life could carry on as before but without Tony. Over 2 years there were reports of aggressive behaviour, including him punching a wall during testing of his memory. Because he resisted services such as day care he was assigned a care worker to accompany him for walks. The woman described his behaviour as odd and sometimes uncooperative during these walks although she coped professionally and well with this. He was admitted to hospital following a crisis with aggressive behaviour with his family.

In the ward Tony seemed both relieved and defensive. He agreed to a full assessment including a neuropsychological profile, and clearly shared the desire to know what was happening to him.

Tony was proud of his working life. He took pleasure in telling about his achievements in developing business plans for his company. As we got to know Tony over a longer time, we could form a better idea of what it was like to be living inside his head. Our idea was that it was like this:

'I know I'm in hospital now, and that's a relief because I can make a good case for myself here. They are all professional people here so I can act like a professional. I used to be so embarrassed to be out in the town with that young woman; she was very pleasant and kind to me but she wasn't a friend and I didn't know what to say or do. I hear them talking about tablets a lot in the ward, and this gives me the idea that I could offer them my expert advice with their business plan – I have done successful sales work with some pharmaceutical companies and this makes me feel a bit better about myself. They'll help me with their expertise and in return I'll offer them mine. So I ask my family to bring in my files from home and I take aside the doctors one at a time and tell them about the deal.'

Should the people who are giving assistance to Tony consider this talk and behaviour as 'behavioural symptoms' of the dementia? Or is there another formulation that would offer more help to understand what is behind them, or what has shaped them.

It is useful to identify the roles that are being acted out. These are roles from Tony's life in which he has felt valued and comfortable, such as breadwinner, boss and admired employee. The roles of 'sick person' and 'patient' have been hard to tolerate – they had given him no status and he did not know how to behave. At home, he rejected these roles, and in the face of no alternatives being on offer became depressed, withdrawn and angry.

Through this understanding of the meaning behind his behaviour, it was possible to develop a workable relationship with Tony. Respect for the 'competent professional' role formed the basis of trust and a way forward other than aggressive resistance. Although Tony's dementia progressed rapidly it was always possible to gain insights into his current behaviours by again trying to 'read' and validate the roles and relationships that he might be transacting – and not trying to 'correct' him into the patient role.

At the age of 93 years Meg was living in a long-term care hospital ward. The dementia with which she had lived for 10 years had left her chairbound and wholly dependent on others. She felt rejected and lost. Meg had grown up in a small village and had been a very popular figure in the village throughout her adult years; she ran the local cinema during the years of the World War II, and was dearly loved for doing so. She had persevered to keep it going, and even after it closed she was busy in the local community, with projects and campaigns. Meg found time in her life to marry and have a family too; and in later life had enjoyed the more sedate pace of bowling as a hobby. What, then, did it mean that she now spent her time calling out repeatedly her brother's name and said little else? It was said that they had never had a good relationship; and he had died more than 10 years ago. Everyone around her held the theory that this was some meaningless behaviour – it was seen as symptom of progressing dementia, a result of loss of orientation, and a nuisance.

Staff then focused their effort on 'Getting to know you', and in the process hypothesized that Meg had come to a point in her life where (irrespective of dementia) she felt compelled to turn to unattended business from the past. Was it that her brother had come into the centre of her attention now precisely because he never had before? Her choices at each point in her life before had led into other relationships, and now they were not present. There was space now for 'what if' thoughts such as 'What if I'd known John better?' In very late life there is often the experience of review and reflection on pathways not chosen. With dementia the person may have difficulty talking about such reflections and need support to process the thoughts openly and naturally. For example, a friend might need to say openly 'You made the very best choices you could at that time in your life – given the circumstances you and John were in'. Once staff saw Meg's behaviour in this light, they could offer her their fuller human understanding for the situation she felt herself to be in. This gave them more job satisfaction than applying only techniques in 'behaviour management'.

> *Jay had lived a seemingly happy and full life in the United Kingdom; no one knew details about his early life, and he had never volunteered much. Towards the end of his life he developed dementia. Having lived in a Nursing Home quite contentedly for some time he became acutely unsettled, lashing out at the nurses and using accusatory names to them, particularly those with fair hair. This behaviour had never been seen before even when his dementia had quite disabled him at home. One of his helpers found out about his early past. Where he grew up in Europe all the people had dark hair; women who dyed their hair fair were viewed with suspicion. He had also been in a prison camp in the war. These two things led to his helpers thinking differently about his reactions to his present accommodation. They realised it was possible that he was interpreting the large rooms as if they were the prison camp, the marching of staff feet along corridors as feet marching people towards their deaths, and the fair-haired women as threats or warders. To minimize this type of stimulation, they moved his room to a quiet end of the home where the sounds of marching feet would not reach and shared his care amongst the non-fair–haired staff. The 'lashing out' behaviour stopped. He died about a year later, having spent his last year free from the torment of the spectre of 'female warders in the prison camp'.*

How the Nature of Stroke and Its Problems Have Been Defined – The Shaping of Societal and Service Responses

Like dementia, stroke is a form of neurological impairment that affects mainly people in the later part of their lives, although some individuals can be affected much earlier in life. In contrast to dementia, however, it is sudden and often is highly visible in its impact. It causes acute discontinuity and potentially catastrophic impact on the person's social roles and relationships. It may appear at first as if nothing can be as it was before. Then hopes may be raised for recovery of abilities often followed by uncertainty, disappointment and having to cope with other people's reactions based on their beliefs about stroke.

Table 5.7 illustrates how some beliefs about the nature of stroke historically have influenced the ways societies have responded to people with stroke-related disabilities, and the service models which these societies have deemed appropriate.

'Struck down'. In times when the soul was seen as the 'animator' of the body, a sudden collapse looked as if the soul was 'struck down by a devil'. Society would try to protect itself against this capricious force by attempting to strike out the 'devil'.

Table 5.7   How beliefs about stroke historically have influenced societal responses and service models

Belief: definition of stroke	Image: person seen as	Society's response	Service model
'Struck down'	Victim of a mysterious force, maybe 'the devil'	Fear of a capricious 'devil' force; pity	Distance, separation
'Act of god'	Victim selected for punishment	Fear	Protection of society from 'them'
Judgement	Deviant, wanting, inadequate	Cleansing, salvation desired	Religious system seen as appropriate
A diseased brain	Broken; not a person any more	Technical; credentialled caregivers	Shut away from the world; medical focus
Accident	Tragic victim; person as 'damaged goods'	Technical; 'find the cure'	Medical; vast resources to cure and research
Trauma: 'vascular attack'	Like a person who's had a heart attack	Accords higher status similar to 'heart attack'	Medically more prestigious; draws resources
Information processing impairment	*Actively engaged in coping with an interruption in information processing*	*Conscious of the person as a person first, living with a limitation in their neurological functioning*	*Personal futures planning; focus on strengths, relationships, reputation and value as a person*
Ecological	*Part of natural range of events*	*Conscious of value of taking care of each other Conscious of well-being irrespective of disability*	*Community strengthening: building everyone's competencies to live with disability*

'*Act of god*'. In some periods of history the image was of the person 'chosen' by god, possibly for punishment, resulting in distancing from the affected person.

'*Judgement*'. The person is seen as judged wanting or deviant in some respect. The associated social response would be 'cleansing', 'correction', 'salvation' or similar – requiring services to bring the person back into the cleansed or saved state. The role of religious rather than health institutions in the society would be emphasized.

'*A diseased brain*' The person is seen as suffering from a pathology, resulting in a less cataclysmic and more benign response from the society.

'*Accident*'. The term 'vascular accident' also conjures a medical pathology image – but suggests more than one variable in the picture.

'*Trauma*'. The term 'vascular attack' draws a comparison with 'heart attack', and emphasizes the physical and personal impact. To see stroke as trauma may bring resources and status into an area of medicine that has been traditionally less prestigious.

'*Information processing impairment*'. The stroke is seen in terms of causing an interruption to information processing channels. The emphasis is on developing alternative channels for processing, including via the assistance of other people.

'*Ecological*'. The event is seen as impacting on the physiological system that is a sub-system of larger systems, such as the family, the community, economic systems and wider environmental systems all of which are inter-dependent. The threat is to the wider systems not just the individual; however, the event is also an opportunity for the wider systems to learn, to predict and to maintain homeostasis.

Current evidence suggests that early focused input aids recovery and that long-term adjustment is benefited by attention to the home and social context (Knapp, Young, House and Forster, 2000; Department of Health, 2001; Rudd et al., 1999). 'Recovery' relies as much on maintaining relationships and roles as on re-establishing instrumental functioning. Hence, psychological approaches, such as Getting to know you (GTKY), strengths/needs and goal planning approaches (see Chapter 6) are relevant here.

The more 'visible' effects of stroke include loss of motor functions and speech. There is, however, a range of potential 'invisible' effects (such as higher executive system and visuo–spatial neuro-processing impairments), which are commonly misunderstood or are not acknowledged.

Understanding the Person with Stroke and Their Behaviour – 'Invisible' Cognitive Disabilities

The information processing model helps us to understand the cognitive processing systems that have been interrupted or have broken down in the aftermath of stroke; this then helps us to work out from basic principles what distortions, interruptions or white noise are affecting the messages the person is receiving from the environment (e.g. in the event of damage to the ascending pathways, the arousal system or the higher executive systems).

The development of anxiety and depression after stroke is a known risk (Astrom, 1996; Burvill et al., 1995a, 1995b), which can interfere with recovery

(Gillespie, 1997; Paolucci, Antonucci, Pratesi, Traballesi, Grasso and Lubich, 1999). Arguably, people with 'invisible' cognitive impairments are more likely to be misunderstood and as a consequence experience alienation, anxiety and depression. A positive approach to preventing and alleviating anxiety and depression will therefore recognize the potential importance of evidence gathering, including neuropsychological profiling, to accurately identify and respond to potential invisible cognitive impairments (Lincoln, Majid and Weyman, 2002).

Impairments in the arousal system and its linking pathways

The arousal system is essential, not only for evoking responses from the higher cortical areas, but also for attenuating the input signals in accordance with their significance to the person. For example, we rely on the nervous and endocrine systems having *different* responses to the signals 'Fire!' versus 'Relax!' In some cases of damage to the ascending activating system this discrimination may fail and the person will experience the same activation of the alarm system (panic and anxiety) equally to all stimuli. It is not uncommon for people after stroke to have difficulty in attenuating arousal responses. For example, a person with neurological damage may respond paradoxically to the instruction 'relax' by responding with *increased* tension and arousal. Such reactions can easily be misunderstood as deliberately uncooperative.

Siobhain was a member of a large close family. She had never married and lived in the large family house along with several other siblings and their families. They ran a family business, and all were happy with this arrangement. Siobhain felt satisfied and content with her life; there was a personal history of coping well with life and its challenges and no evidence of anxiety problems. When she sustained a stroke at the age of 74, she was left with some severe disabilities, which included loss of her mobility. She took this blow with great magnanimity and grace. However, problems began when rehabilitation staff reported that she 'did not co-operate' with therapy goals and exercises. They noticed that, when given an instruction, she would tense up and be unable to carry out an action to command. This was attributed (mistakenly) to anxiety. Attempts that were made to teach her relaxation simply made matters worse. Staff who knew her well reported that she was able to relax and carry out actions when these occurred spontaneously – which was mistakenly taken as evidence that she was uncooperative.

A neuropsychological profile revealed the presence of less visible disabilities, including damage to the systems that relay inputs from the environment and subsequently organize appropriate and purposeful responses. In particular, she could not organize sequences of actions in time and space, such as to copy a design, or to carry out an instruction. This explained why it would be important to avoid using overt instructions when communicating with Siobhain. Staff began to see that impairment of the attentional system mean that all their verbal instructions (even words intended to be reassuring, such as 'relax') were exerting the same high arousal level. (Internal stimuli involved a different pathway.) They found that gentle but clear physical guidance and prompts triggered less tension, and so became more confident in assisting her.

Ina, at the age of 69, had for 10 years been described as having a 'phobia about sitting', which had not resolved with treatment. However, she had other unexplained symptoms, including a tendency to fall, especially backwards, and phases of becoming locked into the standing position when only an external stimulus (such as the telephone ringing unexpectedly) would unlock her flow of actions. The symptoms were not progressive as would occur in Parkinson's disease, Parkinsonian syndromes or Progressive Supra-nuclear Palsy. However, an earlier CT scan had shown small strokes in the same areas that are involved in the progressive brainstem diseases.

Using the 'information processing' model of mind this can be described in terms of errors in linking systems and pathways. For example: damaged connections between the arousal system and the specialized higher functional brain areas could underlie intermittent failures of initiation and loss of coordination; damaged feedback systems could underlie falls or sensations of postural discomfort; and unexpected stimuli from the outer environment could ascend un-modulated and with sufficient intensity to unlock intentional programmes of actions. Making sense of these symptoms in this way (rather than a 'mental illness') helped Ina to feel less ashamed; she felt relief not to be a 'failed phobic' and felt validated that others could accept the 'reality' of her disabilities.

Damage to the links between language and other cognitive systems

A puzzling and challenging situation for many people and for those who assist them arises when the specialized higher cognitive functions appear to survive intact (e.g. the person has well-preserved language and well-preserved motor functions) yet do not function together when required. An example of such a disconnection might be the person is able to fasten a button where this is incidental to an ongoing, spontaneous activity; yet they are unable to carry out the identical action on request. The information processing model helps in rehabilitation because it points to the information pathways likely to be involved and from there to practical strategies for circumventing them (such as physical cueing, modelling or contextualizing).

Elise was a proud and busy grandmother when she had a stroke. At home after several months in hospital, the family noticed changes especially that she 'wouldn't' do what she was told, but 'she can do it if she wants to'. The staff at the day hospital also observed how Elise could go and fetch herself a drink from the fridge but not if asked to do so. This was interfering with good relationships at home, and people were starting to describe her as 'uncooperative', 'stubborn' and 'a different personality'. In fact none of these was the explanation; the impact of the stroke had been to disable the flow of information from the language areas into the integration areas, whilst sparing other pathways linking initiation and intentional functions with integration and procedural planning. Elise and her family found this to be a meaningful and valid explanation, giving them ideas about how to avoid the disabled language–action pathways. They were able to keep their good family relationships and did not allow Elise's lost physical and cognitive abilities to get out of proportion again.

Andrew was a retired accountant who enjoyed playing the stock market until his stroke. From being the centre of activity in the household and taking the lead role in organizing the family's financial and practical affairs, he became the one who needed to be prompted about everything – to get out of bed, to eat, to speak to people, and to walk. It was said that he 'could do' these things but didn't appear to 'be motivated'. Whilst the possibility of depression of mood was being considered, it was discovered on cognitive assessment that there was some damage to the ability to comprehend language and to link language with information from other modalities. This had not been easily detected at first because discrete functions seemed well preserved, including memory, reasoning, visuospatial skills and motor–constructional processes. Subjectively, he would be experiencing difficulty when required to translate others' communications into relevant actions for himself. His family found this to be a practical explanation that helped them accept his true level of disability and to revise their expectations of him.

Language–action disability might easily be taken for lack of motivation and apathy, and thereby raise the question of 'depression', but the person themselves often reports neither low mood nor depressive ideas, and responds to support in achieving graded goals in small steps rather than to interventions that focus on incentives or mood. Rehabilitation will aim to assist structure, through routines and activities rebuilt in graded steps, with the purpose of maximizing (through external environmental stimuli and prompts) the residual ability to maintain action sequences and procedural routines.

Damage to the higher executive system

Complex systems are normally involved in controlling and monitoring the track of thought and attention, and in switching track appropriately to our needs, decisions and the context. Damage to these systems can accordingly be difficult to pinpoint. For example, a person may be able to maintain their ability to monitor and attend to the environment as long as there is a flow of ongoing stimulation. When external stimulation is 'switched off', for example in the dark or when alone, control over the track of attention may not be sustainable. For some individuals being in their own inner world of memories is an aversive experience; add to this a failure of the ability to steer direction or to weigh thoughts rationally, and the experience may become frightening. The person who calls out or cries repeatedly may be seeking environmental stimulation in an effort to release themselves from being stuck on such an inner track.

Tommy shouted at night in his general hospital ward for many hours and was not sleeping. In the daytime it was reported that he was totally appropriate in his behaviour and communication. By his own account the experience he had at nighttime was of being trapped in internal trains of thought from which he could not escape. The purpose of shouting aloud might have been to replace the missing external stimulation, which in daytime helped him to stay 'tuned' to the external environment. With a disabled attention control system he was at the mercy of whichever sources of stimuli predominated, and helpless to switch or re-tune without outside assistance.

Donnie was living at home, not seeming to have sustained obvious aftereffects from his stroke. However, his wife was distressed by his shouting – which stopped when someone else visited the house and occurred only when he was alone or with his wife at home. Attributing it to a breakdown in their relationship, she was on the point of leaving him. On investigation it became apparent that as long as there was a flow of environmental stimuli, his attention kept him responsive and 'on track'; the more unfamiliar the stimuli the greater their power to 'hold' his attention and thereby to sustain appropriate responses. This helped his wife to understand how his shouting did have positive value, for example to help him move on from one step to the next when cleaning his teeth after washing his face. The explanation also helped his wife see how the shouting behaviour was not personal to her, and she and Donnie were able to recover their valued relationship.

Charlie and his wife had retired to another country; when a stroke occurred they came back to their home city for medical help – but were homeless and roleless. Charlie's wife now took charge. She found a new home that was small, practical and designed for disabled people. To Charlie, it was claustrophobic. His wife was so anxious about his safety that she allowed him little unsupervised activity or movement, even to go to the toilet. The house was soon like a hothouse, and his feelings of being smothered intensified as quickly as his wife's anxiety and agitation. Soon, he was being reported as being 'sexually disinhibited', and saying aggressive things. Certainly, the stroke had affected the frontal lobes, and this may have affected his resources to tolerate the stress of change. It may also have been more difficult for him to see the world from another's position, or to hold on to social codes of acceptable behaviour. However, it was clear that his behaviour became 'worse', that is less inhibited, as the pressures to do nothing and be nothing continued. The vicious circle began to close; his wife came to see him as no more than an object of care and as having no feelings. On hearing himself described this way he asked to be taken out of their home to a residential home. In that setting, he was expected and supported to take decisions; he undertook activities by himself with an agreed risk level. The disinhibited behaviour disappeared. He walked outside unsupervised and went to the toilet in the night unsupervised. With this as evidence of how he could function as a self-regulating and autonomous person, despite the stroke, their expectations changed. Charlie and his wife agreed to live together again, as partners and equals.

Definitions of Need in the 'Old' and 'New' Paradigms

A biological focus, and an emphasis on 'cure', has for a long time shaped society's responses to people with cognitive disabilities. People living with disabling conditions for which acute medicine has no remedy are labelled 'untreatable'; this has the consequent risk that the person is seen as of no value simply because of their mismatch with the technology. Yet life with a deteriorating condition, at some part in life, is probably the norm.

The hospice movement challenged this philosophy for people with cancer (Kubler-Ross, 1969, 1975; Saunders, 1959). They re-defined human need in the face of 'incurable' physical illnesses in terms of needs for hope, a place in the community, life with family and friends and general human needs (in place of illness-related needs). The notion of living positively with hope while living with cancer is now largely accepted; it is a result of a sea-change over a period of two to three decades. In contrast, the notion of living positively with hope while living with dementia still challenges a large part of society and the medical community.

In the new paradigm of dementia care the protection and building of *person-hood* is the core of need. Personhood is the *person as a valued part of a living community* – from this stems security, self-worth and a sense of agency. The SRV framework has always placed social roles, relationships and being regarded as worthwhile by others at the heart of both the definition of needs and the social construction of care and service systems. Williams (2003) provides the following SRV definition of need: 'How do I need my community to respond to my experiences, of disablement, oppression, marginalisation, or other suffering, in my best interests, and to create community competence?' Translated into positive action, this means if the response I receive as a person with cognitive disabilities is not *in my best interests,* 'and' *capable of increasing the competencies of my community to deal with disability,* then it should not be happening.

The sanctity of life question

The 'sanctity of life' issue, as it is known, can be understood through the question:

> 'Does a life have value?' (unconditionally and irrespective of disabilities or other difference).

It is not uncommon to hear people who do not have dementia say 'I'd rather be put down than live like that'. Commonly, health professionals talk about 'quality of life' – with the implication that there is a level below which the life is not desirable or worthwhile. However, there is evidence that the people who predict that they will not value life under circumstances of severe disability change their view and seek to continue their life as worth living if it does happen to them (and they have the direct experience).

Each time a person says 'I would rather be dead than have dementia' they are sending a message to and about people with dementia – 'It would be better if *you* were dead'.

If the answer to the question 'Does a life have value, unconditionally?' is 'No', then what follows is discrimination and differentiation of one life from another. When some lives can be seen as less worthy, the way is opened for those individuals to be seen as objects rather than as human, and thereby to be perceived as a nuisance and to perceive themselves as a nuisance to their fellow beings. The answer 'no' paves the way to the belief that some people have lesser, or less important needs, and hence to some people not having their life needs met even where these could be met. For example, needs other than basic biological needs, such as for continuity of relationships, meaningful interactions, love, hope and to have one's concerns taken seriously may be ignored. The individual's expression of unacknowledged needs, emotional or behavioural, is then at risk of being interpreted as further 'symptoms' to be treated – a current example is 'behavioural and psychological symptoms of dementia' (BPSD).

'Death making' as a social process: Wolfensberger (1987, 1998) has described this as an unconscious social process transacted in relation to vulnerable people and named it 'death making' – because the ultimate outcome of loss of person-hood is banishment and annihilation. Wolfensberger's own life experience was of the loss of personhood status of an entire group in his society of origin, whose life path ended in the death camps of 1940s Germany.

The alternative is simple, practical and of benefit to the whole of the society; those around the person with dementia can develop a raised awareness of what it means to be a person, a clear understanding of what it takes to relate to a person with cognitive disabilities and a finely honed capability to communicate with all fellow beings irrespective of differences.

The 'futility principle': (Smith, 2003a, 2003b) has used this to describe the impact on medical and social care systems of the answer 'no' to the sanctity of life question. It happens when interventions which *would* work, for example resuscitation, are *not* applied for some people, specifically for the reason that their lives are seen as being of less value. 'Futility' does not relate to the technique but to the life in question, which is not considered worth giving a future. Often poor quality of life *conditions* (e.g. loneliness and poverty) are transferred to the person, and confusingly named 'poor quality of life'. This label accordingly encourages a response of pity, nihilism and lack of positive intervention. Yet positive practical changes can always be made to the environment, physical or social, to protect against unnecessary risk and accommodate extra life needs. The positive response again is simple and practical; others around the person with dementia can take steps to value the person, and to prevent the person from developing the idea they are a burden.

What follows if the answer is 'Yes'? Society is empowered to create new and different forms of support, and to strengthen citizenship capabilities such as generosity, altruistic action, collaborative action and locally rooted mutual help-ing behaviours. Protecting the personhood of older people with dementia not only assists those individuals, it also fosters a successful inclusive society and the citizenship skills that accompany it.

Finally, a major modern problem is demoralization among staff of services for older people. Evidence, however, indicates that even excellent management skills and training programmes cannot neutralize or stem poor morale in an enduring way; 'hero innovators' may have the capacity to value their own actions but risk 'burn-out'. Logic would suggest that good morale flows from having one's activities positively valued by society; hence, where older and frail people are valued, so will contact with those people be 're-moralizing'.

The Seven Core Themes – Towards Attaining the Goals of Socially Valued Life Conditions and Socially Valued Roles for People at Risk of Being Devalued

Prior to the emergence of positive psychology as such, SRV workers had developed a framework for identifying positive achievements, experiences and social image – and what actions would be required for those to be accomplished for an individual person with special needs – replacing a previous focus on impairments and remedying deficits. The seven core themes are environmental processes that commonly add to adversity in the lives of individuals with special needs. Programme Analysis of Service Systems (PASSING) (Wolfensberger and Thomas, 1983) provided a system for identifying the adversities and the actions that might counter them and support successful fulfilment of valued life goals. Practical actions and insights emerge from applying this thinking in relation to the position of older people with cognitive disabilities.

The role of (un)consciousness in human services

Things that are unpleasant or unpalatable are apt to be denied and repressed into unconsciousness, especially if these things are in contrast to the ideals held in people's consciousness. As a rule, good-hearted and idealistic people work in services; at the same time services are required by society to do things to frail older people that would be difficult to value if they were to happen to ourselves. For example, they often require workers to take people away from their own world, to congregate people together who have little in common other than their disability and to have little to do that is valued. As a result, strong rationalization is needed if workers are to continue; workers need to believe what their service carries out is in the recipients' best interests. Denial of evidence to the contrary is therefore essential.

SRV's positive counter is that consciousness is preferable to unconsciousness. To maintain denial draws constantly on mental energy (hence low morale and high illness levels), while consciousness releases the energy to pursue positive life-goals and is reality-based.

Action point: The process of GTKY and strengths/needs assessment is a key step in identifying the goals that are important *to that person and to promoting positive aspirations about their life in their community*, and in accomplishing these goals. Even if the goals seem difficult to reach, the fact that they are real can lend commitment and courage to all those enlisted in working towards them.

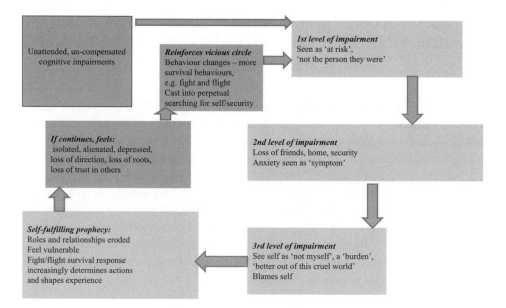

Figure 5.1 Vicious circle in unattended dementia. Based on 'The Relevance of Role Expectancy and Role Circularity to Deviancy-Making and Deviancy-Unmaking', Wolfensberger, W and Thomas, S, 1983, Canadian NIMR. Reproduced by permission of Wolf Wolfensberger.

The relevance of role expectancy and role circularity

The social roles that people adopt or are expected to fulfil exert powerful influences and controls on individual behaviour and beliefs. The self-fulfilling prophecy, or vicious circle (Figure 5.1), can lead to low expectations and restricted roles when a person is viewed as 'older'. For example, it is common for beliefs about later life to be fused with beliefs about dementia, resulting in erroneous expectations and self-derogation.

The fact, of course, is that ageing is a universal reality. The things that can be changed are the social consequences, including increasing community capacity for helping behaviours; developing a new, contributing, image of later life and protecting the valued roles and relationships of a 'good' later life for those who encounter disability. These are within our sphere of control and influence that is we can actually *do* something practical. (To allow human energy to go into unrealistic pursuits, such as 'living for ever' denies and obstructs the development of an age-friendly society). Dementia or not, the way to maintain 'the good things' in life is through protecting valued roles, such as householder/tenant/friend/neighbour/spouse/parent/volunteer/citizen. The sense of being valued, nurtured, fulfilled and future-focused does not depend on being 'disability-free'; on the contrary, feelings of fulfilment and happiness derive from the experience of dealing with real life adversities in the context of a socially competent and enabling community.

When people say that they would want euthanasia rather than dementia, they are more than probably reflecting that they could not bear the fear, rejection, sense of being a burden and losses to dignity, respect, love and being valued that are seen with unattended dementia. However, these losses (the secondary wounds) are not necessary. They are not saying 'I don't want my life'.

When an older person says 'Don't treat me as an invalid' or 'Don't treat me as if I'm stupid' this may reflect that they are having to resist pressures to give up existing roles yet at the same time are having to develop new roles that involve dependency on others. Often with benign motives other people take over activities or press for 'care organizations' to step in. This increases the image of the older frail person as passive and dependent, risking more severe loss of functioning and impairment. Once the person's self-image becomes dominated by the new roles of 'dependent', 'sick', 'disabled' or 'not like other people', then the vicious circle is self-perpetuating.

Action point: Protecting or re-building community relationships, roles and connections is a powerful way of making a positive difference in the life of the person with dementia. It does not preclude clinical interventions aimed at the dementia directly, such as cognitive stimulation; its impact is at another level and potentially of enduring benefit in real-life terms.

Positive compensation for second and third levels of impairment

In mainstream society having a high, or valued, social standing can be greatly protective against the potentially stigmatizing effects of characteristics that are perceived as different or challenging. For example, argumentative behaviour may be seen as 'characterful' in a politician or 'endearing' in a member of royalty; however, in an older person it may be stigmatised as non-compliance, or in the case of dementia as a 'symptom'.

Apparently neutral life conditions can be seen as 'adding value' to status in relation to some groups, yet devaluing to other groups. For example, living in institutional accommodation may be status enhancing in the context of university students, but negatively valuing in the context of people who are old and disabled.

Even generally positive characteristics can become negative when perceived in the context of age and/or dementia. For example, having an interest in a sexual life becomes 'dirty' or in family life becomes 'interfering'; having knowledge becomes 'out of date' and experience is cast as 'living in the past'; offering help can be cast as 'a nuisance' and open communication about life and death can become cast as 'depressing'. The conservatism corollary points to the significance and importance of preventing multiple wounding.

Action point. Reference to the evidence concerning a life is usually effective in neutralizing the negative spin. The GTKY process equips us with facts, and these can counter the blaming script that often takes over when there is no other explanation for challenging behaviour. This can promote positive ways in which people with dementia, and their behaviour, can be described. For example, knowing that a person has a life history of orienteering and climbing mountains can equip helpers to describe current behaviour as 'walking with purpose' or 'seeking exercise' rather than as 'wandering'. The principle of the 'conservatism corollary' is analogous to a balloon that counters the weights that might otherwise stop life moving on; actions and language used with and about the person have power to lighten the burden of negatively viewed status.

Reframing is a positive tool involving identifying needs and goals, clearly, positively and specifically in three steps: 'who', 'needs what – specifically' and 'what would it take to accomplish?'

1. Who: Know the Person
2. Needs what – specifically:

    State needs in place of problems
    Make clear specific statements in place of 'fuzzies'

3. What would it take to accomplish?

    State in clear language what is to be achieved in the interests of the person concerned.
    Provide positive statements of what people and arrangements it would take to accomplish what is desirable, in place of negative statements which just say what is wrong.

An Example:

Who: 'James Bruce enjoys one to one company more than large social gatherings and has a pride in his long career as a successful salesman' rather than 'James Bruce resists social activities and is restless'.

Needs what – specifically: 'James needs one to one company and to have a sense of being successful' (in place of problem statements such as 'James needs to stop resisting activities and to stop being restless').

What would it take to accomplish this (people and arrangements): 'James needs the guidance of Jenny to find his way to the washrooms, and after that needs to be left in privacy to use the toilet then minimal physical prompting to fasten his clothing, before returning to the living room with the minimum amount of attention being drawn to himself; in the living room, he needs Jenny to guide him to the desk where he can read the papers under a good light and have the opportunity to discuss them with Anthony' (In place of a fuzzy negative such as 'James needs to cooperate with toileting and needs to accept help from staff without being aggressive').

The developmental model and personal competency enhancement

Human development has many strands and, unless some barrier gets in the way, will stretch into very late life. Alex Comfort's (1977) seminal work explored this in relation to learning, thinking, reflecting, relationships, roles, occupation, interests, skills and indeed all areas of human functioning. Some limitations, such as reduction in muscle strength, can become opportunities for other talents and interests to grow.

From the earliest psychological investigations about development in later life, evidence showed that the majority of individuals have a positive attitude both to their past life, and to ageing itself (Coleman, 1996, 1997). Longitudinal studies have shown that associated with good self-esteem in later life are having a belief in self as being useful, active, having agency, and having a community of shared belief (Coleman et al., 1993). It seems that resilience features in later life psychology as much as in early development (Lemay and Ghazal, 2001).

Coleman reported a correlation between a detectable drop in self-esteem and earlier death (compared to peers of comparable health status). This raised the question of whether those who are good at resisting the nihilistic attitudes of society are protected against negative stereotypes as they grow into their own later life. This may in part explain the frequent phenomenon whereby older people reject the help of services – 'That is for old people, I don't need that' – may reflect a positive mechanism for protection of self-esteem.

Action point: It will increase the efficacy and acceptability of an instrumental service or other form of practical support if it is acknowledged that 'higher' levels of psychological and social needs are as important. Open communication and listening can validate personal concerns, and pave the way to 'gentle' matching of services with needs later life.

The power of imitation

Imitation is one of the most powerful adaptive mechanisms known. Role models play an important part in identity formation across the lifespan. In some cultures and in some periods in the history of technology dependent societies, older members are viewed in positive roles and as having valued attributes. For example, they may be seen as contributing, productive, wise, strong, growing and having a future (irrespective of frailty or proximity to death). In other (mainly

technologically dependent societies) there tends to be a disproportionately negative representation of older people. For example, commonly older people are
portrayed as intolerant, rigid, uncaring or antagonistic in their relationships with
younger people. This may breed customs and practices that would be unacceptable for other groups in the society, such as institutionalization.

Surrounded by predominantly nihilistic models of ageing, some individuals may easily adopt these negative stereotypes as they learn to deal with
their own ageing. Some may use ageist humour as a protection – but turn it
against themselves – especially about 'memory' and 'dementia'. However, the
evidence shows that many maintain a sense of self despite the negative models
around.

Action point: Where individuals can see evidence of cognitively disabled older
people being treated in ways that are in their own best interests, they also can
hold hope for a future for themselves. Some services have specifically prioritised
protecting the social roles and relationships of older people with dementia, over
and above other goals (Svanberg, Livingston, Fairbairn and Stephenson, 1999;
Svanberg, 1998; Svanberg, Stirling, and Fairbairn, 1998; Dementia Care Initiative, 1995–96). Evaluation indicates they succeed in achieving and maintaining
the personal goals of the person with dementia in the community until the
end of their life (Killeen, 1998). They also demonstrate how communities can
benefit from having individuals in their midst with cognitive disabilities in later
life.

The dynamics and relevance of social imagery

Symbols and imagery convey messages about groups and about individuals
within a society; these shape the responses of others within the community and
wider society to those groups. In some areas of activity there is a high level of
consciousness about the power of social imagery; for example, in marketing
and sales there is conscious effort to construct enhancing images with which
customers of a service will positively want to be associated. Examples include
language such as 'world class' or 'quality' and visual images implying moving up
or forward, speed and happiness. In some areas of human service there may have
been reluctance to acknowledge imagery, partly because of the fear of implying
people are 'like' products. However, the price of ignoring it is that unintended
negative imagery continues unchecked, to the detriment of already vulnerable
people. Images of dementia often represent people as child-like, future-less,
'empty', less than human, constellations of symptoms or even 'dead already'.

Reliance on the assistance of others does not inherently convey a negative
image – for example, celebrities and royalty may find their status enhanced by
virtue of relying on helpers and this is strengthened by calling these helpers

housekeepers, managers or even servants. There will usually be changes to visual image or language, used in relation to older people with dementia, which could be protective or positively enhancing of their personhood and standing in their community.

If the fact is accepted that words and visual images have power, there follows a responsibility to prevent unnecessary damage to vulnerable older people through neglect of negative imagery.

For example, what does it 'say' about a person if their relationship slots are exclusively filled by paid 'carers' or by 'smart' houses technology? Is this the image that valued others in the society would seek? Or would they seek to mix with and receive assistance from 'housekeepers' or 'butlers' with whom they can form a natural relationship?

Language is powerful in that it paints visual images immediately, is within our full conscious control (if we choose) and costs nothing (other than some thought). Words commonly used in connection with a person with dementia might include for example, 'patient', 'client', 'disabled', 'challenging', 'severe', 'non-compliant' – choosing alternatives can be the most healing action another person can take. In contrast, when a person is described in terms of their personal history, needs, strengths and goals, this creates a positive image, maintains a sense of the person as a unique individual, and points to ways to work that are both realistic and in partnership *with* the person.

Action point: Reframe negative depersonalising uses of language and other imagery, choosing person-centred language and images to convey the same information, and avoiding unnecessary potential damage to social image. Here are some examples of reframing:

'Joyce is an agitated wanderer who is aggressive in groups and doesn't recognise her family now'

Reframe as 'Joyce Davies is a lady who has previously been a suffragette, and had a career in teaching as well as raising a family of three boys. She has a sense of humour and enjoys feeling that she is useful; she relates well to the staff and has more difficulty in relating to others who attend the day centre. She has always liked to take daily exercise, and after half an hour of walking each morning she needs a clear prompt to guide her to a new activity. Joyce's family are aware that she was the one to run the household and they feel upset when she appears not to recognize them; they have welcomed the reassurance that she enjoys being given responsible jobs at the day centre and feel encouraged to continue this at home.'

'Please assess for residential care, due to the fact that the family cannot manage the strain any longer and have latterly rejected all help offered'.

Reframe as 'This is a this lady who has led a most interesting life, including having been a suffragette and a working mother, and is now having difficulties in coming to terms with impairments in communication and mobility. Her family would like to support her at home and need a sense of contributing to her care, of working in equal partnership with other assistance, and of being able to support her in her expression of feelings of frustration. The family may benefit from their own assessment of needs. It will be valuable to identify friends and people who have known her in various roles in the community in order that planning for her future be fully informed'.

The importance of personal social integration

The process by which we each 'hold' our sense of identity has roots in how we relate to each other, and how we take care of each other; this provides a continuous source of validation of our sense of self. The person with dementia can have difficulty in 'holding' a sense of self and of personal identity, not just because of memory changes, but more dramatically if they are disconnected from the places and roles in the community that are their sources of identity and validation.

An older person has an identifiable history of roles; despite this, our societies have found it easy to dismantle these roles and to detach people from them. Many people with dementia are made to experience, possibly for the first time in their lives, a discontinuity with previous life experiences. This can often involve physical separation from home and from key roles and relationships. Serial relocation thereafter is not uncommon, with major consequences for sustaining identity and a vision for the future (other than static).

Action point: In small steps it is possible to construct ways of providing support for people with dementia that protect and champion their integration within the natural community. Having older people with cognitive disabilities in the midst of the community helps everyone to learn about living with disabilities for themselves including increased tolerance. By using GTKY and a person-centred approach the older person with dementia can fulfil a 'real life' and avoid a 'limbo' existence.

Whilst Nancy had been in hospital she had missed her home life badly. When she was discharged to home, it was said that it was 'to see how she got on'; she was full of trepidation and anxiety. The thing she wanted most was on trial, it seemed. Nancy had difficulties with dressing herself as a result of a tremor, and she was quite disabled by the fact her memory and her motor skills were now poor. She felt she could learn to live with these things, if only she could be safe in the security and love of the family home again. But she was to be disappointed. Her husband insisted that, for ease, she be dressed in socks and carpet slippers each day and use a commode in the living room. In terror she refused to allow her grandchildren to visit the house. The mornings were fraught, as she tried to insist on dressing in stockings and shoes, but this led to argument, tears and failure. Things reached a point where she blamed herself for what was wrong – here she was, in her own home, but more miserable and ashamed than when she had been in hospital.

The staff who helped her in her home carried out a GTKY and identified that Nancy had always had the role of head of the household; she ran the family finances, dressed and groomed herself smartly every day without fail in a particular order, and enjoyed her grandchildren's visits. From this, they hypothesised that Nancy's reactions were because she sensed the loss of her previous social roles – even though she was 'physically' present in the community this was not sufficient to make her feel a part of that community again. In fact the opposite had happened – the old social roles had been stolen away and replaced by the new role of 'patient' or 'object of pity', and it was through this that she experienced herself as alienated and disconnected from the very roles that her life had depended on. As a result of the GTKY the staff introduced a change in the care plan, with the purpose of re-establishing the social roles that had been core to Nancy's life. She was given control in respect to her dressing in the morning, and assisted in this by a staff helper (to enable her husband to remain in his natural role, and to avoid a role reversal between Nancy and her husband). The conflict between them diminished; they returned to their previous relationship. Nancy's anxiety subsided sufficiently to enable her to take a large part in dressing herself, albeit with the continued presence and support of another; she felt well enough dressed to resume the role of grandmother and had enough pride in herself again to act as host to her family visitors. The family found it much easier to visit and to discuss news other than the 'illness' and all the problems that the dementia caused. They found comfort in being able to carry out the 'old' roles; they could see Nancy thrive in this context, even despite her disabilities. She had come close to giving up the struggle, when she first thought that life as she had known it was gone - made the more unbearable because physically she was where she wanted to be, but she could only see herself as a burden and as failing to grasp the apparent opportunity to re-make her life. Through GTKY and through others being willing to work to reconstruct and support the core roles in her life, she was able to have a sense of being a person again – through having a social presence and social roles.

Each of us seeks to hold an identity through our transactions with others. We cope with threat, change and loss because we continue to have the social and personal meaning of our life validated. However, if we lose our social identity we lose a major reservoir for our natural resilience; we exist in a psychological 'no man's land', like a refugee.

Depression and anxiety affect a high proportion of older people living in care homes (Copeland et al., 1992). Disturbed behaviour is common and increasing (McGrath and Jackson, 1996; Ballard et al., 2002). And staff morale is low and growing more difficult to sustain in these kinds of settings (Allen-Burge, Stevens and Burgio, 1998). Small steps to maintain valued lives within the natural fabric of the community seem worth the effort.

6
New Paradigm Principles of Service Design

New paradigm principles of service design focus on matching individuals' needs to community support and services; they are particularly relevant for services for older people with ongoing disabilities that are associated with dementia, stroke, cardiovascular or musculoskeletal disease, severe mental health problems or with social isolation. The new paradigm principles can be defined as follows:

1. *Person centred*. The person-centred approach is based on identifying the individual's characteristic patterns of coping, their strengths, preferences, roles, relationships and social identity based on getting to know their life. It increases the likely success of meeting current needs by understanding them in a context of the characteristic patterns of the individual's life and of what is valued in the person's culture. For example, if a person's culture of origin valued rising at dawn or taking a bath once a week, then a personal support plan will have more success if these needs are met (and others' values not imposed). Despite disabilities, or nihilism in the surrounding community, it focuses on the individual's unique remaining capabilities, on active living and on moving forward with various levels of life and fulfilment. Since commonly the staff who care for frail older people struggle to find a positive reward in their work, the person-centred approach provides a tangible means to making a discernible difference – it is reality-based and therefore positively achievable. At the heart of the 'person-centred' approach is the idea that later life disability provides the whole community with the opportunity to see fellow citizens as courageous and fighting (instead of damaged and weak), and to learn from them how resilience and happiness flow from adverse circumstances.

2. *Relationship centred.* The individual's need to have valued and special rela-
    tionships is seen as of central importance – over and above even biological
    needs such as for food and water. The culmination of a life's achievements is
    commonly described in terms of the individual's special meaning and value
    to others in their various communities (of work, interest, family, friends and
    beliefs). Reciprocity in roles and relationships lends meaning to individual
    lives. Accordingly, if a service is to be successful in supporting a person with
    significant and continuing disabilities, it is most likely to do so through at-
    tention to how it can support, sustain and prevent damage to, the individual's
    standing in the eyes of important others.
3. *Flexible and responsive.* 'Making services fit people (not making people fit
    services)' is one way this principle has been portrayed. *Responsive* services
    will increase and reduce their level of support as the individual's needs vary.
    This differs from the more traditional approach where the person is required
    to move on when their needs increase (with attendant discontinuities and
    potential demoralization for staff and sense of rejection for users).
4. *Life planning.* A life planning approach acknowledges general developmental
    life goals, alongside special needs arising from disabilities. Often in crises,
    general human needs go unacknowledged and/or unmet because attention
    has to be given to acute immediate needs. In dementia, many immediate
    needs may have to be attended to. However, if these take over in the long-term
    life becomes static, and emotional and behavioural problems can arise. As a
    general principle, the older person with long-term disabilities, particularly
    if these arise from a dementia, will benefit from having life goals included
    and addressed openly within their support and care plan. Life goals may be
    developmental, such as to develop capacity for reflection, but often late life
    goals are social goals such as to contribute to one's community and to be
    valued for their contributions.
5. *Person centred is not 'making the institution cosy'.* By definition, to work
    in a person-centred way is to work to identify those dimensions of life
    that make for a valued and worthwhile life in the mainstream community
    shared by all. These dimensions of life would include at least the following:-
    having a place considered unique to me (as home); having places to share
    and opportunities to meet and mix with a wide range of (valued) other
    people; opportunities to participate in real productive activities, leisure or
    interests and opportunities to be held in high regard by my fellow citizens.
    Where special assistance is needed because of disabilities, this would be
    provided in the individual's best interests including all of those above, and
    at the same time would contribute to the community's caring competen-
    cies. Maintaining a sense of self as a whole person is a continuous process
    of interaction and engagement with mainstream community, risks and all.
    An institution can be made to look like a homely place, and community

facilities can be replicated inside the institution (such as shops, hairdressers or social clubs); however, by definition the institution cannot provide the opportunities to achieve the social dimensions of personhood identified above. This is achievable only within natural mainstream community life, with minimal barriers between disabled older people and valued other citizens.

Person-Centred Service Principles in Practice

If a service is operating on person-centred principles – whether it be a service for housing, health, social, personal, occupational or leisure needs – the service will first and foremost focus all of its resources on four life areas, with the purpose of enhancing both the instrumental aspects of the person's life (what actually happens for the person) and the symbolic aspects (how the person is regarded in the eyes of others, as a result of what happens). These are the following:

- Relating people to places
- Relating people to people
- Relating people to activities and time
- Relating people to symbols and images (e.g. language used about and with the person, how others perceive the places they spend time in, the people they spend time with and the activities occupying their time)

Relating people to places

The person-centred service supports the person with dementia in accessing and spending time in places frequented and desired by other mature people in the community, that is:

- the same exemplary facilities as other adult people use throughout the day, week and year;
- where the person meets and mixes with valued people in a dignified and non-stigmatizing way;
- which are in attractive surroundings appropriate to people of mature status;
- where any buildings, staff and procedures used by the service are generally regarded in a positive light;
- where risks and associated safety features are comparable with those acceptable to older and younger citizens of status.

Relating people to people

The person-centred service supports persons with dementia in meeting, mixing with and sustaining relationships that typical and valued other mature persons in the community would want to have in their own lives, and through whom life enrichment, status and a positive self-identity can be derived.

- Meaningful, busy activities are pursued with valued other people.
- Support away from other cognitively disabled people is maintained and it can play a significant part in sustaining personal identity.
- The person is defined as fully human and is supported first in meeting their general human needs and secondarily in meeting their special needs.
- The person spends time away from natural places and people only for intensive episodes of special assistance to do with their specific disability.
- The person does not spend the main part or all of their time with specially credentialed persons who are paid to be with them.
- The person derives status and life enrichment from mixing with a variety of people, including people who have a meaningful role and an unpaid relationship with them.

Relating people to activities and time

The person-centred service supports the person to fulfil activities and routines, which would generally be appreciated as worthwhile. This will include the following:

- An appropriate separation of leisure, home, occupational, family and friend-ship activities – not all under one roof, for example, going out to socialize, for entertainment, to the bank, to the doctor or to the shops, as opposed to having the entertainment or the local service brought to the person.
- As intensive as possible real activities, and avoiding watered down or pretend activities, for example, to attend the local church service, not have a 'special' service brought in for disabled people only; to go to real shops, including at ordinary busy times of day, not have 'special' goods brought in for sale to only other disabled people.
- Having material possessions that a mature, respected person would value having and which are commensurate with the person's ability to use them, for example, using a clock or photograph album, which would be desirable to many people as objects of interior design, *instead of* a specially made clock or

calendar designated 'for visually impaired people', or as a 'reminiscence aid' or 'orientation aid'.

- Being supported to exercise choice about the 'small' things in life (e.g. the order of getting dressed in the morning) and the 'big' things in life (e.g. who to have as friends, and who to live with).
- If need be, having the support of someone who has the time to get to know the person concerned, to take their concerns seriously and to act on their behalf with no other conflicts of interest that is, who is not a member of their family or from a service they use.
- Having daily opportunities to maintain familiar interests and to develop these and different ones if desired, for example, to listen to preferred music or drama and not have this called 'stimulation therapy' or 'art therapy'.
- Having daily, weekly, monthly and yearly opportunities and appropriate support to follow activities that would generally be appreciated as worthwhile, for example, to follow one's preferred diet; go out to shops, the hairdresser, church, etc.; to consult a medical practitioner where and when others do; to contribute genuinely to one's community ('voluntary work'); to attend entertainment, cultural and leisure events and at the times others do for example, go to the theatre, or Christmas shopping, when others do and not at specially reserved quiet times for 'disabled people'.
- Having support in activities that identify the individual as a person of masculine gender or feminine gender (and avoiding interpretations that the person is 'of no gender') for example, maintaining interests in grooming, appearance, dress, occupation and pastimes appropriate to the gender role the person has occupied in their life.

Relating people to symbols and images

The person-centred service finds ways to support the person that protect and enhance the way the person is perceived and understood by valued others in the natural community. Choices can be made about the places where we spend our time, the people we spend our time with, the activities we become engaged in and the forms of support we have – that can enhance our image, or standing, in eyes of our fellow community members. In the natural social world people deliberately associate themselves with certain places, people and activities to change the way others regard them. Things that are generally regarded as likely to enhance the image and dignity include the following:

- Respectful language used to address the person and to refer to the person for example, 'Mary MacLean who is a retired teacher and was a suffragette;

she now relies on our service to assist her to live her chosen life, including assistance with her cognitive disabilities as a result of dementia'.

- Respectful language used to refer to the behaviour of the person with dementia, which clearly signals our understanding that there is meaning behind such behaviour and that we are willing partners with the person with dementia in trying to 'read' that meaning and respond accordingly and graciously, for example, describing the specific behaviour in terms of unmet needs, feelings or attempts to problem-solve ('Mary MacLean has drawn much fulfilment from her life as a teacher and on occasions now when she is made aware of her dependence on others to read and write she can feel embarrassed and show her frustration'); this avoids labelling a person as 'challenging behaviour' that can make inappropriate associations with other groups not valued in society, for example, 'aggressive' or 'violent' conjures associations with criminal or damaging behaviour.

- Receiving needed support from personnel who are deliberately described in terms of 'assistants', and who describe their work in terms of 'the accomplishment of specific valued life activities and roles', and not from personnel who describe their job in terms of, for example, 'management of problem behaviour', 'control and restraint', 'de-escalation' or 'high-level care', which reinforce the image of the person as difficult, problematical, abnormal or incapable of having positive life experiences as a person living with dementia.

- Avoiding any images that might suggest the person is like a child, or a burden, or is only known in terms of pathology; for example, avoiding language such as 'gone back to childhood' and instead saying 'enjoys things that are familiar from earlier life experiences because these are meaningful and lend a sense of validation as a person'; avoiding association with possessions that would be more commonly associated with young children for example, soft toys (even if these are liked, and even if people who are not vulnerable to image degradation can get away with it) and instead encouraging associations that unambiguously draw attention to the responsible and dignified status of the person as an adult.

- Accessing support from services, whether health, social, personal, housing or other, which are at least as varied, excellent and highly thought of, as adult people without dementia expect; in cultures where mainstream services for people of an older age group (or similar age to the person with dementia) are not regarded as desirable, varied or enhancing (e.g. where housing or health services are limited or stigmatized) this should not be considered as 'good enough' for the person with dementia – instead, the housing, health, etc. supports needed by the person should be sought from the range that is considered more desirable for adults irrespective of age and commensurate with good standing in the society more widely.

Clearly, a person with dementia commonly requires *special* forms support, particularly as their condition progresses; it would be a misrepresentation of social role valorization (SRV) if the above-mentioned points were misinterpreted to mean that the person's special needs are to be ignored or denied. In fact, the opposite is the case, since to apply SRV and to pursue person-centred solutions requires a capacity for complex thinking, a high level of consciousness and well-practiced problem-solving skills. Practically speaking, support that avoids damaging the person's existing social network and avoids implying to them or others that they are 'not like other people' or 'not the person they were', is more likely to be successful.

To experience adverse events and disability is commonplace if not universal. The majority of individuals cope with these without expert therapeutic assistance, given that natural social networks and community are available to them (Lemay and Ghazal, 2001). The person-centred approach points to how to minimize or prevent secondary damage, such as stress, anxiety, depression, anger and isolation – by supporting rather than supplanting natural supports in the community.

The Principle of the 'Least Intrusive Option'

There are usually a number of options available to us when setting about achieving a goal. Whichever is chosen will convey a message (or image) about the persons involved. The least intrusive option principle suggests that in supporting a vulnerable person, the greatest benefit and least harm comes from choosing first the most dignifying and most status-protecting option. Only if this proves not to be sufficiently effective would the next, more intrusive, option be tried. For example, the most dignifying and most status-protecting option to assist a person with travel might be to provide a travel companion who dresses in ordinary clothes and accompanies the person on ordinary transport that is valued by and used by a wide range of other citizens. Only if this proved to be ineffective for example, the person had falls or could not negotiate a step would a special form of transport be considered for example, a bus with a lowering step. Options such as travelling in a bus with special writing on the side, such as "Disabled" or "Dementia Day Care", would be considered in the general population as odd and unusual. If an option is not valued by others in the community for themselves, then it is likely to have an intrusive and potentially image-negative effect for a vulnerable person.

As a rule, least intrusive options are barrier-free, naturally and frequently occurring in the community, valued, without special physical adaptations and not requiring specially credentialed or uniformed staff to operate (e.g. joining the local singing group, with a companion who also wants to sing). More intrusive options on the continuum would be those that require separate activities or buildings away from the mainstream environment (e.g. going to the singing group that is specially for 'older people' at a different time or in a different place). The most intrusive options would include, for example, using special buildings (e.g. going to the Dementia Day Care to join their singing group) or specially trained staff (e.g. nurses or care workers who run a singing group for disabled people exclusively).

The principle helps us to work to stay at the lower end of the 'intrusiveness' continuum, in the interests of preventing loss of place in the natural community. Asking this question can help assistants become more conscious about the importance of social image in balance with instrumental functioning when selecting means towards ends in providing support:

> *Have I considered the least intrusive option for meeting this need i.e. as far towards the 'least intrusive' end of the continuum as is possible? Have I considered the possibility of using, or harnessing, natural means, ordinary environments and non-specialized personnel before any other option is considered?*
>
> *I can consider moving to the next more intrusive, form of assistance if, and only if, every effort has been made to try to achieve the objectives at the lower level of intrusiveness.*

Sometimes the 'least intrusive option' is criticized by the suggestion that it could expose a vulnerable person to risk or humiliation (e.g., it may be argued that it will be stressful for a person with dementia to go to their local post office because they cannot cope with counting money and communication). However, this would only result if insufficient levels of support were offered that is, if the principle were misapplied. (The person with dementia accompanied by a companion who knows them well can be given the experience of coping with dignity and subtle support at crucial moments, and so can continue to see themselves as a welcome member of the local community.) In addition, the phenomenon of 'rising to the occasion' (i.e. resilience) cannot be experienced if the person with dementia is kept away from mainstream community places. Risk management plans can support effective person-centred solutions, where risk avoidance is likely to aggravate stress.

Technology and the Principle of the Least Intrusive Option

The person with dementia functions with limited information processing capacity and is vulnerable to overload. Accordingly, introducing novel stimulation can cause an increase in anxiety, and careful consideration is therefore required in introducing environmental management technology, such as alarms, remote or automatic controls, or other unfamiliar technological appliances.

There is evidence that technology that enables constant monitoring can be experienced as stressful and anxiety provoking. Information-processing theory would understand this as the absence of a 'safety signal', meaning that the receiver's arousal system cannot be 'switched off'. For example, a carer receiving monitoring signals may find the chronic anticipation of sleep disturbance as stressful as actual disturbance.

'Smart' technology alleviates this problem to an extent as the information system itself makes and enacts decisions, without depending on a human party. For example, a 'smart house' might switch on lights to the toilet in the night and 'lead' the person back to bed the same return route, in response to the trigger of a bedside pressure mat.

Wherever technology is being considered as a means of meeting the needs of disabled people, ethical questioning is always of benefit – specifically the questions are the following:

1. Is the technology being proposed typical and widely desired by valued people in the wider culture?
2. Is there a risk the technology will replace or reduce valuing interpersonal contacts in the life of the person?
3. Will it enhance the positive regard with which the person is held in the eyes of valued others in their community?

If the answer is 'no' to any of these, then a less intrusive option would be preferred since it might be both successful and less 'labelling' or stigmatizing. Less intrusive options would be closer to the norms and mainstream conditions by which ordinary people live their lives. (A minority of people in a society choosing high levels of technology in their lives is not evidence of it being a valued means to valued ends in the wider society.)

Going Beyond the Concept of Instrumental Effectiveness

Quality services must be conscious not only of what they *do* but also of *the messages they send* about the people they serve, if they are to be effective. For example, having automated curtain-closing devices within 'an intelligent house' may be effective in maintaining daily routines; however if it presents an image of 'I don't need neighbours' then it may damage social integration. A helpful process when considering any intervention is to weigh the instrumental benefit expected against the likely damage (or enhancement) to image for the individual or group concerned.

A person-centred approach will consciously choose means for assisting the person, which are the closest possible to the mainstream ways in the culture, which risk least damage to the person's social role and which minimize intrusion on the person's natural relationships – even where there are *more effective means* available including effective special technologies. For example, if there is a special service that is effective in dealing with challenging behaviour in dementia, a person-centred philosophy will nevertheless choose in preference an approach that is not stigmatizing and capable of protecting the person's roles, relationships and connections in their community, even if it is less effective in eliminating the challenging behaviour. This challenges the old paradigm 'rule' that symptom control is always most important. It replaces it with the possibility that some people with dementia with challenging behaviour may always live with the behaviour – and at the same time can have a valued life in their community.

Quality of life may be like happiness in that neither are elements or experiences in their own right – they are emergent properties and only exist in so far as the activities from which they flow exist. Hence 'happiness' does not exist except as an experience arising from some activity – which is as likely to be an ordinary everyday activity as a special or unusual one.

By the same argument 'quality of life' does not exist as a dimension of someone else's or our own judgment; it is an emergent property of the experiences of daily life. Those activities that are sometimes described as 'drudgery' are the same activities from which emerge happiness and quality of life when we undertake them – such as feeding ourselves, keeping ourselves warm, clean and safe, caring for our immediate and wider environment, working and caring for our family and friends.

The Consequences for Family and Friends of People with Dementia

Family and friends of people with dementia have several tasks – the need to understand the behaviour and responses of the person they know who now lives with cognitive disabilities; the need to sustain their natural relationship with that person for example, as partner or parent; the need to understand their own fears about dementia (to avoid projecting these on to the person with dementia) and the need to live with their society's beliefs and attitudes about dementia, which can be nihilistic and depersonalizing – and strongly persuasive.

Through the 1980s and 1990s, the voice of the carer was listened to with much greater attention than before – so much so that the balance may have shifted away from the person with dementia (Goldsmith, 1996; Killick and Allan, 2001). Despite the relative carer 'power', in the absence of a highly valued option for the care of people with dementia, carers may find themselves pressured to accept what is there, and fearful of making suggestions in case of appearing critical and losing whatever help there is.

There is now a conscious recognition that the needs and concerns of the carer or family are distinct from that of the person with dementia, and need to be identified separately. A person-centred framework assists us to define 'in the best interests of the person', in a way that is practical, immediate, transparent, open to scrutiny, does not depend on long delays in the name of research, and is not disproportionately influenced by single-issue viewpoints.

The person-centred route to identifying the person's 'best interests' involves

- examining and getting to know the person's needs,
- gaining a full knowledge of their life, the choices they made and the ways they coped,
- identifying what typical valued adults at a similar point in their lives find desirable in their lives, and
- identifying aspirations for their future, irrespective of disability.

The Constructs of Capacity and Incapacity

The spirit behind United Kingdom legislation concerning capacity is to place the wishes of the person concerned at the heart of planning any care they may require, and to ensure that the means selected to provide the assistance are the least intrusive on the person's life (as they would wish it to be) (Scottish Executive, 2000, 2004; Department of Health, 1997).

Legal protection for the person who is deemed as having "incapacity" requires that

- any action should be of benefit to the person,
- the least restrictive intervention is selected,
- the person's wishes and feelings are taken account of,
- the views of relevant others are taken account of,
- the independence of the person is encouraged.

Crucial to the implementation of the above-mentioned points is the definition of key terms, in particular 'of benefit to' and 'least restrictive intervention'.

'*Of benefit to*'. It may help to ground the interpretation of this in a historical context. During the period up to and including the World War II and within the culture of Eastern Germany, it was asserted that to end their lives was 'of benefit to' the occupants of the women's and children's psychiatric wards in the Stadtroda Hospital (The Scotsman, 2004). First hospitals and then concentration camps undertook 'mercy killing' of mentally impaired and mentally ill adults and children. Death was 'for the benefit of those people'. The same words are still sometimes used in contemporary societies when speaking about euthanasia; it is presented as if 'for their benefit'.

Does 'of benefit to' mean 'prevent from coming to further harm' (which may include death as a potential removal from suffering), or 'pursue some positive state'? The person-centred working definition of 'of benefit to' would include only those interventions that are congruent with the positive life goals of person – not 'protection from harm by life ending'.

'Least restrictive intervention'. In a person-centred framework 'least intrusive' would include protecting the image or standing of the person with disability in their community. In addressing needs for special care, restrictions will not be put on important life goals – such as choices about where we live, who we live with and who we count as friends.

The meaning of "incapacity" and its implications. In the ('bad old') past, an assessment that deemed a person not to have capacity was a licence to override the wishes of the person, whereas, in the ('good new') present world, legislation ensures the person's wishes are supported. The implementation of legislation is of course not this easy; it relies on change in expectations, for example to counter the old belief 'Everybody knows that people with significant dementia will have to go into institutional care one day – it's just a matter of when'. The key to successful implementation lies in how much creativity exists within the community to inspire new ways of supporting severely disabled people without institutionalizing them.

Issues of Self-Esteem, Security and Identity in Dementia and Other Cognitive Disabilities

In a seminal study of self-esteem in late life, following the same individuals over 10 years, Coleman, Aubin, Robinson, Ivani-Chalian and Briggs (1993) found that the two most highly predictive factors of maintaining self-esteem were having valued relationships other than family and having positive beliefs about self. Examples of the latter would be feeling useful, feeling capable and having a positive attitude to past life and to ageing. Those low on these two factors were more likely to undergo a drop in self-esteem over the period and to die earlier. We might conclude that a 'healthy' environment for ageing is one that provides a sense of continuity with the past and where values are openly shared with a circle of friends. In person-centred language a happy late life is highly dependent on the social context.

In dementia, the focus of attention is often on helping the person with the facts and realities of daily functioning, such as how to remember when to eat or how to orient safely from place to place. However, of more concern to the person may be the experience of feeling cut off from the flow of information that normally holds and sustains a sense of identity and security.

In the social interactionist model, social signals from our environment are as important for life as air, water and nourishment. Feelings of annihilation and alienation can motivate extremes of behaviour. Killick (1997) has shown that a priority for the person with dementia is to share a meaningful personal and social dialogue about their experience. Spending time with people with dementia can enable both communication partners to harness new abilities – such as to create poetry. In dementia, what was individual and internal is made over to the interpersonal (Kitwood, 1997) – others anchor our tangled thoughts and validate our memory and identity.

Positive Futures Planning

O'Brien's (O'Brien and Lyle, 1986; O'Brien and Lovett 1992) 'Five Accomplishments for Services' framework guides us to focus on positive accomplishments in all important life areas – not to be limited to alleviating or minimizing the symptoms or pathologies. It draws our attention to such questions as 'What would it take to protect or strengthen this individual's life in respect of relationships, places, contributing and respect?' Each life is seen as having value, and as having potential to develop and grow in these important life areas – irrespective of disability.

O'Brien's (1986) five accomplishments in relation to late life

The 'Five Accomplishments' identify what it takes to move towards living a valued life, irrespective of disability. In terms of 'old age', it draws our attention to the fact that some dimensions of development do not even begin until late life – and require a social context in which to be fulfilled.

- To help people discover and move towards desirable personal futures in their late life – irrespective of whether old age is devalued in the culture, and *even if* there are effective means, such as chemical or behavioural agents, that

can control, limit or eliminate the problems (e.g. pharmacological control of difficult behaviour, special care facilities, or euthanasia).
- To offer needed help in ways that protect and promote those desirable, valued experiences and developments now.

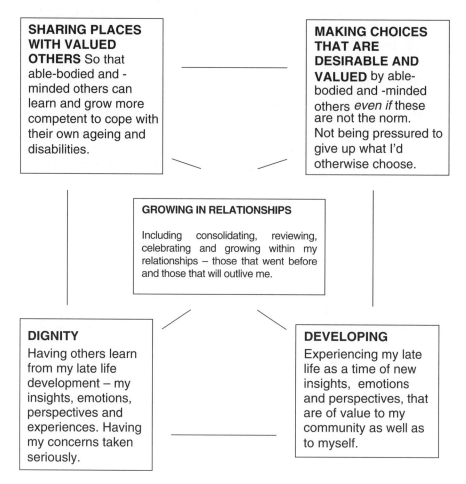

Figure 6.1   Five accomplishments in relation to later life

Even if limited, there are always choices about different ways to provide support. For example, there is choice about whether a person is introduced to other people and their reaction listened to, before they are asked to live with, or accept help from, those people. When considering how best to help a person with dementia, this question can help 'Will this take the person in a positive direction in respect to one or more of these essential accomplishments?' If the answer is '"no', then it should not be considered, and it is likely that the possible 'intervention' was for the benefit of someone else. If the answer is 'yes', then it is possible to go forward with this step in a positive spirit even if it is very small.

A New Kind of Service: Dementia Care Partnership

In Newcastle upon Tyne in the United Kingdom a pilot project was developed in the 1990s to test out the process of care management (Department of Health, 1990) with people with dementia in a British inner city (described in Killeen, 1998). The aim was to enable people with significant disabilities as a result of dementia to live in their own homes for life with whatever personalized support was required. As part of this an independent supported living scheme was developed (Svanberg, Livingston, Fairbairn and Stephenson, 1999; Svanberg, 1998; Svanberg, Stirling, and Fairbairn, 1998; Dementia Care Initiative, 1995–96), which aimed to provide an effective alternative to residential forms of care when living at home is no longer possible. These pilot services included an independent living house; they were later extended and included in mainstream service provision under the name of Dementia Care Partnership.

The philosophy on which the project was founded came out of several years of previous experience with consulting people with dementia locally, and was as follows:

- People with dementia should be fully involved and informed about all aspects of their care, such as who provides it, possible re-housing, and their agreement must be sought.
- The commitment given must be 'for life' that is irrespective of changing needs and dependency, and this should be true for the person who moves to an alternative supported 'home for life' as well as for the person in their own home.
- Continuity of care would be provided by a team of support workers, recruited locally wherever possible, who would work towards enabling the person with dementia to re-establish and retain links with their own communities, to keep to their own 'normal life' routines and to retain optimal control over their own affairs – for example, keeping their own bank account, paying their bills, attending church and so on, with all the supervision and help necessary.

Carers' full participation was encouraged from the beginning. Information about the person's patterns, routines, significant events, likes, dislikes, interests, strengths and abilities was gathered with the assistance of the carer. Early on carers were involved in designing the information about the project and the assessment protocols, and with recruiting support workers. Later they were brought together with the support workers for their relative in individual care planning meetings, and with carers of other prospective independent living house tenants to play an active role in the furnishing, décor and other matters relating to the house.

Other local services, including neighbourhood housing, the multidisciplinary mental health team for older people, and the legal services of the NHS Trust gave practical advice and assistance, for example on drawing up tenancy and lease agreements.

Neighbours were consulted from the beginning, including the local Police, social services, voluntary agencies, general medical practitioners and primary care teams, and in the case of the house, the local housing committee. Apart from the concern that people should have the help of support workers at all appropriate times the proposal was accepted and welcomed.

In practice the people either continued living in their own homes with support, or were consulted about the choice of moving to the independent living house (the criteria for this are described below). The recruits to the support worker positions were expected to have some experience of dementia care, preferably personal, and were provided with further training particularly in the philosophy of the project and in personal caregiving.

The independent supported living house was agreed as an option to be considered if some of the following criteria were relevant:

- Living alone
- A high degree of vulnerability in the community due to risk behaviour
- Multi-disciplinary assessment indicating a confirmed diagnosis of dementia, moderate or severe
- Carers being unable to cope and experiencing a high degree of stress
- The recommendation of residential care not meeting with the agreement of the person with dementia and their carer.

The house comprised a pair of neighbouring flats. Adaptations were only installed according to the needs of the individuals – that is, there were no batch installations of special aids or adaptations – and security, fire and other alarm systems, furniture and soft furnishings were installed on a domestic scale with full involvement of the tenants. An early idea to have one bedroom used for respite care was dropped when the carers argued that the proposed respite bedroom in the house would be an intrusion on the privacy and usual patterns of life of the permanent tenants. Instead, an upstairs bedroom was retained for use of overnight family guests. Support workers were able to provide an 'awake' service overnight for both flats by means of installing an internal connecting door linking the two flats and this was the only alteration made. Each flat operated as an individual household, each with two tenants and their own front door.

The concept of shared living is different from a small-scale staffed home. Its distinguishing features include the following:

- The move is preceded by an introductory period in which tenants choose the person with whom they will live and get to know them.

- Each person has their own tenancy agreement.
- Each person is responsible for how the house is run day to day.
- The function of the support worker is to provide help and guidance not to determine how life will be lived.
- The tenant is encouraged to continue their own activities, household tasks, shopping and outings with whatever support is needed.

In the subsequent three years Dementia Care Partnership (DCP) developed five supported independent living projects in the city, including one for younger people with dementia, although the core work remains supporting individuals with dementia living in their own homes by means of individualized care plans and local support workers who are trained to consider supporting local social integration as a main purpose of their work.

Getting to know people was seen as a crucial foundation before any decisions were made about people's futures. After initial crisis needs were assessed and dealt with, a further long-term needs assessment was carried out. This was for the purpose of planning realistic personal goals and patterns of life. If there was any disagreement on any proposed goals or means, for example between the person and their family, this was identified and help with conciliation was offered. Attention and time was given to explaining the reasons for optimizing the person's control and continuity in their life throughout the process. The local advocacy service could be introduced at individual planning and review meetings to assist in identifying the solution optimal for the person. In advance of setting up the independent supported living house, an informal day club was set up to bring the referred people together once a week in a social setting over a period of 8 weeks. The support workers were able to accompany the prospective tenants; the strength of relationships and friendships that had developed along with the likes, dislikes and interests of the people were taken as the basis on which tenants were invited to live together.

Support workers were recruited with local knowledge and continuity of care in mind. Training emphasized a person-centred model of care, with an underpinning concept that they were substitute carers carrying out the activities undertaken by a family carer. Their function was to provide guidance and help as necessary, not to tell people how life should be lived or fit them into routines. Each individual's history reveals the domestic routines and activities valued by that person and this makes it easier to see the practical things that will need to be arranged by supporters. One person may like to sit at the fish quay early in the morning while another person's favourite part of the day may be listening to the children coming out of school in the afternoon.

The underpinning principle of support worker training was that that for people with dementia, 'community care' is not *living in* the community but is *living as part of* the community. The support role, accordingly, is an enabling one; it is to enable the person who may be withdrawing, because of illness or disability, to re-establish links and to encourage a sense of being part of their community. A part of the support workers' job was to show neighbours and shopkeepers in the locality how successful they could be in relating to the person with dementia. The worker for example would involve the person in decisions and support the person to make their own choices and ensure the person could cope successfully.

Because the support role requires creating a more 'dementia-competent' environment, it was important to select people who were familiar with and part of the local culture, so that they could 'buddy' the person concerned with ease and subtlety within this community. In practice this minimized stress and optimized normal functioning for the person who was cognitively disabled.

Support workers were recruited who had some previous experience of caring for a person with dementia, preferably someone in their own family, but some had been employed in domestic or other services. The job specification was akin to a blend of 'homemaker' and 'family carer'. Workers were employed by the board of DCP, whose membership was carers and ex-carers of people with dementia (who wanted to provide an alternative to institutional forms of care). Ongoing experience showed that support and training in loss and bereavement was a core issue both for supporting family and support workers in the event of death.

The PEACH philosophy was developed to capture the essential purpose and actions of DCP:

- **P**artnership and person-led services
- **E**mpowerment
- **A**ttachment
- **C**ontinuity
- **H**ope

Financing

The first step is a maximization of income, by accessing benefits, for housing, for social care and for health/disability needs, according to the policies prevailing at the time. A second step for this programme was to separate housing issues from care management and care provision. This empowered the tenants by making it possible to advocate for better standards, or to change provider if the quality does not meet the required standards

Evaluation showed that the costs for a person supported on this programme were *not* greater than if that person went to large group services such as residential or nursing home care, contrary to common belief. The costs were met by a combination of benefits and client contribution. Care manager pressures were different, since financial assessment was more detailed and the 'case' had to be kept open, not handed over, as in the residential care package. In terms of user outcomes, the evaluation concluded that people functioning with moderate to serious levels of cognitive disability could be successfully supported by flexible care packages and in independent living, with a reduction in behaviour disturbance, a reduced use of medication, a better chance of a home for life, and in a way that is affordable and good value in the broadest sense (details are described by Svanberg, Livingston, Fairbairn and Stephenson, 1999).

The service is now in demand with the health and social care providers locally. It has strengthened its integrative role by developing a 'family centre' so that it now serves the community more broadly.

7
Psychological Therapies with Older People

What does it mean to have a fulfilled life? Where do late life and ageing come in to this? The ageing of an individual is a process at the interface of several systems – physical, social and psychological. Ageing offers opportunities for fulfilment and expression of such positive psychological developments as resilience and self-efficacy. Indeed, it is increasingly the case that loss, disability and illness are compressed into a narrow window of the lifespan (where previously these experiences would be encountered throughout life). Accordingly, the resilience that grows from encountering these experiences may not be realised until later life. Two particular psychological therapies are considered here because they focus on the person in context. The cognitive behavioural approach is consistent with social role valorization (SRV) in recognizing the importance of beliefs (or thoughts) in shaping responses and feelings – and the power of seeking evidence to challenge negative beliefs and low expectations. Cognitive analytic therapy offers a tool to understanding the interface between systems (such as parental family and peer relationships) and their influence throughout the lifespan on psychological development.

The Ecological Context of Ageing

Historically, ageing has been thought to be a result of irretrievable deple-tion of physical and mental resources. For example, Freud proposed that 'overuse' of specific mental or physical energies (such as sexual activity) was life-shortening.

More recent evidence however contradicts these traditional beliefs (Kirkwood, 1999, 2004). Kirkwood's 'disposable soma' theory views the phenomenon of ageing as the result of random molecular changes that accumulate in the course of normal cellular DNA repair. (We are not programmed to die, but to carry out DNA repair.) Long-lived species may be programmed to maintain a high level of repair in particular throughout the reproductive years to ensure sufficient energy investments to cover all resource uses. In this theory, we would expect hostile environments (such as pollutants, poor nutrition, an absence of clean water and sanitation) to provoke more and earlier 'ageing' effects. The increase in longevity over the last few decades in certain societies has certainly been correlated with environmental improvements: (a) the widespread implementation of public health measures especially clean water and sanitation and (b) the introduction of antibiotics targeted on specific micro-organisms. Together with nutrition and lifestyle, these wider environmental factors measures are now believed to account for over 75 per cent of the positive changes in individual ageing in recent decades (Kirkwood, 2000, 2004).

Kirkwood argues that the remaining toxic environmental influences to be addressed are negative attitudes and hostile social responses (stereotyping), which continue to exert damage and set limits on longevity.

The Social and Psychological Consequences of Mainstream Longevity

Longevity is a change that has taken place *faster* than any other major change in human history that is, over only a few decades and one or two generations. It seems that the societies gifted with this transformation have not yet updated their perception of life. They continue to measure worth or fulfilment in terms of economic role and material productivity. Hence 'retirement' is still perceived as a drop in status and increased lifespan seems to cause anxiety and fear in society.

Martha's entire adult life had been spent living with the image of herself as a victim of terror and suffering, as the abused child of a violent and cruel father. She had married a man who turned out to have behaviour much like her father; her second marriage was to a man she insisted was perfect and who looked after her ideally and perfectly. When he died she perceived herself as a double victim – (still) of her father, and now also an abandoned wife bereft of her saviour. Relating to others in any other way she found almost impossible, and repeatedly re-created for herself situations where she was again the victim, this time of 'failed medical treatments', 'uncaring friends' and a world where 'nobody needs me because I'm old'. All of these were reminiscent of her earlier preference for illusory comforts – her beliefs that medical treatments should fix everything and that being needed ideally (as by her second husband) is the 'saviour' of life. She could not 'get better' because that would mean giving up her victimhood and relinquishing her belief in her second husband as a spiritual angel whose activities revolved around her. In Martha's case, later life itself did not bring the anxiety-provoking situations; her anxiety came from the failure of lifelong 'comfort' mechanisms, and her inability to see herself other than as an object of (victim of) the activities of others. To contemplate a place in which she was truly alone, and solely responsible for her own self-worth and identity, seemed to her more terrifying; it was a place she avoided right through her later life. She continued to pursue her 'comfort' beliefs by as extreme means as it took, visiting spiritualists for 'contacts' with her 'guardian angel' deceased husband, and thereby rejecting other paths open to her in later life. The fact that this brought no real comfort or sense of relief from anxiety was of no account, as Martha had no experience of changing her 'delusion'.

See Figure 7.1 for a cognitive analytic understanding of Martha's circumstances.

With later life come more opportunities to enter unmapped territory. Although giving up comfort myths and illusions can be terrifying, on the other hand, loss, change and disability can free the person to develop real psychological and social well-being. Persons who have lifelong seen themselves as 'victims' can see themselves for the first time as persons in their own right, with all the responsibility that this involves. The person, whose psychological life has been dominated by regret about an action, or shame about some un-fulfilled material ambition, can move on to a different psychological plane. The experience of changes and disabilities in later life may introduce a future focus that goes beyond own lifespan, and the opportunity for pro-social behaviours.

In Smail's (2001b) analysis, life experience brings the potential to increase our emphasis on subjective truth and on unself-conscious absorption. These are not the prerogative of the older individual, but the process of living can bring with it a move in this direction, away from the world of material accomplishments and towards the subjective (sometimes, perhaps mistakenly, called the spiritual).

To make proper use of the opportunities opened up by the acknowledgement of distress is to take one of the few paths open to us to develop and assert our subjectivity. (Smail, 2001a, page 210)

Keyes and Lopez (2005) identify 'going beyond baseline' (i.e. the development of well-being and hope) as a potential psychological outcome in the human response to adverse circumstances. Positive psychology would challenge the idea of late life as a time of multiple pathologies and instead would see it as rich in opportunities for positive psychological growth – especially in such social attributes as nurturance, altruism, responsibility, responsiveness and other civic values that outlive the individual.

The Relevance of the Social Context of Ageing

In this chapter the roots of anxiety and depression in later life are traced to factors in the social environment (negative attitude to ageing) and to internal factors (self-constructs about ageing). Mental well-being in later life is understood in terms of the prevailing societal beliefs about ageing and later life, and the available roles and relationships within the social context. 'Mental health collapse' in later life is understood as a failure of the core self-constructs of earlier life in the face of a social context that offers weak and unworthy social roles for older people, complicated for many individuals by significant losses of competence, image and opportunities.

Resiliency is present throughout the lifespan (Weiss and Kasmauski, 1997). Perceived social support is shown to have a role in resilience by moderating the impact of stressors (Davies, 1996; Ingersoll-Dayton and Talbott, 1992). The evidence also shows that having valued social roles gives self-esteem, self-identity and a buffer against events (Cheston and Bender, 1999). In summary then, the social context for the individual's ageing and development is an active force in promoting resiliency and coping.

Understanding both earlier life and later life socialization experiences will be necessary to our understanding of the person's coping styles and patterns. The formative experiences, roles and relationships from earlier life, including the primary family, are important because of the shaping influence on the person's ways of responding to the demands of the environment. Hence we look at Davies' (2000) development of attachment theory and how it relates to patterns of coping in later life with adversities and disabilities. The person's later socialization experiences account for another significant proportion of the variability in patterns of ageing – for example, their formation of and maintenance of adulthood relationships, and what and how needs have been met through these relationships.

The New Paradigm Gerontology

Kirkwood (2000) argues that lifespan is more malleable than had ever been imagined (contrary to earlier beliefs that it is programmed and pre-determined). He posits evidence about four factors in the variability in individual ageing:

1. *Genes* influence the mechanisms of cellular DNA repair, accounting for 25 per cent of variability. The remaining 75 per cent is accounted for by environmental variables as follows.
2. *Nutrition* in the form of a balanced natural diet (rather than added vitamins) promotes protection against the effects of free radicals on cells.
3. *Lifestyle* in the form of natural exercise has a major protective effect at any time.
4. *The physical environment* – clean public water supply/sanitation and the use of specific antibiotics have made the largest difference in the past century.
5. *The social environment* – still to be tackled, and identified by Kirkwood (2004) as the need to neutralize and challenge attitudes about ageing and later life specifically fatalism, denial, negative stereotyping, tunnel vision, failure to take personal responsibility and fantasy.

Table 7.1 traces how these negative attitudes about ageing have a disabling effect and how knowing the facts has a protective and a positive effect on the individual's own ageing and mental well-being.

'Good ageing' therefore seems to be related via gerontology research and models to an age-friendly culture (i.e. one capable of sustaining positive attitudes about ageing). Ultimately the challenge seems to be to social and applied psychology to develop models that incorporate disability and ageing as positive dimensions in the realisation of individual and community good.

The Relevance of Proximity to Death

Stereotyped beliefs about ageing (see Table 1.1) carry potential detrimental effects for the mental health of the group to whom they are attributed. Some groups are doubly labelled with potentially damaging perceptions, notably older people with dementia or other cognitive disabilities – being seen as 'close to death' and 'lost their mind'. This group traditionally has had enacted against it powerful societal forces for institutional containment and socially engineered separation from mainstream society. The social processes that Wolfensberger (1987) has identified as death-making culminate in the ultimate social control over those seen as a threat in our technologically dependent societies – those

Table 7.1 The seven tasks for positive mental health: turning distorted beliefs into rational beliefs about ageing

Distorted belief about ageing	Effect on mental health of distorted belief	Rational evidence about ageing	Effect on mental health of rational belief
Fatalism 'I can't change it anyway'	Lost sense of agency. 'It's all in the genes, so why look after myself'.	Ageing is malleable; exercise and nutrition make a difference. Genes account for only 25% of variability in ageing.	*Sense of agency.* Knowing that activity, nutrition and having positive attitudes around me make the biggest contribution to well-being.
Denial 'It won't happen to me'	Witnessing rejection and dismissal of 'old people' from society, I feel discomfort at this but keep it suppressed and dare not explore why I feel it.	Ageing is part of a universal whole of which I am a part. Much of value is yet to be accomplished. Society does change e.g. doesn't tolerate prejudice against people with disability compared to a few decades ago.	*Consciousness.* Sense of discovery, optimism, and acceptance, knowing that most people choose life when faced with disability and difficulty.
Negative stereotyping 'All old people are losers'	Lost sense of self. 'I'm a loser' 'On the downhill'.	Later life is a unique opportunity to develop and model hope, morality, ethical behaviours, altruism, empathy and resilience.	*Positive personal identity.* Sense of being a necessary part of a cycle of life, helping to shape a society that will survive and contribute good.
Inevitability 'This is how it has to be'	'My ageing will be just like my parents' and grandparents'	A revolution in understanding ageing is underway. It has a unique purpose in the cycle of life.	*Choice.* Sense of freedom from the material and production concerns of earlier adult life.

Table 7.1 (*Continued*)

Distorted belief about ageing	Effect on mental health of distorted belief	Rational evidence about ageing	Effect on mental health of rational belief
Negation of personal responsibility 'Someone else will find a way to sort it out for me'	Loss of self identity and sense of agency. Blaming. Disappointment. Abandonment of control.	Later life provides me with the opportunity for the development of positive psychological traits and competencies such as reflection, responsiveness and pro-social behaviours – this is my investment in the future.	*Personal responsibility.* Knowing I have the opportunity in later life to invest in my community and promote positive values such as future focus and capacity for reflection, irrespective of adverse life conditions or disabilities.
Disease fantasy 'Someone will fix it with a pill'	Ageing labelled as a disease instead of a social process. Unstable, passive dependency on drugs. Burden.	It doesn't need fixed. There are no age limits to resilience and human growth.	*Normality.* Later life is a different and purposeful part of ordinary life. It isn't just 'extended' adult life – on the contrary it brings opportunities to transform the future for succeeding generations.
No hope Old age is different from youth and other times of life	'I might as well pack up my life and sit in death's waiting room' or 'I want to be put down if I get like that'.	Later life provides opportunities for dealing with new challenges in new ways – older people are often valued by succeeding generations for their different values and greater experience.	*Hope.* Survival and sustainability in global terms may depend on our success in transforming our expectancies about consumption and our reliance on technology – the values and competencies characteristic of later life are crucial to this success.

seen as 'unfixable' and (in the traditional terms) 'hopeless'. Until relatively recently this was the culture in cancer care. People with cancer were seen as without hope, to be rejected, feared, and shut away from view particularly when they were approaching death. Then the new era of hospice care in the community brought a new paradigm in cancer care. In the new philosophy of cancer care, hope is the foundation stone and a worthwhile life (irrespective of time left) is the objective of care. At one time it was not expected that mental well-being and cancer could exist together. Following the sea-change in attitudes about cancer, which started only a few decades ago (Cartwright, Hockey and Anderson, 1973), now palliative care services focus on supporting hope and effective pain control (Nolen-Hoeksema and Davis, 2005). A similar sea-change has yet to take place in relation to dementia and other long-term disabling conditions; palliative care would require positive and assertive technologies to help individuals to adapt and communities to give support. The purpose of services would change from pathology limitation to hope and the pursuit of life goals. People with dementia would receive support that affirms hope and their unique place in community life.

Common Distorted Beliefs About Human Ageing and Their Effect on Mental Health

Table 7.1 lists the attitudes that are most likely to have a dampening or damaging impact on individuals in later life (if internalized) – and the seven tasks that, if accomplished, can benefit well-being and protect mental health in later life. The widespread nature of negative attitudes about ageing in our technologically dependent societies, together with publicity about inadequate services and poor care, distorts expectations about growing old. Some of the roots of anxiety and depression in later life can be seen here. Each task involves challenging a distorted belief about ageing and replacing it with a rational belief based on the evidence. The accomplishment of each task has potential implications for establishing positive mental health traits and dimensions, possibly for the first time or to a new level in the individual's lifespan: for developing a sense of agency, consciousness, personal identity, choice, personal responsibility, normality and hope.

The Seven Tasks: Helping People Challenge Distorted Thinking About Ageing

One: fatalism versus agency

The belief that 'old age' is all 'downhill' and 'all in the genes' can result in failure to sustain adaptive health behaviours. Such beliefs can be used as an excuse to continue with health-damaging habits, such as smoking, poor nutrition and lack of exercise. The facts are that genes account for around 25 per cent of the variability in individual human ageing – and that exercise, cessation of smoking and developing a nutritional pattern that minimizes free radicals in the body make a difference as soon as they are instigated.

Two: denial versus consciousness

The anti-ageing movement thrives in technologically dependent communities. Some scientists believe that death can be overcome. From using anti-ageing skin preparations to undertaking reconstructive surgery to paying for cryogenics – all contribute to the collective denial of ageing. On every occasion we laugh at an ageist remark we deny its potential to harm. Taking a stand against the irrationality of the anti-ageing movement, choosing acceptance and tolerance of all individuals irrespective of age-related appearance or disabilities, and raising consciousness about the sense of purpose, self-acceptance, empathy, warmth and satisfaction in relationships with others that can accompany later life uniquely – are ways of raising consciousness about our individual responsibilities to each other and our community. Society can and does change. For example, society does not now tolerate prejudice against people with disabilities to the extent it did only a few decades previously. There is also the fact that most people, despite their own earlier life prejudices (e.g. horror about dementia or frailty), find that when it happens to them *their* life is undoubtedly still worth living.

Three: negative stereotyping versus personal identity maintained

There is a stereotype of later life as a time of loss. Yet, the fact is that uncertainty and loss in many forms occur across the lifespan. Many older people actually experience a strengthening of personal identity, and feel empowered to express ethical, altruistic and empathic behaviours. They have the sense of being a necessary part of the life cycle, and a belief they can help to shape a society that will survive and will contribute net good to the world they leave behind.

Four: inevitability versus choice

To our parents and grandparents, in an industrialized and production-focused society, late life may have been seen as inevitably intertwined with the idea of being scrapped, dumped or in the way. However with improved environmental conditions (assuming these can be sustained and shared with all) living longer now gives opportunities to re-prioritize subjective life over material production and to make choices accordingly.

Five: negation of personal responsibility versus personal responsibility

When medical technologies are highly developed, people come to expect more. Doctors are blamed if the technology fails to save life. Surgeons are expected to do repairs to replace worn joints and damaged arteries. The individual's own sense of responsibility for maintaining healthy joints and cardiovascular function may not be well developed. The consumer model of health can significantly undermine a sense of individual personal agency. The pursuit of institutionalized complaints against the health system can be a substitute for health-seeking behaviour. Providing people with the evidence that nutrition, lifestyle and attitude account for a large proportion of health and longevity can help recover a sense of personal self-control. Also, as more people of the post-industrial societies grow older they are likely to look for opportunities for subjective reflection, and a sense of 'spiritual' connection with and investment in the future.

Six: disease fantasy versus normality

There is a dark belief that we all become diseased in old age, and all have the same diseases (Comfort, 1977) – probably cancer and dementia. Actually, normal ageing is as varied as individuals are varied and ageing doesn't need to be a fixed pattern. Later life is not just extended adult life; on the contrary it can bring different priorities and insights, and the opportunities to express these and perhaps transform the future for succeeding generations. There are no limits – other than those that come from societies' prejudices and avoidance of awareness about death.

Seven: no hope versus hope

Later life used to be viewed as empty and unproductive – a 'waiting room' for death. But new insights within biogerontology show that organisms are programmed for survival, not pre-programmed for decay. The hospice movement challenged the belief that there could be no hope in the life of a person with cancer, by recognizing that hope lies in taking care of each other and the world we rely on. It may be that mental health, just as much as survival and sustainability in global population terms, depends on our success in transforming our expectancies about consumption and our reliance on technology; the values and competencies characteristic of later life may be crucial to this transformation to a new society.

Eleven Tasks for Identifying and Treating Anxiety in Later Life

Many people manage the business of growing older, whatever the culture that surrounds them, and cope with the psychological sequelae of growing older in a way that is satisfactory for themselves. However, there are individuals for whom the process is fraught with experiences that become problematical.

There is evidence from primary care research that 40 per cent of older people have mental health problems (Goudie and Richards, 1993). Although a wide range of difficulties is represented, anxiety-based problems are probably the most common (McGarry, Bhutani and Watts, 1997; Krasucki et al., 1999; Watts et al., 2002; British Psychological Society, 2002). They are also underdetected and unattended (Audit Commission, 2000) despite the existence of valid clinical technologies to enable us to detect, assess and provide intervention.

If not treated anxiety can lead to severe reductions in functioning (Fifer, Mathias, Patrick, Mazonson, Luebeck and Buesching, 1994), more risk of developing physical problems (Hotopf et al., 1998) and failure to recover from physical illness (Haga et al., 1991). In essence, there is evidence that anxiety exacerbates health problems, prolongs recovery and contributes to disability.

Positive therapy means going beyond baseline, to develop or restructure thoughts about mastery, growth, purpose, autonomy, self-acceptance, and relations with others. Well-being therapy has an impact on anxiety related pathology and symptoms, but is more than symptom management. Its aim is to foster those conditions of life that enable natural resilience (Maddux, 2005).

Eleven commonly encountered sources of anxiety in later life are identified below. They stem from either actual adverse experiences or beliefs that these events will inevitably accompany ageing. In a therapy situation they could be used as a basis for systematic enquiry, to help elicit constructs important to the individual and subsequently as a basis for individually tailored treatment. As in Personal Construct Theory (Kelly, 1955) the therapeutic value comes through gaining insight into (and challenging) our own core constructs and their predictive value.

1. *Loss of control, autonomy and individuality versus self-acceptance.* As we age we are increasingly exposed to the risk of being 'stamped' as 'old', 'disabled' or 'sick'; we are increasingly defined in terms of shortcomings and may develop as a result chronic self-criticism and negative self-evaluation. Psychological interventions can help first by exploring the particular distorted

beliefs about ageing by using a counselling and validating approach. For example, if inevitability is identified ('This is how it has to be'), then it is helpful to start with a humanistic counselling position (e.g. 'This is a very painful and difficult place to be – to feel that life is spoilt'). A cognitive behavioural approach will then help by (a) identifying specific triggering thoughts (e.g. 'My life is worthless now I can't do what I used to do') and (b) introducing a new habit of thought – to identify the true facts about what *can* be expected in this new situation.

James was a farmer and used to think about himself as capable and competent, happy in his own company and reliant on no one. In his seventh decade he retired, just at the same age his father before him had done. His father had not wanted to retire, and died a few months afterwards. James had neither thought about 'retirement' nor relished it, but accepted it. Very soon he became perturbed and frightened; these were unfamiliar and bewildering emotions for him. There was a series of episodes in which, immediately after going to bed, he had experienced severe palpitations, sweating and thoughts that he would die. He would get up from bed, and feel too frightened to go back. It worsened until he was fearful of going to bed at all, as he could never be sure of when another episode would strike. He told no one the full story until, forced by exhaustion, he went to his family doctor, and consequently consulted a psychological practitioner.

Exploration of his expectancies about retirement revealed his thoughts preceding his retirement had been predominantly of emptiness and death. His response had been to 'hide them' but they had intruded again in a more pressing way while he was trying to fall asleep. Early thoughts were 'There is nothing to my life if I can't be farmer' and 'I'm just like my father'. On one occasion his heart started racing on going to bed, and the thought came 'I'm going to die'. He developed hypervigilance to changes in bodily sensations, especially noticeable at bed time and before sleep. He began to interpret these as life-threatening signs and symptoms ('Just like my father'). At such times, he wanted to die. However, the thought 'There is nothing to live for' contradicted his moral beliefs; so at the same time he wanted not to die, and in fact during a panic attack was terrified of dying. He judged his thoughts to be cowardly and this caused shame and further disintegration of his sense of self.

He developed the safety behaviour of getting up from bed, reinforcing the thought 'Unless I get up from bed I will suffocate'. As a result of this process, James had arrived in a place in his life unlike any he had encountered previously; he had no experience of turning to others to share his thoughts, and so had no opportunities to challenge these negative views about retirement. Other people may share their thoughts and at-tendant fears about ageing and retirement more readily and so find a way to challenge and replace their 'demon' distorted thoughts from ear-lier life. Such people might counter distorted thoughts with, for example: 'I'm not like my parents, the world is so different now'; 'Retirement is an arbitrary term'; 'What other people think retirement should be is of no matter, I will make of it what is right for me'. James used his opportunity of interactions with the psychologist to improve accurate recognition of body sensations, to practise alternative behaviours to replace avoidance be-haviours, and to develop new health promoting skills and knowledge such as auto-relaxation.

2. *Seen as a burden, particularly a social burden, versus positive relations with others.* In a society that sees life as a commodity, and places material wealth to the forefront as a life-defining concept in terms of human value, the strong possibility is that many people will internalize this idea, and as a consequence will be vulnerable to self-deceptions such as 'If only I could work again I would be fine' or to damaging self-evaluations such as 'I will never be as useful again and so I might as well turn my face to the wall'. The core belief 'I am being a burden' emerges as a recurring theme in clinical work with anxiety in later life. Ideas of self-harm may accom-pany this belief. Unchecked, the process may progress to deeper levels of depersonalization – for example, thoughts such as 'I am not the person I was'. The person's behaviour may become uncharacteristic; the sense of alienation means previously altruistic and community-conscious persons express 'demanding' or 'self-centred' behaviours. Then the self-fulfilling prophecy is completed – the stereotype of the older person as selfish and demanding is reinforced. Effective intervention is likely to require change in the environment rather than in the individual's cognitions alone. All individuals, no matter what age or stage in life, thrive if their fellow citizens find their presence worthwhile and act in ways that signal this.

Joan valued her life in terms of her work as a mother and in later years as a carer in the family. She had even nursed her adult son through ill-ness and dying, and had been known as 'strong' even after his death. When it came to living with the aftermath of a stroke, however, she began to behave 'unlike herself'. She became focused on her disabilities and shortcomings; being told that her recovery was in fact relatively complete and successful did not allay her anxieties. She saw herself as fallen from her position of grace – now deposed from the 'strong' position she despised the position of 'weakness' that she felt she now occupied. Internalizing society's values meant constantly striving to achieve the state of 'perfect carer', and avoiding relying on others. While in good health this self-deception could be sustained. With a change in health, and the possibility of being less than perfect as the caregiver of the family, she was filled with terror. Where others may have been in a social context that helped them to internalise a different way of valuing themselves, Joan was rigidly dependent on her care giver role. In a material world context, care givers experience positive status and power; by implication care receivers are 'other', 'not me', and 'dependent'. To be in the care-receiving position seemed to her an intolerable switch of position. Self-esteem that depends on either materially or socially perceived 'superiority' in society is likely to be fragile in old age, when such positions are challenged by circumstance. The therapist explained to Joan that the person's way of coping with disabilities or changed roles is often to resist the changes and to try to continue as previously. This is the signal that it is time to stop and review the meaning of what it is the person is reluctant to give up or change. For example, acting as a caregiver was giving meaning to Joan's life, and the anxiety appeared to be maintained by worry thoughts along the lines of 'I'm not me if I'm not taking care of others' or 'I'm not worth anything if I'm not doing things for other people' or 'I'm just a burden now and can never be worthwhile to anyone'. The therapist introduced cognitive behavioural therapy principles and language to identify these thoughts, and to develop evidence-based truths as alternatives and means of deflating the power of the worry thoughts. For example, 'I am me, and in a new situation; when I have been in new situations before I have set myself realistic goals no matter how overwhelmed I felt and have stuck to them', 'I can think of occasions previously in my life when I have received help and this was really needed and I appreciated it', or 'I have experienced the privileged position of looking after other people, so now I can relax and know that other people want that opportunity too'. For Joan the intensity of the worry process itself had become more disabling than the residual effects of the stroke. Thoughts such as 'I'm a nuisance' flag up the presence of core distorted beliefs about interpersonal relationships. The work carried out by the therapist and Joan focused on her understanding of how overgeneralization and dichotomous thinking served to fuel the worry escalator. They spent time revising and updating Joan's beliefs particularly about caregiving, and exploring alternative bases on which to base roles and relationships, including active involvement of Joan's partner.

3.   *Rejection and treachery versus social acceptance.* A widespread fear amongst older people is that of being tricked by fate into institutional care. Sometimes people are actually tricked (e.g. being told by relatives that they are to visit a residential home and then being left). In other cases, we trick ourselves by pretending it cannot happen to us; as a result we take no steps to prevent it happening. But there is also a double treachery; rejection from mainstream society is commonly described as 'for our own good'. The risks of normal life are now judged to be unacceptable (usually to society). But when older disabled people are taken out of their place in the community it is the community that is deprived. Others become anxious about their own fate in later life, and manage to suppress this by avoiding thinking about the matter.

Penelope had retired as a schoolteacher and cared for her parents until their deaths. She continued to live in the parental house and to give support to various aunts and other ageing relatives. Where she had previously seen herself as capable, busy and satisfied with her life, at the age of 71 she found herself in a dilemma. She was experiencing disturbed sleep, intrusive worry thoughts about her future, and a crisis of her previously strong religious beliefs. She had a repeated dream in which she was following a hearse when the back would open and the coffins would fall out on the road with no one caring about them but herself. In the dream, she was unable by herself to collect and lift back the coffins; this dream experience left her with sensations of panic and a deep despondency. She had been able to keep going as long as other areas of her life allowed some distractions; but soon these were spoilt too by the panic and worry feelings. In therapy discussions, it became clear that Penelope was viewing her earlier life as having been entirely worthless; she felt she had become isolated in looking after her family and that this now had no meaning. These doubts about her past life seemed to her a sin and a betrayal of her faith. Worry now welled out of the belief that she had lost her faith and been alienated from her god. It seemed she had no safe haven and no one to save her from the institution. Guilt emanated from such thoughts as 'Perhaps my community is not benign and caring, as I had always believed; perhaps my god is not forgiving of my weakness and shortcomings; perhaps I am being rejected for being weak and inadequate.' Tracing the process by which worry thoughts regenerate and renew themselves in a vicious circle of worry and self-blame was a crucial part of work with Penelope. Rather than work with the rational evidence on a worry by worry basis, she was asked to learn about the worry cycle and to intervene in the worry process, by thought stopping and relaxation. Once she had experimented and experienced for herself the fact that the worry process could be changed, the worry became un-hooked from her

> *core beliefs. These were then not under threat. Of course the situation did not change – that is, she was alone, and in a world that showed relatively little concern for older people on their own. However, she had learnt to live with her new state of 'the scales have fallen from my eyes'.*

4. *Segregation and congregation versus social integration.* The experience of ageing in an ageist society can be many people's first experience of being on the receiving end of prejudice. As protection against prejudice and discrimination many older people appear to segregate themselves away from the mainstream community. Others choose to remain living in houses that are physically integrated within the community, but become socially separate – perhaps excluded from or restricting themselves from opportunities to mix and meet with a wide range of others. Many see later life as an invalidating experience, and so fail to achieve the sense that ageing is a key part to our understanding the meaning and purpose of life itself (Sapp, 2004; Kirkwood, 1999). 'Therapy' can include education in the facts and reality of ageing, for example identifying evidence that older people are least likely to be victims of crime and that 80 per cent of people in later life do not develop dementia.

> *Donald and Myra were partners of 53 years of marriage. But Myra now lived in a residential home and barely recognized Donald when he visited. Donald's own health was frail as a result of damage to his cardiovascular system and he also experienced involuntary muscle spasms. He continued to be active in the daytime but in the evenings he closed the door on the world and felt intensely isolated. Then the worry process would gain a grip; he had repeated worry thoughts about Myra, about how he couldn't help her now, and about his failure to appreciate the visits and support of his daughters. Donald was a war veteran of Dunkirk, and couldn't understand his inability now to take control of his life. His anxiety caused rapid breathing, the fear of a heart attack and a retreat to bed in the belief that this would help. Donald was fearful about therapy to help manage his anxiety symptoms because he didn't want to stop thinking about Myra. Therapy began by establishing with him that thoughts about Myra would always be there, including the sad ones about their separation, but that these were distinct from the worry thoughts. He began to spot 'self-blame' thoughts (e.g. 'I should be more grateful') and catastrophizing thoughts (e.g. 'That spasm means I am going to have a heart attack'). He worked to identify the 'truth' and rational evidence in its place (e.g. 'I express my*

> *gratitude to my daughters well; however, it is natural to think about Myra as my relationship with her is unique' and 'Muscle spasms occur for mainly physical reasons and although unpleasant will not harm me or cause a heart attack'). He also practised a self-relaxation technique, and it was evident that his spasms were more quickly dispersed when relaxed. Donald could not change the circumstances of separation from Myra nor the consequent irreversible challenge to his previous lifestyle; however he learnt to spot the worry thoughts, and to replace them with focus on relaxation and thoughts about his positive ways of coping in the here and now. All this was achievable, even though Donald had hearing difficulty and some mild cognitive impairment from his circulatory problems.*

5. *Dehumanization versus personal growth.* If we mix with people who view older and disabled people as unproductive and useless, many of us may come to view ageing as a time of becoming more object than subject – of relinquishing one's full humanity and personhood. Media and political images allege a tidal wave of financial cost to the country as the population ages. Once internalized, such thoughts maintain much anxiety. It can often be the most robust, successful and confident of persons who have the worst fall – as they have never before encountered the dehumanization precipitated by retirement or disability. The opportunity for reflection with a neutral other can reveal the truth: long life brings the possibility of a deepening understanding of many aspects of life; it places a person in the position of potentially experiencing and sharing richer and more diverse dimensions to life than were possible in earlier life.

> *Alan and Sheila had had a finely balanced relationship. They had succeeded in sustaining a marriage even though they had significant doubts about each other's commitment. There had been hurt, betrayal of trust and accusations of affairs. With work to focus on, and then children and grandchildren they had soldiered on, thinking that nothing much could change. Alan developed a progressive muscular illness however, and ended up relying on a wheelchair. He spent increasing amounts of time at home. Sheila felt invaded, and disliked what felt like his contamination of her space. Alan's chair at home was identifiable by the mat placed under his feet and the towel over the chair seat to protect the upholstery. He talked with anger as if he were aware of being the 'dirty object'. He refused to be taken into public places in his wheelchair because he felt shunned by people, as if they saw a*

> 'lump' instead of a person. Sheila's feelings mirrored these; she felt she was looking after a physical entity but not a person, and she resented what she named as her new 'job for life'. Their relationship, fragile at its best, could not withstand the drift towards dehumanisation of Alan. Following a year in which each sought support in their different and separate ways, Alan finally arranged to leave home.

6. *Denial of true feelings/ invalidation versus environmental mastery.* As Kirkwood (1999) says, ageing is neither inevitable nor necessary from a biological point of view. So the important question is 'What is the function of longevity?' not 'What do we do about the problem of ageing?' A function of longevity for example might be understood in terms of increased potential for achieving moral behaviours and states such as happiness, humility and the like. The mismatch between this potential and the kinds of restrictive environments in which many people find themselves in late life is clearly a source of invalidation and stress. Examples of such environments include the following: being offered soft toys and expected to accept these in place of real relationships; being given medical and other tests that are said to be 'for your own good' but which undermine you and get you to comply with others' intentions for you; being talked about, not with; your own adult offspring insisting that you are causing them worry, so much so that you end up feeling guilty and an embarrassment to them; offering to share your 'wisdom' and experience, and looking forward to extending your own philosophical dimensions, only to be met with the insistence that you are out of touch, not able to understand the world as it is now and even just like a child.

> Sean was worried that he would be taken into hospital when his cancer finally worsened and had expressed his clear wish to be allowed to remain at home. His 'worry' was based on the reality that nearly everyone he knew who'd had cancer had ended up too ill to argue the point and had died in hospital. His other cause for (realistic) concern was that his wife was under some strain, and the solution being pressed on her was to allow Sean to be hospitalized. Instead of taking his intent seriously, Sean was dubbed 'a worrier' and this only added to the arguments being stacked up against him. The culmination came when a nurse suggested to him that he would probably worry less in hospital. Unused to having disputes with the caring professionals Sean felt desperate, alone and resentful at having his feelings

> *dismissed. How could running away from the situation help his anxiety, he thought? He really needed people to support him and his wife through the process of his dying. Instead of being able to process his emotions about the prospect of leaving behind all he had known, he was being forced to fight just to hold his position. Resentment, disappointment and fear might have been the final emotions he experienced before the end of his life. Instead, a specialist cancer care organisation was contacted and Sean was supported at home with full access to the technical help he needed for pain control. In this way he was validated as being a caring and thoughtful person, and was able to live his final days with the dignity of knowing that his feelings would be taken seriously.*

7. *Discontinuity in the physical environment versus social actualization.* Despite the rhetoric of 'community care' and 'fitting services to the needs of the individual' older people continue to be expected to move from home if they are to have certain needs met. Once in the care system, they are then required to move on, sometimes serially, as needs increase or change. An acute event such as a fall and hospitalisation can result in 'no way back' and blinkered expectations about future well-being and desire for social integration.

> *Violet had cognitive disabilities and shared a home with her daughter. Violet had a carefully planned support package at home which allowed her daughter to pursue her career. One day she had a fall in her home, and was hospitalized with a fractured femur. Following traditional lines of thought the hospital team recommended that she be transferred to a residential home. She became anxious and agitated, to a point where the hospital team predicted a very poor life prognosis and recommended a nursing home. However, her daughter and care manager were committed to supporting her at home in the belief that this was in keeping with Violet's wishes. At increased cost in the short term Violet was provided with the nursing care and support that she needed at home. Despite the medical prognosis Violet recovered her mobility at home, and continued to live another 3 years. Her anxiety had disappeared once at home – not only in familiar surroundings but also supported by familiar trusted persons who believed that her future at home was meaningful and right for her (and the associated costs of support also diminished).*

Alex had had episodes of depression in his adult life but each time he had sought treatment from his family doctor or psychiatric services and had recovered. When in his sixties he experienced various changes never before encountered. He retired, and his wife was diagnosed as having cancer; he gave up driving through a loss in confidence, and moved into another episode of his depression. This time, however, none of the treatments that had appeared to help previously helped now. His thoughts shifted to guilt – about his failure to get better. He became too anxious to do most routine activities for example, drive, occupy himself, or go outside. He was admitted to hospital where further treatments were tried and failed. By this time his thoughts were thoughts of self-derogation; he saw the future as filled with unknown terrors, unmapped and unremitting. Agitation took over his behaviour and worry took over his thinking. Society's only answer was further discontinuity; Alex saw his life as finished and was moved to a nursing home. Ironically he was deemed a fraud for being more able than expected, and so never found the solace he needed.

8. *Discontinuity in relationships and social connections versus social contribution.* Facing a disability for the first time ever in later life, the person may be unprepared for the strong pressures that come to bear on them. After a stroke, for example, the person may be rejected by their partner as unattractive, altered or even 'not the person I married'. The person who 'fails' to rehabilitate after a fall or illness, for example, may be made to feel worthless. When a move out of our own home is suggested or put forward as an offer that cannot be refused, the message is, of course, not simply a practical one but a comment on our (reduced) worth and value to our society. (The message may be 'society is unwilling to take the risk or make the effort to maintain me within it'.)

Natalie faced the aftermath of her stroke with courage. A hospital discharge statement was positive concerning her recovery of abilities. She continued to suffer a loss of expressive language however. Despite the optimism of Natalie's therapists, however, her daughter emphasized the risks – so much so that Natalie was prevented from doing even tasks she was capable of. As her confidence ebbed way, anxiety and self-loathing took over. With time Natalie came to believe her daughter's view – that she should give up her home and move into a residential home. As with so many Natalie's distress was not seen as meriting therapy. She was left to worry. She became restless, agitated and uncooperative. Soon there was talk of her needing care in a

> *special unit for mentally disturbed older people. However a new service had been set up in Natalie's city whose purpose was positive support in the person's own community. Natalie was supported to accept this; it enabled her to be mum, granny and neighbour again, and there was soon plenty of evidence that she was again a welcome and contributing person in her local area.*

9. *Seen only in terms of ageing or disability versus in resilience-fostering relationships.* The fact is that only around 20 to 25 per cent of variability in ageing can be attributed to genetic factors (Kirkwood, 2004). The rest has to be accounted for by environmental factors, including attitudes about ageing. There is pressure from society to conform to the stereotype of 'all old people are the same for example. 'grumpy', 'slow', 'bad memory' or 'ungrateful'. To resist this requires personal enlightenment about ageing, understanding that all life phases have limitations and later life has just different limitations – as well as opportunities for experiencing happiness, purpose and optimism.

> *Tom's wife developed dementia, and with it a relaxation of her lifelong reserve about sharing her feelings and thoughts. They developed a close and trusting relationship during their last years together, and with this came a satisfying sense of stability and calm for all their family and friends.*

10. *Having one's life 'wasted' versus purpose in life.* Some individuals may give up activities, roles and responsibilities at a time when it is expected by tradition for example at 'retirement' age. Or they may think of the age of their own parents' death as a marker, perhaps experiencing themselves as being in the waiting room of disability or death from that age on.

> *Bob's father had died when he was 14 years old, leaving the family to struggle for a livelihood and an education. His mother died at the age of 70. In the year that Bob met his 70th birthday, his own grandson had his fourteenth birthday. From that time Bob's life had shrunk to encompass very little; he had stopped going out and was consumed with worry about his grandson. Objectively there was nothing to worry about. However, Bob was deeply disturbed and could not enjoy his cherished grandson's happiness. Bob eventually identified that he had a long held fear about reaching the*

> *age of 70. He saw it as the marker of the end of his useful life; in addition, in his experience bad things could happen at the age of 14. In therapy discussions, Bob was able to see the erroneous basis for such thoughts, to see the process by which his fears were engendered by them, and to replace them with thoughts based on truth, such as 'Chronological age is not as important as the environment a person is in' and 'Irrespective of whether I am here my grandson will take control over his own life and decisions'.*

11. *Blamed for the problems and intimidated versus seen as socially contributing.* Having identified the wounding process, by which people with learning disabilities come to be blamed and to blame themselves for the difficulties, Vanier (1982) went on to create communities in which people who have learning disabilities can live as fully participating and equally valued members in their communities. In contrast, our mainstream communities seem to tolerate older people being intimidated in ways that would not be acceptable for people with learning disabilities in our society. For example, forgetting to put off the cooker, losing one's temper, or insisting on independence might be regarded as inexcusable in an older person. Commonly the succeeding generation blames the preceding generation for 'the bad things in life' (such as wars and environmental disasters) – but apply different standards to themselves for example do not expect themselves to achieve major change within one generation. Blaming previous generations can act as another mechanism for avoidance of change and failure to grasp the real systemic issues.

> *Gordon came to hospital agitated and anxious about everything in his life. He had been depressed before but this felt different. He saw himself as a person always able to control his demons – although he really had only placed them to the side and avoided them. He was a high achiever and continued to be active in social movements to benefit others. He had obsessional thoughts about global catastrophes, and reinforced these with compulsive watching of TV news. He felt his compulsions were taking control – his future beliefs were exclusively about disorder, helplessness and destruction. The realisation of our own mortality does not always bring such catastrophic thinking, but in Gordon's case having a sense of control and power over fate had been his mainstay. In therapy sessions the pattern of catastrophizing thoughts and feelings was examined; for the first time in his life Gordon learnt how to examine the rational evidence and not avoid it.*

Rational alternative thoughts were openly addressed such as 'The negative incidents reported on the News are vastly outnumbered by caregiving and helping actions'; 'No one person can control events'; 'Each action has a value and an impact that reaches into the future'. He became able to enjoy again the 'here and now' experiences in his life and discovered how a focus on his relationship with his wife was bringing him a much-sought sense of reward and self-respect.

Core Issues Related to Depression and Thriving in Later Life

Depression: shame and personal identity in later life

The experience of shame can be defined as the experience of perceiving, or believing, that others value the self badly, or as inferior or flawed. Shame and humiliation exist purely in the interpersonal domain; that is, they do not exist without two 'actors' – the self and the other, and the reflective interaction between these. Shame is linked to a range of behaviours that serve to conceal the flawed self (Gilbert, 2001) and hence it may persist undetected over a lifespan. However, later life is a time of many changes that might threaten these defences and concealments; if physical attributes, for example, have been depended on to sustain a sense of self then loss of physical attractiveness may be experienced as a crushing blow to core role structure (Kelly, 1955) or to core role states (Ryle and Kerr, 2002).

External shame is to be found in the ways others behave and in the language used towards the older person. For example, jokes that imply asexuality/childishness such as 'You'll be getting yourself a date tonight then', or being described as 'severe', 'complex' or 'multiple problems', may infantilize the person. *Internal shame* is to be found when older persons themselves carry internal schema, such as 'asexual', 'severe problem' or 'worthless'. Such self-derogation can elicit humiliation behaviours from others resulting in a self-perpetuating circle.

Practitioners working with older people in distress are aware that, for some people, serious and often catastrophic conditions of deep distress only emerge in later life, and there is a growing body of evidence to this effect (Morse and Lynch, 2000). Cognitive analytic therapy (CAT) helps us to understand this phenomenon in terms of the construction and de-construction of the self in later life (Hepple, Pierce and Wilkinson, 2002; Sutton, 1997).

Depression: core role states and the experience of late life

CAT (Ryle and Kerr, 2002) recognizes that patterns of interaction with others are powerful and have a persisting effect on the developing self. However it is more than social constructionist theory; it explicitly links the evolving self with the social ecology. For example, the concept of the 'seed self' (those roles that are not actualised) can throw light on the origins of unexpected behaviour in late life (Hepple and Sutton, 2004; Hepple, Pierce and Wilkinson, 2002; Sutton, 2000; Ryle, 1997). *Reciprocal role states* remind us of Kelly's bipolar personal constructs (Bannister, 1981; Bannister and Fransella, 1971) in emphasizing the social construction of the self. Personal construct psychology (PCP) proposes that individuals construe the world in terms of their own unique personal constructs (their core role structure), and that experience leads to continuous validation or reconstruction of these as they attempt to anticipate the demands and events in an ever-changing environment. Using PCP clinically with people in later life has shown how, in a context of extreme adverse life conditions and disabilities, re-construing and re-valuing constructs supports well-being and life satisfaction (Robbins, 2005).

The CAT concept of bipolar states similarly helps us clinically to understand those individuals who, in late life, show sudden and unpredictable changes in patterns of behaviour. In striving to escape from the core pain of earlier life (maladaptive) relationships or experiences, the individual idealises the polar opposite and strives to achieve this state. For example, the person may have had the bipolar constructs *good versus bad* or *loved versus criticized* as core constructs of their self-identity throughout life. However, previous lifelong patterns of behaviour may be suddenly abandoned when this is no longer sustainable – often when an idealized partner dies. The individual in this transition in later life is in a fragile state – probably experiencing personality de-construction and identity. Their efforts to re-construct identity may put unrealistic demands on others, such as family or services, to a level that becomes intolerable and is usually inappropriate. For example, they may present symptoms persistently so that they are in a constant position of seeking perfect care.

The self may 'escape' from an early life abused state by idealization; for example, a marriage partner is placed in the reciprocal opposite (saviour) role and the relationship may be trapped in an eternal loop whereby all energies must sustain the distortion of the partner as perfect. Later in life, with own disabilities or changed circumstances, the fantasy may become too challenging to sustain resulting in exit from the loop i.e. an unpredicted change in lifelong behaviour patterns (Hepple, Pierce and Wilkinson, 2002). Such a person may be particularly challenging in a long-term care-dependency situation.

The CAT approach can lead to insights into complex and challenging situations that seem resistant to other therapeutic formulations, such as the following:

- The borderline template describes the lifelong caregiving and idealizing personality who enters a rapid descent into hopelessness, disillusion and somatization when their role becomes care-receiving – their customary striving for idealized, uncritical mirror relationships through caregiving becomes unsustainable.
- Borderline traits may be quiescent through adult life because the individual channels all their energy into surviving within the 'loop'; in later life, with a reduced reservoir of energy or loss of the reciprocating partner, this survival state may become unsustainable.
- Cumulative life events may limit the individual's coping repertoire, but this may not have catastrophic effects until dependency comes along, potentially resulting in a late life collapse.
- People may disclose childhood abuse for the first time in late life as a consequence of an attempt to exit from the enforced silence, perhaps triggered by the death of other key players. Or if cognitively disabled the person may react to personal care with unrestrained emotions reminiscent of the earlier experience.
- The narcissistic template describes the personality who strives for idealized admiring relationships. Catastrophic collapse into self-neglect, depression, and even pseudo-dementia may be observed in the narcissistic individual in late life. In CAT terms, such individuals fail to tolerate loss of those social and occupational roles that previously sustained their need for unqualified admiration.
- The *contemptible versus contemptuous* split core state may be related to earlier life experiences involving humiliation. An early survival strategy may be to seek visible success in life as a protection against the feared humiliation, often at the cost of open and authentic relationships. However, faced with disability and dependency such a strategy collapses, precipitating the reciprocal state of self-derogation.
- The *rejected versus rejecting* split-core state may be related to earlier life experiences of unsatisfactory attachment behaviours. Although anxious attachment may be survived by developing aggressively independent behaviour patterns throughout a large part of adult life, this may be hard to sustain in late life. Disability, anticipated or actual, may activate deeply needy patterns of behaviour. Hence a characteristically stoical, self-sufficient person may switch to an unquenchably needy state in later life even in the absence of significant disability.

Figure 7.1 illustrates the CAT Core Role states for the Borderline and Narcissistic templates.

Originally as a child and younger person	Core pain	Early survival strategy
Terrorising experiences	Paralysed with fear	Numb; no feelings
Shut in a cupboard; beaten	Shock	Idealised brother
Brother 'murdered' by father	Un-expressed fears	Un-expressed feelings of rejection and
Humiliated, degraded, abused		humiliation; 'not worth saving'

{In adult life married abusive man; remarried idealised man, whose death brought a slide into collapse and spiritualism.}

Now – most of the time	Regressed state	Survival state
Perpetually perceives people to be against self	Humiliation of self	Protects self from more harm
People tell 'bad things' about me	e.g. vomits, refuses food, obese,	Strives to please, then feels martyred
Suspended animation, 'The Wall', unreachable	stutters, won't talk about past	Seeks and rejects medical help, angry
	Can't remember or feel	Idealised husband ('snag' of life not
		worth living without him), spirit world

Occasionally	Seed self or real self state
Beaming 'earth mother', beautiful, warm	Real self – a 'good child', feeling loved
	Giving love, deserving to live, nourishing to self and others

Martha's attempts to escape from the core pain are to seek idealised relationships, resulting in split states that are ultimately unsustainable (Borderline Template)

Striving for ideal care — Ideally caring vs Ideally cared for / Abused vs Abusive

Seeking uncritical minor relationship — Wanted vs Wanting / Abandoning vs Abandoned

Figure 7.1 CAT core role states

Originally as a child and younger person

Core pain

Early survival strategy

Father a village policeman
Set an example/had to please
Humiliation
Fear

Obsession about stealing
Fear of 'being bad' and locked up
Unexpressed fears
Paralysed

Striving (successful career)
No recall of bad times
Feeling criticised, rejected, humiliated, contemptible

{At 66, retires, wife diagnosed with cancer – severe depressive episode – rapid slide into vegetative state.}

Now – most of the time

Regressed state

Survival state

Perpetually perceived threat
'Will be caught'
'Useless'

Humiliates and degrades self
e.g. can't dress, can't walk
can't write, soils

Numb
Sense of time standing still
Sense of living superficially and 'not in touch with feelings'

Occasionally

Seed self or real self state

Real self – a boy wanting to grow whole
Deserving to live, nourishing to self and others, tending to plants

David's attempts to escape from the core pain are to seek idealised relationships, resulting in split states that are ultimately unsustainable (Narcissistic Template)

Striving for real care — Ideally caring vs Ideally cared for / Contemptous vs Contemptible

Striving for admiring relationship — Ideally admired vs Ideally admiring / Striving vs Critical

Figure 7.1 (Continued)

Borderline Template: Martha

Martha collapsed into self-neglect and self-humiliation over a period of years following the death of her idealized second husband. Her behaviour patterns included vomiting, refusing food, stuttering, refusing to talk of her past and perceiving everyone to be saying 'bad things' about her. She came to the attention of the psychological services as a consequence of her repeated pattern over years of seeking medical help then rejecting it. At discharge she would produce new symptoms then reject treatments or remedies.

Martha's memories of childhood were of being beaten, locked in a cupboard and terrorized by her father. To survive her early fear she developed a way of becoming 'numb', and feeling paralyzed. When her brother died at the age of 10 she blamed herself – she had failed to protect him. In adult life, she first married an abusive man, presumably recognizing in him the behaviour patterns that were familiar and for which she had readymade survival strategies. She found a worthwhile role in defending her family against him. Her second marriage was to a man she cast as 'wonderful' and her idealized husband. She continued to seek the idealized caregiver role – pursuing spiritualism to make contact with her husband, and bestowing hand-crafted goods for fund-raising in the hospital departments she attended. Occasionally, the 'seed self' or real self in Martha could be seen; a 'good child', a nourishing mother, and an equal and fascinating conversation partner. However, this was transient and generally not retrievable during the therapy meetings.

Martha continued to cycle through phases of self-degradation (her regressed state) alternately with phases of demand/rejection of help. One difference was noted, however, and that was that her stutter disappeared in the months following her first ever disclosure about her childhood experiences of abuse. She never relinquished her pursuit of the role of idealised caregiver. Through contacts with spiritualists she sustained the belief that her husband still needed and admired her. She believed she had visions of her brother – when he appeared as a 'little angel' in her home. Despite some alleviation of the symptoms that had brought her into contact with medical services, Martha's core role states had not shifted and she continued to live her life in a fragile and shifting mental state.

Narcissistic Template: David

Growing up as the son of a village policeman, David was not appreciated in the company of the other children. He went to school in another town, and compensated through hard work and high achievement, becoming a successful professional person and successful husband and father. With retirement, however, came a catastrophic collapse into non-functioning and 'depression'. With his

> *wife's diagnosis and treatment for cancer, David took on the role of carer with as much perfectionism as he had his job and his garden previously. However, as she responded to treatment and needed less of David, he was unable to find a reflection of himself in her. A deeper catastrophic collapse ensued, to a point where he was admitted to psychiatric hospital unable to carry out even basic self-care skills. He never returned home, but after 2 years moved to nursing home care where he remained sheltered from the dilemma's of life and from the fact of the narcissistic collapse of his relationships.*

Depression: regret

Davies (2004) reports that regret is a common experience affecting up to 65 per cent of people. Regret is a negative appraisal of some part of one's past life. Cognitive errors maintain regrets – counterfactual thinking for example, 'If only I hadn't done that', critical thinking for example, 'I shouldn't have done that' or labelling for example, 'I'm a bad person for having done that'. The problems arise when the person cannot continue to suppress from memory the regretted event, and this may interfere when new and current decisions have to be made. For the person whose thinking is already dominated by critical self-doubt, to be faced with new key decisions over difficulties in later life can trigger a retreat into panic, ruminations and avoidance of decisions. In a therapeutic relationship, the aims would be to transform the thoughts that mediate the regret and so remove the need to suppress the memory of the event. A factual thought to be identified and reinforced might be 'Only what is known at the time can influence choice or actions, not information discovered later'

> *As a child Maisie had been sexually abused over a number of years by a family friend. Fearful of her parents' reaction, she had never disclosed this abuse. She saw herself as fundamentally different from other people, a victim, tainted, and undeserving of her 'good husband', her 'good children'. Her regret was that she had taken no action to try to stop the abuse. She recognized that she had been overprotective of her own children. She saw all children as potential victims, and was highly sensitized to News items about children. She had passively endured episodes of depression spanning her adult life. The therapist discussed with Maisie the context of her choices as a child. There was evidence that her parents would not have believed her; they may well have punished her for 'lying'. Alternative thoughts were identified such as 'I didn't have the choice to tell anyone'. Gradually she began to not expect a return episode, a new experience for her.*

Depression: attachment patterns and later life

Attachment theory points to a meaningful link between the individual's early life experiences of secure relationships, and their patterns of coping with insecurity and loss later in life (Davies, 2000). It has opened doors to the appreciation of late life as being primarily concerned with negotiating (and re-negotiating) the self in a context of past and present relationships. In attachment terms, later life is a continuing dynamic of internal emotional and cognitive processes, working and re-working issues of trust, dependence and separation in the face of new 'strange situations' (Ainsworth, Blehar, Waters and Wall, 1978).

Bowlby initially set out the notion of attachment as

> . . . a pattern of behaviours which is care-seeking and care-eliciting from an individual who feels they are less capable of dealing with the world than the person of whom they are seeking care. (Bowlby, 1969)

And later as

> The biological need to establish long-lasting and enduring affectional bonds with other that are able to provide the individual with a sense of security, safety and comfort. (Bowlby, 1980)

This definition sees attachment needs as on a par with human needs for water, food and shelter. The child grows to become fully adult only if these needs are met.

> Evidence is accumulating that human beings of all ages are happiest and able to deploy their talents to best advantage when they are confident that, standing behind them, are one or more trusted persons who will come to their aid should difficulties arise. The person trusted, also known as an attachment figure, can be considered as providing his or her companion with a secure base from which to operate. (Bowlby, 1988)

Insecure attachment patterns arise where a child does not receive the message that they are loved deeply and unchangeably. If the child felt they had to work to earn love, they may become an adult high in neediness, dependency and feelings of *insecurity*. If the child felt others to have been distant, inconsistent or uncaring, they may become denying and dismissive of attachment needs in adult life. If the child felt insecure in their attachments, they may become avoidant of close relationships in adult life.

Cognitive disability: Miesen (1993, 1999) considers Alzheimer's disease as like a 'strange situation', which activates these same attachment behaviours. This may explain how individuals with the same level of cognitive disability can show very different behaviours.

Loss and bereavement: Bereavement can be understood as not only the emotion of grief but also a loss depriving the individual of the security object on which they rely (Parkes, 1972).

Dependence: It may activate early-life attachment styles, with caregiving and care-receiving needs taking over as sources of security and identity. Caregiving institutions may attract insecure attachment behaviours, and have difficulty in discharging those individuals.

Depression: learning and later life

Being part of a learning community promotes a sense having a valued life, irrespective of age. Learning to lead, teach and share can be a positive experience of later life. For example, the Beth Johnson Foundation demonstrated how older people could contribute through reminiscence to social history (Bernard, 1998). Universities, archivists, educationists, social historians and local community groups came to value the memories, reflections and stories of older individuals through the Age to Age (2000) programme. Such activities emphasize the interpersonal, and intergenerational, value of the older citizen.

A key dimension of quality of life in a community is the relationships that exist across the generations. Reduced social contact, isolation, and segregation are undesired states by any age grouping in a community. The conscious and deliberate continuation of learning in old age, as exemplified by formal grandparent classes and by the 'University of the 3rd Age', are noted for not only promoting physical and mental 'productiveness' in older people, but also for promoting well-being and quality of life.

The lifelong learning paradigm is also relevant to the prevention of loneliness. For example 'Kindred Spirits' successfully matched shared interests and provided opportunities for mutual helping among older people, without the intervention of a traditional service (Wurr, 1999).

Depression: ageing and happiness

Greater longevity presents more opportunities for members of communities to learn the psychological skills of 'looking after each other' (Smail, 2001b). The more people with disabilities living within the community the more opportunities the members of that community have to become competent in sharing places and making life choices that integrate rather than isolate. Arguably, a measure of the viability and positive strength of a community lies in how it transacts its business towards its older members.

Table 7.2 The nine tasks for an ecology-focused society and how these may influence well-being

Area of individual or social functioning	Technology-focused society	Ecology-focused society
Occupation/work	Wealth production; continuous growth	Production harnessed to sustainability
Personal	Immediate, intense, artificially produced on demand	Natural, dependent on environment
Model of social 'progress'	Battery farm: selection and culling, for perfect individual Single dimensional.	Complex, multiple, interdependent, all forms of life have their place Multi-dimensional, round
Model of ownership of societal resources	Individual – given rights based on attributed merit (may not be linked with responsibilities)	All – share responsibilities in an interdependent complex system (rights)
Health	Cure	Well-being
Mood state	Seeking to maintain high mood and stimulation levels; 'happiness' seen as an objective in itself	Flexible; coping with changing levels of mood and connection with the environment
Relationships	Focus on consumer ideal; social life seen as measure of self-worth	Focus on authenticity, insight, self and other awareness and tolerance
Family	Narrowly defined; distinction made between 'mine' (biological or cohabiting family) and 'not mine'	Broadly defined; consciousness about links with other human groups and other species
Roles and status	Hierarchical, 'upwardly' aspiring; status associated with material possessions and wealth production	Global, 'outwardly' aspiring; status associated with life patterns that are not damaging to other human groups or species.

With advances in technology over the last decades, societies have focused on the creation of the 'perfect individual' and 'eternal life', thereby fuelling denial and defensive eugenic measures against frail older people (and other life forms that are at odds with this goal). In this 'old paradigm' technological advances have been driven by consumer values that are short term and unsustainable.

As we move forward into the 'new paradigm', technologies are looked to for help in managing and reducing the human footprint on the environment. The emerging global imperative on societies is for cooperation on achieving sustainable patterns of personal and pro-social behaviour. A 'new' positive psychology of ageing can help to open and expand a new understanding about the interdependency of generations, species and resources within a complex living system. Changing patterns of behaviour will not happen through threats of global catastrophe. It will depend on creating a compelling picture of a desirable future for individuals into later life. The new paradigm will involve inviting all people to value low-consumption patterns of life. It can be assisted by inviting all people to look on later life as a special opportunity to enjoy happiness and hope (free from consumer imperatives) and personal well-being (irrespective of adverse health or circumstances).

The 'new' positive psychology of ageing could help support and expand sustainable future patterns of human behaviour. It represents an ecological perspective in which individual ageing (Table 7.2).

- □ can provide opportunities for developing psychological and social well-being,
- □ is viewed as the 'full circle' of life,
- □ symbolizes the interdependency of all forms of life, in a highly complex living system,
- □ demonstrates that at every phase of life, early and late, happiness relates to a sense of being a meaningful part of a regenerating system,
- □ points to the highest principle of all which is that life requires us to adopt sustainable means of existence within our natural environment and with this comes sustainable happiness.

References

Age To Age (2000). *A Learning Activities Project for Older People.* Institute of Human Ageing, University of Liverpool.

Ainsworth, MDS, Blehar, MC, Waters, E and Wall, S (1978). *Patterns of Attachment: Assessment in the Strange Situation and at Home.* Lawrence Erlbaum, Hillsdale, NJ.

Allen-Burge, R, Stevens, AB and Burgio, LD (1998). Effective behavioural interventions for decreasing dementia-related challenging behaviour in nursing homes. *International Journal of Geriatric Psychiatry*, 14, 213–232.

Astrom, N (1996). Generalised anxiety disorder in stroke patients. A three-year longitudinal study. *Stroke*, 27, 270–275.

American Psychiatric Association (2000). *Diagnostic and Statistical Manual of Mental Disorders*, 4th edition, text revision, American Psychiatric Association, Washington, DC.

Atkinson, RC and Shiffrin, RM (1968). Human memory: A proposed system and its control processes. In Spence, KW and Spence, JT (eds). *The Psychology of Learning and Motivation*, Vol 2, pp. 89–195. Academic Press, New York.

Audit Commission (2000). *Forget Me Not: Mental Health Services for Older People.* Audit Commission Publications, London. Available at http://www.audit-commission.gov.uk/ac2/NR/Health/nrmhsop.pdf

Baglioni, AJ (1990). Residential relocation and health of the elderly. In Markides, KS and Cooper, CL (eds). *Ageing, Stress and Health.* John Wiley and Sons, Chichester, England.

Bailey, D and Kavanagh, A (1998). Valuing the person: Getting to know their life. *Journal of Dementia Care*, Sept/Oct, 26–27.

Ballard, C, Powell, I, James, I, Reichelt, K, Myint, P, Potkins, D, Bannister, C, Lana, M, Howard, R, O'Brien, J, Swann, A, Robinson, D, Shrimanker, J and Barber, R (2002). Can psychiatric liaison reduce neuroleptic use and reduce health service utilization for dementia patients residing in health care facilities? *International Journal of Geriatric Psychiatry, 17*(2), 140–145.

Bandura, Albert (2001). The changing face of psychology at the dawning of a globalization era. *Canadian Psychology/Psychologie canadienne, 42*(1), 12–24.

Bannister, D (1981). Construing a disability. In Brechin, A, Liddiard, P and Swain, J (eds). *Handicap in a Social World*, pp 230–236. Hodder and Stoughton, London.

Bannister, D and Fransella, F (1971). *Inquiring Man. The Theory of Personal Constructs.* Penguin Modern Psychology, Middlesex, England.

Barrowclough, C and Fleming, I (1985). *Goal Planning with Elderly People. Making Plans to Meet Individual Needs.* Manchester University Press, Manchester, UK.

Bender, M (1998). Shifting our focus from brain to mind, *Journal of Dementia Care,* January/February, *6*(1), 20–22.

Bender, MP and Wainwright, A (1998). *Model of Mind in Dementia.* Paper presented at the Annual Conference of the Psychologists Special Interest Group Working with Older People (PSIGE), Napier University, Edinburgh, 2 July.

Bernard, M (1998). The Beth Johnson Foundation: A quarter of a century of research with, for and about older people, *Education and Ageing, 13,* 143–162.

Bond, J, Dittman-Kohli, F, Peace, S and Westerhof, G (eds) (2007). *Ageing in Society: European Perspectives on Gerontology*, Sage, London.

Bowlby, J (1969). *Attachment and Loss. Vol 1: Attachment.* Hogarth Press, London.

Bowlby, J (1973). *Attachment and Loss. Vol 2: Separation: Anxiety and Anger.* Hogarth Press, London.

Bowlby, J (1980). *Attachment and Loss. Vol 3: Loss: Sadness and Depression.* Hogarth Press, London, Basic Books, New York.

Bowlby, J (1988). *A Secure Base: Parent–Child Attachment and Healthy Human Development.* Basic Books, New York.

British Psychological Society (2002). *Clinical Psychology Services for Older People in Primary Care.* Division of Clinical Psychology Occasional Paper No. 4, British Psychological Society, Leicester, UK.

Brost, NN and Johnson, T (1982). *Getting To Know You. One Approach to Service Planning for Individuals with Disabilities.* Wisconsin Coalition for Advocacy, Madison.

Burvill, PW, Johnson, GA, Jamrozik, KD, Anderson, CS, Stewart-Wynne, EG and Chakera, TMH (1995a). Prevalence of depression after stroke. The Perth community stroke study. *British Journal of Psychiatry, 66,* 320–327.

Burvill, PW, Johnson, GA, Jamrozik, KD, Anderson, CS, Stewart-Wynne, EG and Chakera, TMH (1995b) Anxiety disorders after stroke. The Perth community stroke study. *British Journal of Psychiatry, 66,* 328–332.

Cartwright, A, Hockey, L and Anderson, J (1973). *Life before Death.* Routledge and Kegan Paul, London.

Carver, CS and Scheier, MF (2005) Optimism. In Snyder, CR and Lopez, SJ (eds). *Handbook of Positive Psychology.* Oxford University Press, New York.

Cheston, R and Bender, M (1999). *Understanding Dementia: The Man with the Worried Eyes.* Jessica Kingsley, London and Philadelphia.

Clegg, A, Bryant, J, Nicholson, T, McIntyre, L, De Broe, S, Gerard, K and Waugh, N (2001) Clinical and cost-effectiveness of donepezil, rivastigmine and galantamine for Alzheimer's disease: a rapid and systematic review, *Health Technology Assessment*, 5(1), 1–137.

Coleman, P (1996). Identity management in later life. In Woods, RT (ed). *Handbook of the Clinical Psychology of Ageing*, pp. 93–113. John Wiley and Sons, Chichester, England.

Coleman, P (1997). Personality, health and ageing. *Journal of the Royal Society of Medicine*, 90 (Suppl 32), 27–33.

Coleman, P, Aubin, A, Robinson, M, Ivani-Chalian, C and Briggs, R (1993). Predictors of depressive symptoms and low self-esteem in a follow up study of elderly people over 10 years. *International Journal of Geriatric Psychiatry*, 8, 343–349.

Comfort, A (1977). *A Good Age*. Mitchell Beazley, London.

Copeland, J, Davidson, I, Dewy, M, Gilmore, C, Larkin, B, McWilliam, C, Saunders, P, Scott, A, Sharma, V and Sullivan, C (1992). Alzheimer's disease, other dementia's, depression and pseudodementia: Prevalence, incidence and three-year outcome in Liverpool. *British Journal of Psychiatry*, 161, 230–239.

Craik, FIM (2000). Age-related changes in human memory. In Park, DC and Schwarz, N (eds). *Cognitive Aging: A Primer*. Taylor and Francis, Philadelphia.

Davies, ADM (1996). Life events, health, adaptation and social support in the clinical psychology of late life. In Woods, RT (ed). *Handbook of the Clinical Psychology of Ageing*. John Wiley and Sons, Chichester, England.

Davies, S (2000). *Beginning and Ending Loving: Lifetime Implications of Attachment Theory for Clinicians, Services and Societies*. Workshop held at the Annual Conference of the Faculty of Psychologists Working with Older People (PSIGE). Division of Clinical Psychology, British Psychological Society, Birmingham University, 12 July.

Davies, S (2004). *All Possible Worlds? The Ageing of Regret*. Paper presented at the Annual Conference of the Faculty of Psychologists Working with Older People (PSIGE). Division of Clinical Psychology, British Psychological Society, University of Durham, 9 July.

De Hennezel (1997). *Intimate Death: How the Dying Teach Us to Live*. Little Brown, London.

De Souza, RM, Williams, J and Frederick, ABM (2003). *Critical Links: Population, Health and the Environment*. Population Reference Bureau, Washington, DC.

Dementia Care Initiative (1995–96) *Annual Report*, Newcastle upon Tyne. Now Dementia Care Partnership: admin@dementiacare.org.uk

Dening, T (1994). *Is Alzheimer's a Disease?* Alzheimer's Disease Society, July, 6.

Department of Health (1990). *National Health Service and Community Care Act*. HMSO, London.

Department of Health (1997). *Who Decides? Making Decisions on Behalf of Mentally Incapacitated Adults*. Cm3803, HMSO, London.

Department of Health (2001). *National Service Framework for Older People*. HMSO, London. Available at http://www.doh.gov.uk/nsf/olderpeople.htm

Department of Health (2005). *Mental Capacity Act*. Crown Copyright.

Featherstone, M and Hepworth, M (1990). Images of ageing. In Bond, J and Coleman, P (eds). *Ageing in Society. An Introduction to Social Gerontology*, Sage, London.

Fifer, SK, Mathias, SD, Patrick, DL, Mazonson, PE, Luebeck, DP, and Buesching, DP (1994). Untreated anxiety amongst adult primary care patients in a health mainte-nance organisation. *Archives of General Psychiatry, 51,* 740–750.

Finch, C and Kirkwood, TBL (2000). *Chance, Development and Ageing.* Oxford University Press, New York and Oxford, UK.

Gilbert, P (2001). Shame. Workshop held at University of Edinburgh, May. (Based on Gilbert, P (1997). The evolution of social attractiveness and its role in shame, humiliation, guilt and therapy. *British Journal of Medical Psychology, 70,* 113–147.)

Gillespie, DC (1997). Post-stroke anxiety and its relationship to coping and stage of recovery, *Psychological Reports, 80,* 1059–1064.

Gilligan, R (2000). Adversity, resilience and young people: The protective value of positive school and spare time experiences. *Children and Society, 14,* 37–47.

Goldsmith, M (1996). *Hearing the Voice of People with Dementia: Opportunities and Obstacles.* Jessica Kingsley, London.

Goudie, F and Richards, G (April 1993). *The psychological needs of older adults and their carers in primary are settings.* Unpublished report, Community Health, Sheffield NHS.

Haga, H, Shibata, H, Ueno, M, Nagai, H, Suyama, Y, Matsuzaki, T, Yasumara, S, Koyano, W and Hatano, S (1991). Factors contributing to longitudinal changes in activities of daily living (ADL): The Konganei study. *Journal of Cross-Cultural Gerontology,* 6(1), 91–99.

Hamarsnes, C (2002). *Friends as a ource of social support for older persons.* Progressive Alternatives Society of Calgary, Calgary.

Hazan, C. and Shaver, PR. (1994) Attachment as an organisational framework for re-search on close relationships, *Psychological Inquiry, 5,* 1–22.

Hepple, J, Pierce, J and Wilkinson, P (eds) (2002). *Psychological Therapies with Older People.* Brunner-Routledge, East Sussex, UK.

Hepple, J and Sutton, L (eds) (2004). *Cognitive Analytic Therapy and Later Life. A New Perspective on Old Age.* Brunner-Routledge, East Sussex, UK.

Hotopf, M, Mayou, R, Wadsworth, M and Wessely, S (1998). Temporal relationship between physical symptoms and psychiatric disorder: Results from a national birth cohort. *British Journal of Psychiatry, 173,* 255–261.

Holden, U and Woods, RT (1995). *Positive Approaches to Dementia Care,* 3rd edition. Churchill Livingstone, Edinburgh, UK.

Ingersoll-Dayton, B and Talbott, MM (1992). Assessment of social support exchanges: Cognitions of the old-old. *International Journal of Aging and Human Development,* 35, 125–143.

Jerrome, D (1990). Intimate relationships. In Bond, J and Coleman P (eds). *Ageing in Society. An Introduction to Social Gerontology,* Sage, London.

Kelly, GA (1955). *The Psychology of Personal Constructs.* Norton, New York.

Kerridge, RK, Glasziou, PP and Hillman, KM (1995). The use of "quality-adjusted life years" (QALYS) to evaluate treatment in intensive care. *Anaesthesia and Intensive Care, 23* (3), 322–331..

Keyes, CLM and Lopez, SJ (2005) Toward a science of mental health. In Snyder, CR and Lopez, SJ (eds). *Handbook of Positive Psychology*. Oxford University Press, New York.

Killeen, J (1998). Home care: can it be a real choice? *Journal of Dementia Care*, Jan/Feb, 12–14.

Killick, J (1997). *You Are Words: Dementia Poems*. Hawker Publications, London.

Killick, J and Allan, K (2001). *Communication and the Care of people with Dementia*. Open University Press, Buckingham, UK.

Kirkwood, T (2004). *Positive Ageing*. Paper presented at the Annual Conference of the Faculty of Psychologists Working with Older People (PSIGE), Division of Clinical Psychology, British Psychological Society, University of Durham, 8 July.

Kirkwood, T (1999). *Time of Our Lives. Why Ageing is Neither Inevitable Nor Necessary*. Phoenix, London.

Kitwood, T (1993). Towards a theory of dementia care: The interpersonal process. *Ageing and Society*, *13*, 51–67.

Kitwood, T and Bredin, K (1992) Towards a theory of dementia care: Personhood and well-being. *Ageing and Society*, *12*, 269–287.

Kitwood, T (1997). *Dementia Reconsidered: The Person Comes First*. Open University Press, Buckingham, UK.

Knapp, P (on behalf of the Intercollegiate Working Party for Stroke) (2000). *The Psychological Care Provided to Stroke Patients in Hospital – The Results of a National Audit*. Paper presented at the Annual Conference of the Psychologists' Special Interest Group Working with Older People (PSIGE), Division of Clinical Psychology, British Psychological Society, University of Birmingham, July.

Knapp, P, Young, J, House, A and Forster, A (2000). Non-drug strategies to resolve psychosocial difficulties after stroke. *Age and Ageing*, *29*, 23–30.

Knight, BG (1996). Psychodynamic therapy with older clients. In Woods, RT (ed). *Handbook of the Clinical Psychology of Ageing*. John Wiley and Sons, Chichester, England.

Krasucki, C, Ryan, P, Ertan, T, Howard, R, Lindesay, J and Mann, A (1999). The FEAR: A rapid screening instrument for generalized anxiety in elderly primary care attenders. *International Journal of Geriatric Psychiatry*, *14*(1), 60–68.

Kubler-Ross, E (1969). *On Death and Dying*. Tavistock, London.

Kubler-Ross, E (1975). *Death. The Final Stage of Growth*. Prentice-Hall, New Jersey.

Leipzig, RM, Cummings, RG and Tinetti, ME (1999). Drugs and falls in older people: a systematic review and meta-analysis. *Journal of American Geriatrics Society*, *47*, 30–39.

Lemay, R (1999). Roles, identities and expectancies: Positive contributions of role theory to normalization and social role valorization. In Flynn, RJ and Lemay, RA (eds). *A Quarter Century of Normalization and Social Role Valorization: Evolution and Impact*. University of Ottawa Press, Ottawa.

Lemay R (2001). A synopsis and review of Bandura, Albert. "The changing face of psychology at the dawning of a globalization era". *Canadian Psychology*, *42* (1), 12–24.

Lemay, R and Ghazal, H (2001). Resilience and positive psychology: Finding hope. *Child and Family*, *5* (1), 10–21.

Lincoln, N, Majid, MJ and Weyman, N (2002). Cognitive rehabilitation for attention deficits following stroke (Cochrane review) In *The Cochrane Library*, Issue 3. Update Software, Oxford.

Maddux, JE (2005). Stopping the "madness" positive psychology and the deconstruction of the illness ideology and the DSM. In Snyder, CR and Lopez, J (eds). *Handbook of Positive Psychology*. Oxford University Press, New York.

McGrath, A and Jackson, GA (1996). Survey of neuroleptic prescribing in residents of nursing homes in Glasgow. *British Medical Journal, 312*, 611–612.

Meadows, D (1995). Who causes environmental pollution? *International Society of Ecological Economics Newsletter, 1*, 8.

Miesen, B (1993). Meaning and function of the remembered parents in normal and abnormal old age. In Pollock, GH and Greenspan, SI (eds). *The Course of Life*, Vol *viii*. International Universities Press, Madison, CT.

Miesen, B (1999). *Dementia in Close Up*. Routledge, London.

Morse, JQ and Lynch, TR (2000). Personality disorders in late life. *Current Psychiatry Reports, 2*, 24–31.

Nakamura, J and Csikszentmihalyi, M (2005). The concept of flow. In Snyder, CR and Lopez, SJ (eds) *Handbook of Positive Psychology*, pp 89–105. Oxford University Press, New York.

Nolen-Hoeksema, S and Davis C (2005). Positive responses to loss: Perceiving benefits and growth. In Snyder, CR and Lopez, SJ (eds). *Handbook of Positive Psychology*. Oxford University Press, New York.

O'Brien, J and Lovett, H (1992). *Finding a Way Towards Everyday Lives: The Contribution of Person Centered Planning*. Pennsylvania Office of Mental Retardation, Harrisburg, PA.

O'Brien, J and Lyle, C (1986). *Framework for Accomplishment*. Responsive Systems Associates, Decatur, GA.

Osburn, J (1998). An overview of social role valorization theory. *International Social Role Valorization Journal, 3* (1), 7–12.

Paolucci, S, Antonucci, G, Pratesi, L, Traballesi, M, Grasso, M G and Lubich, S (1999). Post-stroke depression and its role in rehabilitation of inpatients. *Archives of Physical Medicine and Rehabilitation, 80*, 985–990.

Park D and Schwarz, N (2000). *Cognitive Ageing. A Primer*. University Press, E Sussex, UK.

Parkes, CM (1972). *Bereavement. Studies of Grief in Adult Life*. Penguin Books, Middlesex, England.

Pattie, A and Gilleard, C (1979). *The Clifton Assessment Procedures for the Elderly (CAPE)*. Stoddart and Houghton Educational, Kent. (Fourth impression 1995.)

Princen, T, Maniates, M and Conca, K (eds) (2002). *Confronting Consumption*. MIT Press, Cambridge, MA.

Race, D (ed) (2003). *Leadership and Change in Human Services. Selected Readings from Wolf Wolfensberger*. Routledge, London and New York.

Robbins, S. (2005). Looking forwards towards the end – Working with older people. In Winter, DA and Viney, LL (eds). *Personal Construct Psychotherapy: Advances in Theory, Practice and Research*, pp. 296–319. Whurr, London.

Rottenberg, DA and Hoffberg, FH (eds). (1977) *Neurological Classics in Modern Translation*. Hafner Press, New York.

Rowe, JW and Kahn, RL (1998). *Successful Aging*. Pantheon, New York.

Rudd, AG, Irwin, P, Rutledge, Z, Lowe, D, Wade, D, Morris, R and Pearson, MD (on behalf of the Intercollegiate Working party for stroke) (1999). The national sentinel audit for stroke: A tool for raising standards of care. *Journal of the Royal College of Physicians London*, *33*, 460–464.

Ryle, A (1997). *Cognitive Analytic Therapy and Borderline Personality Disorder. The Model and the Method*. John Wiley and Sons, Chichester, England.

Ryle, AR and Kerr, IB (2002). *Introducing Cognitive Analytic Therapy*. John Wiley and Sons, Chichester, England.

Sapp, S (2004). Well-being in older people: The role and importance of religion and spirituality. *Signpost*, *9* (2), 9–14.

Saunders, C (1959). *Care of the Dying*. Macmillan and Company, London.

Schacter, DL and Tulving, E (1994). What are the memory systems of 1994? In Schacter, DL and Tulving, E (eds). *Memory Systems 1994*. MIT Press, Cambridge, MA.

Scottish Executive (2003). *Mental Health and Well-Being in Later Life. Report of a Workshop held at the Stirling Management Centre*, 10–11 March.

Scottish Executive (2004) *Guidance to the implementation of the Adults With Incapacity (Scotland) Act*, Edinburgh.

Seligman, M. (1991). *Learned Optimism*. Knopf, New York.

Seligman, MEP (1975). *Learned Helplessness: On depression, development and death*. Freeman: San Francisco.

Seligman, MEP (1998). *Learned Optimism: How to Change your Mind and Your Life*. Pocket Books, New York.

Seligman, MEP (1998). *Learned Optimism: How to Change your Mind and Your Life*. Pocket Books, New York.

Seligman MEP (2002a). *Authentic Happiness. Using the New Positive Psychology to Realize your Potential for Lasting Fulfilment*. Free Press, New York.

Seligman, MEP (2005). Positive psychology, positive prevention and positive therapy. In Snyder, CR and Lopez, SJ (eds). *Handbook of Positive Psychology*, pp. 3–9. Oxford University Press, New York.

Seligman, MEP and Csikszentmihalyi, M (2000). Positive psychology: An introduction. *American Psychologist*, *55*, 5–14.

Sixsmith, A and Stillwell, J (1993). Rementia. Challenging the limits of dementia care. *International Journal of Geriatric Psychiatry*, *8* (12), 993–1000.

Smail, D (2001a). Illusion and reality: The meaning of anxiety. Reprinted in *Why Therapy Doesn't Work*, pp 3–223. Robinson, London.

Smail, D (2001b). Taking care: An alternative to therapy. Reprinted in *Why Therapy Doesn't Work*, pp 225–445. Robinson, London.

Smith, WJ (1999). "Rational suicide" as the new Jim Crow. In Werth, JL (ed). *Contemporary Perspectives on Rational Suicide, Series in Death, Dying and Bereavement*, pp. 54–62. Brunner/Mazel Inc., Philadelphia, PA.

Smith, WJ (2003a). *Issues of Deathmaking and SRV*. Paper presented at Third International Social Role Valorization Conference: Leadership and Change. University of Calgary, Canada, 7 June.

Smith, WJ (2003b). *Forced Exit: The Slippery Slope from Assisted Suicide to Legalized Murder*. Spence Publishing Company, Dallas, TX.

Snyder, CR (1994). *The Psychology of Hope: You Can Get There from Here*. Free Press, New York.

Snyder, CR and Lopez, SJ (eds) (2005). *Handbook of Positive Psychology*. Oxford University Press, New York.

Stirling, E (1990). Getting to know you. In Brent, P (production ed). *Golden Opportunities: Better Communication with Older People* and *A Practical Guide to Reminiscence with Elderly People*. Video-assisted training packs. Pavilion Press, Winslow Press, Bicester.

Stirling, E (1996). Social role valorization: Making a difference to the lives of older people? In Woods, RT (ed). *Handbook of the Clinical Psychology of Ageing*. John Wiley and Sons, Chichester, England.

Stokes, G (1990). Behavioural analysis. In Stokes, G and Goudie, F (eds). *Working with Dementia*, pp. 66–72. Winslow Press, Bicester, UK.

Stokes, G (2000). *Challenging Behaviour in Dementia. A Person Centred Approach*. Manchester University Press, Manchester, UK.

Sudnow, D (1967). *Passing On. The Social Organization of Dying*. Prentice-Hall, Upper Saddle River, NJ.

Sutton, L (1997). Out of the silence: When people can't talk about it. In Hunt, L, Marshall, M and Rowlings, C (eds). *Past Trauma in Late Life. European Perspectives on Therapeutic Work with Older People*. Jessica Kingsley Publishers, London.

Sutton, L (2000). *CAT in Later Life: "No Final Word"*. Paper presented at the Annual Conference of the Psychologists' Faculty Working with Older People (PSIGE). Division of Clinical Psychology, British Psychological Society, University of Birmingham, 13 July.

Svanberg, R (1998). Rising to the challenge of radical change. *Journal of Dementia Care*, Nov/Dec, 18–20.

Svanberg, R, Livingston, M, Fairbairn, A and Stephenson, C (1999). Popular solution that can offer "best value". *Journal of Dementia Care*, Jan/Feb, 24–28.

Svanberg, R, Stirling, E and Fairbairn, A (1998). An ordinary house in an ordinary street. *Journal of Dementia Care*, Sept/Oct, 12–14.

Taylor, SE. and Brown, JD (1988). Illusion and well-being: A social psychological perspective on mental health, *Psychological Bulletin, 103*, 193–210.

The Scotsman (2004). German professor charged with killing disabled for Hitler. p. 17, 29 January.

Vanier, J (1982) *The Challenge of L'Arche*. Darton, Longman and Todd, London.

Victor, CB (1987). *Old Age in Modern Society: A Textbook of Social Gerontology*. Croom Helm, London.

Watson, J (2003). Interview given to BBC World News, 'Fifty years commemoration of the discovery of the genetic material DNA', May.

Watson, J and Crick, F (1953a). Molecular structure for nucleic acids; a structure for deoxyribose nucleic acid. *Nature, 171*(4356), 737–738.

Watson, J and Crick, F (1953b). Genetical implications of the structure of deoxyribonucleic acid. *Nature, 171*(4361), 964–967.

Weiss, R and Kasmauski, K (1997). Aging: New answers to old questions. *National Geographic, 192* (5), 2–31. (Photographs.)

Williams, P (2003). *Incorporating SRV into Wider Frameworks for Teaching Anti-Oppressive Human Service Practice.* Paper presented at Third International Social Role Valorization Conference: Leadership and Change. University of Calgary, Canada, 6 June.

Williamson, GM (2005). Aging well: Outlook for the 21st century. In Snyder, CR and Lopez, SJ (eds) (2005). *Handbook of Positive Psychology.* Oxford University Press, New York.

Wolfensberger, W (1987). *The New Genocide of Handicapped and Afflicted People.* Training Institute for Human Service Planning, Leadership and Change Agentry, Syracuse University, New York.

Wolfensberger, W (1994). Let's hang up 'quality of life' as a hopeless term. In Goode, D (ed). *Quality of Life for Persons with Disabilities. International Perspectives and Issues,* pp. 285–321, Brookline Books, Cambridge, MA. (Reprinted in Race, D (ed). *Leadership and Change in Human Services. Selected readings from Wolf Wolfensberger,* pp. 197–203. Routledge, London and New York.

Wolfensberger, W (1998). *A Brief Introduction to Social Role Valorization as a Higher Order Concept for Addressing the Plight of Societally Devalued People, and for Structuring Human Services.* Training Institute for Human Service Planning, Leadership and Change Agentry, Syracuse University, New York.

Wolfensberger, W (2000). A brief overview of social role valorization. *Mental Retardation, 38,* 105–123.

Wolfensberger, W (2003). *Issues of Change Agentry in the Dissemination of SRV.* Paper presented at Third International Social Role Valorization Conference: Leadership and Change. University of Calgary, Canada, 4 June.

Wolfensberger, W and Glenn, L (1975). *Programme Analysis of Service Systems (PASS): A Method for the Quantitative Evaluation of Human Services,* 3rd edition, Vol II. Field manual, National Institute on Mental Retardation, Toronto. (Reprinted 1978.)

Wolfensberger, W and Thomas, S (1983). *PASSING: Programme Analysis of Service Systems: Implementation of Normalization Goals,* 2nd edition. Canadian National Institute on Mental Retardation, Ontario.

Worldwatch Institute (2004). *State of the World.* Earthscan Publishers, London.

Wrzesniewski, A (2005). Jobs, careers and callings. In Snyder, CR and Lopez, SJ (eds). *Handbook of Positive Psychology,* pp 761–762. Oxford University Press, New York.

Wurr, S (1999). *Kindred Spirits: An Alternative Way to Reduce Isolation – The Full Evaluation.* Paper presented at the Annual Conference of the Psychologists' Faculty Working with Older People (PSIGE). Division of Clinical Psychology, British Psychological Society, Bat Spa University College, July.

Zarit, S and Edwards, AB (1996). Family caregiving: Research and clinical intervention. In Woods, R (ed). *Handbook of the Clinical Psychology of Ageing,* pp. 333–368. John Wiley and Sons, Chichester, England.

Index